T0312264

Men
at
War

Men at War

[A Soldier's-Eye View of the
Most Important Battles in History]

EDITED BY

BILL FAWCETT

BERKLEY CALIBER, NEW YORK

THE BERKLEY PUBLISHING GROUP
Published by the Penguin Group
Penguin Group (USA) Inc.
375 Hudson Street, New York, New York 10014, USA
Penguin Group (Canada), 90 Eglinton Avenue East, Suite 700, Toronto, Ontario M4P 2Y3, Canada
(a division of Pearson Penguin Canada Inc.)
Penguin Books Ltd., 80 Strand, London WC2R 0RL, England
Penguin Group Ireland, 25 St. Stephen's Green, Dublin 2, Ireland (a division of Penguin Books Ltd.)
Penguin Group (Australia), 250 Camberwell Road, Camberwell, Victoria 3124, Australia
(a division of Pearson Australia Group Pty. Ltd.)
Penguin Books India Pvt. Ltd., 11 Community Centre, Panchsheel Park, New Delhi—110 017, India
Penguin Group (NZ), 67 Apollo Drive, Rosedale, North Shore 0632, New Zealand
(a division of Pearson New Zealand Ltd.)
Penguin Books (South Africa) (Pty.) Ltd., 24 Sturdee Avenue, Rosebank, Johannesburg 2196,
South Africa

Penguin Books Ltd., Registered Offices: 80 Strand, London WC2R 0RL, England

The publisher does not have any control over and does not assume any responsibility for author or third-party websites or their content.

PRINTING HISTORY
Berkley Caliber trade paperback edition / December 2009

Library of Congress Cataloging-in-Publication Data

Men at war : a soldier's-eye view of the most important battles in history / edited by Bill Fawcett.—
Berkley Caliber trade pbk. ed.
    p. cm.
  ISBN 978-0-425-23013-8
  1. Military history—Anecdotes. 2. Battles—History—Anecdotes. 3. Soldiers—Biography.
4. Combat—History—Anecdotes. 5. Strategy—History—Anecdotes. I. Fawcett, Bill.
  D25.5.M454 2009
  355.0209—dc22   2009022412

[CONTENTS]

A Roman Legionnaire at Alesia

A City Within a Wall Within a Wall

BY DOUGLAS NILES

For the first two thousand years of recorded warfare the infantryman armed with some version of a spear or sword dominated the battlefields. Perhaps the ultimate development of the "spear carrier" was the Roman legionnaire. What made him different was not his weapons, which would have been familiar to any warrior of the last two millennia, but his organization and discipline.

DOUGLAS NILES is the author of some fifty novels in the various genres of adventure. He has designed award-winning miniature battle games, including two versions of the official Dungeons & Dragons mass combat games. As a historian he has penned alternate histories and contributed to a wide range of military anthologies and historical collections.

[*]

"Look! Lucius Fabius gains the wall!"

The cry echoed through the cohorts of the Eighth Legion as the veteran centurion, trailed by three men of his company, hauled himself over the parapet on the rampart of Gergovia. Two Gauls charged the burly legionnaire, who raised his shield with his left arm to deflect the first as he stabbed his *gladius* hard with his right. The sturdy, wide-bladed short sword caught the second Gaul in the side of his belly, piercing his chain-link armor and gouging deep into the flesh. As that defender went down, Fabius pivoted. Like every legionary, he knew how to use his heavy *scutum*, the curved shield that was a Roman trademark, as a weapon as well as a defense. The centurion drove the boss of that shield into the face of the first Gaul. Flailing, that one toppled backward, off the rampart.

From his position thirty paces to the side, Titus Mocius joined in the cheer. He'd heard Fabius boasting earlier that he would be the first over the wall, the first to claim the fabulous spoils of Gergovia that the Gauls had—presumably—stored within the fortified city. Now the centurion, one of the most well-known veterans in the Eighth Legion, had staked his claim to a section of the wall. One by one he helped his three companions over the lip of the parapet, and they stood firm against the Gauls who rushed to overwhelm them.

The pent-up frustrations of a long siege at last came boiling to the surface, and Titus felt an exhilaration he had not known in weeks. Although his legion had not, technically, been ordered to attack, the men had seen the opportunity and it had proved too much to resist. The *Legio VIII* had rushed toward a gap in the enemy's infantry formation, the charge carrying all the way to Gergovia's walls.

"To the gates! Follow me!" This cry came from Mocius's own centurion, Marcus Petreius. With two dozen legionaries of his company following Petreius, the centurion fought his way to one of the many gates in the city wall and smashed the wooden planks with his *gladius*. Titus followed. Like many others, he still held a *pilum,* and he launched the javelin at one of the Gauls on the rampart over the gate. Then, drawing his sword from its scabbard at his right waist, he charged forward to do battle at his centurion's side.

The Gallic defenders swarmed everywhere, as many of them outside of the city as within. The army of Vercingetorix was encamped on all the heights around Gergovia, and the Gauls wasted no time in coming to the city's aid. They pressed from both sides, and Titus Mocius felt a glimmer of misgiving. He and the rest of his legion had charged eagerly, anticipating victory, but now he realized that they were terribly exposed.

More Gauls, bearded and whooping, swinging axes and swords, swarmed toward Marcus Petronius in his position at the gate. Titus stood beside the centurion, blocking and bashing the Gauls with his *scutum*, but more and more of the enemy warriors closed in. Soon the small detachment was surrounded by hundreds of howling barbarians. More of them lined the wall above, dropping rocks, blocks of wood, and even feces on the hated Romans, perhaps a dozen of whom still survived around their Marcus Petronius.

"This is no good—you've got to get away! Fall back!" shouted the centurion. "Gather around the eagle—leave these walls!"

Titus stabbed with his short sword, holding the hilt of the *gladius* low and driving the tip up under a Gaul's shield. The enemy leaped back, avoiding a wound, while Marcus Petronius spun on his heel and stabbed another foe. "Retreat, by Jupiter!" the centurion roared. "I will hold them as long as I can!"

Responding by instinct to that commanding voice, Titus Mocius was compelled to obey. Together with the rest of the survivors of his company, he battled his way out of the gate's shadow, through the ditch that the Gauls had excavated around the city of Gergovia. He looked back at the top of the wall and saw Lucius Fabius go down, buried under the weight of a dozen Gauls. Marcus Petronius, still before the gate, spun around like a dervish. Blood streamed down his arms, staining the chain link of his mail shirt, but he roared a challenge and, like magic, drew the Gauls to him. That distraction gave Titus and the others the chance to escape.

The last Titus saw of his centurion, Petronius was still fighting, but he fell beneath the onslaught of a dozen stabbing blades. Now the Romans of *Legio VIII* ran for their lives, sprinting away from the wall, pursued by hundreds, even thousands of madly howling Gauls. Another legion advanced up the hill, from the vicinity of the Roman camp. The cohorts spread into open formation, leaving gaps for the retreating legionaries to retreat through. The Gallic pursuit was finally deterred when the men of the fresh legion hurled their *pila*, the lethal javelins showering down in two quick volleys. The intervention was quick, disciplined, and courageous— and it was enough to allow the reeling survivors of the onslaught to reach the safety of Caesar's lines.

* * *

The next morning, all of Caesar's army was assembled in the open field before the camp. They stood in ranks with the citadel of Gergovia looming above them. Titus Mocius stood with the men of his cohort. The ten cohorts of the Eighth Legion stood to one flank of the army, with the rest of the legions arrayed in similar formation. Like everything Roman, the legion was a precise, logical formation.

Ideally, each legion would include some 4,500 men, organized into ten cohorts, each of which was commanded by the senior centurion of that cohort. The cohort was the basic unit of tactical maneuver, though each of them was broken into smaller groups for organizational purposes. A *century* was 100 men, commanded by a single centurion; the centurion would have assistance from an *optio* (second in command) and *tesserarius* (guard sergeant), who served as assistant century commanders. Within each century were ten or twelve *contubernia*, which were sections of eight men who shared a tent in camp and the use of a single mule on the march. In battle formation, or as today, when drawn up for a parade or ceremony, each cohort presented a front of some fifty men, organized in eight or ten ranks. The cohorts of a given legion would be organized four abreast in the front, with two ranks of three cohorts behind. They would stand, march, and fight in a checkerboard pattern, leaving as much space between the cohorts as was occupied by the block of men in each formation.

The legionaries themselves were all professional soldiers and Roman citizens—though not necessarily from Rome itself. (In the case of Caesar's legions, most of the men hailed from different provinces in Italy.) They were sturdy, physically fit, and hardy men who signed up generally for a term of sixteen years of duty—a term that was often extended for centurions and other career soldiers.

Each legion was commanded by a legate, who was almost invariably a member of the aristocracy—though Caesar, and many other generals, selected their legates for command abilities and courage more than family connections and wealth. The legate would be aided by a quaestor, who handled many of the unit's administrative duties, as well as a *tribune laticlavius*, a young nobleman appointed by the senate who served as second in command. Five additional officers, *tribuni angusticlavii*, were of equestrian rank, slightly lower than aristocrats, but they tended to be seasoned veterans and the legates often relied heavily upon them as lieutenants.

Each legion proudly presented its colors on a standard, which included the bronze image of an eagle. The eagle was carried, both on the march and in battle, by the *primus pilus*—that is, the senior centurion of the entire legion. Now it was the *primus pilus* who stomped the eagle standard on the ground, and thus conveyed the command for each man to give his attention to the *imperator*, or general, before him.

Before them the legionnaires could make out the figure of the army commander, standing upon a tall wooden platform to address his soldiers. Though the tiny figure was indistinct, his bright red cloak made him easy to identify.

Gaius Julius Caesar was nearly half a mile away, and Titus could not hear his words directly. But a series of lieutenants were deployed across the field, and as the great man spoke, they repeated his words, their voices carrying clearly to the ears of every man in the formation.

"Legionaries of mine! You are like my own children! Your valor and your great deeds cause me pride. I know you can accomplish great things, with discipline, patience, and a plan. Yet when greed and impetuousness rule your hearts, your disobedience and your failures cause me shame, and disappointment."

There was a pause as the words were carried through the ranks of the army, and a soft, rippling sigh as the men absorbed the rebuke, shame welling up in every legionary's heart. There was nothing that could cut them so much as criticism from their beloved, and thus far invincible, leader.

"It causes me great sadness," Caesar said, after a pause to make sure that his words were carried to every legionary, "to see that my men think themselves wiser than their general. To think that they would attack a city that I did not order them to attack. To observe how the lust for treasure, the impetuous rush toward violence, like a pack of angry boys, could break the discipline of mighty legions."

Titus burned with shame, for he knew that his leader spoke the truth. And the *Legio VIII* was the prime offender.

"My soldiers, my children: I admire your courage, and your willingness to carry war to the Gauls. Neither the formidable defenses of the city, nor its position on such a high hill, nor the number of foe, shall cause you to falter or know fear. Yet at the same time, I must censure your arrogance, for it would appear that you think you know more than your general!

"And this is not the case! Be aware, my legionaries, that I require from my soldiers obedience and self-command in every measure equal to that of valor. Yesterday's action cost us more than seven hundred brave men, among them more than forty centurions—and this is a loss we shall feel for the remainder of the campaign!"

All through the cohorts, through all the legions, shoulders slumped and spirits sagged. Titus could not meet the eyes of the men around him, nor did they seem in any way eager to look into his face. Shame consumed him—not so much for his own failures to carry the city, nor even for the bold comrades who had fallen at the walls of Gergovia. His shame, like that of the rest of the legionaries, had to do with failing his beloved commander, for performing in a way that caused Caesar distress.

Certainly sensing this chagrin, this guilt, the great general concluded his speech with words of comfort and hope.

"My bold soldiers!" he cried. "I speak thus to you so that you may learn from your errors, but I do not wish to chide you, to make of you lesser men than you are. I want you to understand the reasons for yesterday's failure. And those reasons are *not* due to any great competence on the part of the foe, nor to any lack of valor on the part of the Roman legions! No, my men: the fault lies in the disadvantage of position, in the ramparts of the enemy and the heights he commands. These are faults that your general perceived, and these were the reasons he did not command a general assault!"

"So learn from this error, my men. Do not repeat it. Listen to your general, to your officers, and we will, we *must*, prevail!"

* * *

The following day Caesar ordered his legions out of their camp, into the field below Gergovia's height. Here the Roman infantry drew up in order of battle, cohorts spaced evenly across the ground, javelins at the ready, in plain view of the Gallic host on the summits and elevations surrounding the city. Some forty thousand veteran legionaries stood ready to give battle, on level ground that would offer no advantage to either side. The Gauls, who had the advantage of numbers in perhaps as much as a two-to-one ratio, were restrained by their own general—the clever Vercingetorix— who declined the invitation to battle, as Caesar no doubt had known he would.

Even without a battle, the long hours under the summer sun, standing in battle formation, looking at the great host of the foe so obviously unwilling to fight, did great things for the morale of the Romans. They retired to their camp again that night, and when, the next morning, the order came to march, the legions prepared to move with the memory of their audacious challenge, and the enemy's timidity, foremost in their minds.

Titus Mocius, like his fellow legionaries, would be heavily

laden for the march. He was part of an eight-man section, called a *contubernium*, which was awarded the use of a single mule to carry the large leather tent that sheltered the legionaries at night. In addition, the beast was burdened with some other jointly shared equipment, including a large kettle and great coils of rope. The mule was also saddled with a bag of grain, from which the soldiers baked their hard bread around the evening fires.

Mocius himself, like his fellows, would march ready for battle, as was typical when moving through territory where enemy troops were known to be present. His sword was girded at his waist, on the right side as always. The *gladius* was a splendid weapon with a steel blade about twenty inches long and a hilt cared with grooves for each of the legionary's fingers. The scabbard swiveled easily at his belt, so that he could quickly draw the weapon by inverting his right hand, seizing the hilt, and pulling the sword forward to release it for action. He wore his shield on his left arm. This was a curved barrier, formed with three layers of wooden strips covered with tightly bound leather. A metal boss in the middle of the shield served as a decoration, but also as a formidable blunt instrument in battle.

On the march in hostile territory, the legionary would also wear his helmet on his head. This protective cap was a bowl-shaped piece of bronze, with a brim running around the side and two sturdy side plates dropping to protect the wearer's cheeks and ears. A horsetail plume usually topped the helm. In his right hand the legionary carried a long pole, a shaft that would be used to help form the barricade around the camp at night. When on the march, however, the pole served to support the bundles of his personal kit, including a spare cloak and pair of sandals, a waterskin, and a few tidbits of personal food—in Titus's case, a small slab of salt bacon and a piece of hard cheese.

A second bundle, counterbalancing the pole, contained his excavation equipment, including a basket, a saw, and a shovel. Other men carried axes, picks, hammers, and other items, so that, among the *contubernium*, the legionaries possessed at least one or two of every standard digging, cutting, and building tool. After striking the camp, taking down the palisade to use the poles for the march, the army moved out shortly after dawn. The Romans marched on foot, but they were accompanied by several thousand German auxiliaries, fierce cavalry who rode in several divisions along each flank of the marching column, with one detachment leading the way. The infantry strode along at the full pace, a marching step that involved long strides and a steady, unfaltering pace. Here in Gaul they did not have the benefit of a good Roman road, but even along the dirt tracks leading through woods and across pastureland, the legions made excellent time.

The cavalry scouted far and wide, flushing out a few Gauls, but encountered no organized resistance. By mid-afternoon, the general called a halt, and the legions moved into the area of the new camp. The place had already been surveyed and marked by the pioneers who marched ahead of the full army column, so the erecting of the evening's shelter proceeded according to the standard, and very familiar, drill.

The surveyors had erected a large flag at each side of the rectangular camp, and each legion, each cohort, even each *contubernium*, knew exactly where to go. While some of the men pitched the tent, others, including Titus, went to the perimeter of the camp, where the bases of their wooden posts were buried a foot or more into the ground. These stakes were lashed together around the entire periphery, except for four gates, with leather straps, so that they created a sturdy, if not especially tall, barrier. On the outside of the fence the legionaries dug a trench several feet deep, using the excavated dirt to help bolster the stakes. The streets within the camp were arrayed in a cross pattern, with a terminus at each of the four gates, which fell in the midpoints of the four walls. The street running the long axis of the camp was called the *via praeto-*

ria, while that road crossing the long axis and connecting the other two gates was called the *via principalis*.

Finally, the camp was made, and by sunset the men, those not posted to guard duty, gathered around their cook fires, chewing hard bread. Titus shared a few scraps of his cheese with his tent mates, while another man, Sextus Rufius, passed around some slices of apple, from the small bag of fruit he had managed to forage while the army had been encamped at Gergovia.

"Where do you suppose we're going from here?" Sextus asked.

"I heard the legate say we're going back to the Province," Titus offered. "There's revolt brewing even down there."

"You mean the damned Gauls who've suckled at the Roman teat for a hundred years have decided they've had enough?" grumbled another legionary. "You'd think they'd see the value in sticking with Caesar."

"Well, he'll show them soon enough," Titus declared.

But he wished he felt as confident as he sounded. In fact he, like most of these legionaries, had been serving in Gaul for many years. During each campaign season they'd marched across the countryside, and fought to subdue some tribe or another of the barbarians who inhabited every corner of this rich, fertile land. Frequently it seemed that they had no sooner pacified some band, such as the Senones or the Treverii or the Helvetii, than another would rebel. The Gauls would kill the Roman merchants and citizens who had taken up residence and started up businesses in their towns, then battle the legions that came to exact vengeance. In every case, Caesar had prevailed, quelling the rebellion, punishing the enemy ringleaders, and then, in his astonishingly forgiving way, allowing the newly subjugated—or resubjugated—tribe to once again establish an alliance with Rome.

Yet now, after some eight years of war, the rebellions had erupted across the whole of Gaul, including in those regions such as the Province, which bordered on the Mediterranean Sea, and the lands of the Aedui. Both areas had long and profitably been allied with Rome, and it was only the goading and revolutionary influence of Vercingetorix that had persuaded nearly all of the tribes of the Gauls to take up arms against the legions.

Already this year Caesar had crossed snowy mountains to surprise the enemy with a quick start to the campaign. They had routed the Gauls in every pitched battle where the two armies met. The Romans had sacked and burned great cities, including Cenebum, where the rebellion had first flared to life, and Avaricum, where the legions had erected a great hill next to the lofty city and finally carried the place by storm.

Only at Gergovia had the legions been checked, and now the men knew that the failure rested on their own childish impetuosity and not upon their leader's lack of judgment. So they resumed the march with high morale and grim determination. Yet Titus Mocius was not alone in hoping for some kind of cessation to the ceaseless war.

And yet, when the legions broke camp the next day, and the next, they continued to march south, and it seemed that the rumors were true: they were abandoning barbarian Gaul and returning to the Province, which by all rights should have been thoroughly pacified.

Throughout the march, there was no sign of Vercingetorix and the Gallic infantry. The barbarian cavalry, however, which greatly outnumbered the German riders serving Caesar, made a real nuisance of itself. Titus and his fellows never ventured away from the army without being well armed and ready for trouble. A full cohort, some four hundred men, needed to venture forth simply to collect firewood, and even then they were not free from harassment. Still, when the Gaul horsemen showed up, the Romans would form a defensive square behind the shields. They would cast their *pila* if the enemy riders came too close, and the barrage of javelins was usually enough to hold the enemy at bay long enough for the legionaries to do their job.

This was the course of the march for some ten days, as the legions moved away from Gergovia and toward the Province. Apparently the sight of this retreat was enough to embolden Vercingetorix, for he finally made an effort to halt the Roman progress. As with his harassment, this resistance was accomplished with his cavalry.

On the eleventh day of the march Titus joined the rest of the legionaries in forming up, fully girded for battle, as the Gaul cavalry charged from both flanks and against the front of the Roman column. Yet Caesar, as always, employed his own forces with great skill. While the men in the legions watched, the outnumbered German horses charged to counter each Gaul advance. Once, when the enemy threatened to turn the flank of the German cavalry, the Eighth Legion was ordered to advance, which the men did in formation, marching at the short, clipped military pace with javelins poised.

But it was the cavalry that carried the day. Titus joined his fellow legionaries in cheering lustily as they watched the Germans rout the Gauls from the top of a commanding hill, driving the enemy from the field in great disorder. In the camp that night they heard tales of great slaughter, as the Gallic cavalry fell back to the main body of Vercingetorix's army and the German horses wreaked great havoc among all the enemy's men.

True to his pattern, Caesar showed no reluctance to change his plans. Every legionary noticed the alteration the next morning as, now, the legion column pivoted to march north, pursuing the Gauls, who continued to fall back from the formidable Roman army. No longer were the legions heading toward the Province—instead, they would carry the war into the very heart of Gaul, pursuing the great host of Vercingetorix until they could bring that wily fox to a den.

Several days later more legions, under the command of Caesar's most trusted lieutenant, Titus Labienus, joined the main body, resulting in a force of some sixty thousand men. They pursued an even greater number of Gauls, but the Romans maintained the initiative, and the enemy continued to retreat.

So it was that, ten days later, the two great armies came to Alesia.

* * *

"I remember when I joined the legion," Titus Mocius observed wryly. "I thought my most important tool would be my sword."

He drove the blade of his shovel deep into the fertile soil of Gaul and hoisted another load of dirt out of the rapidly growing trench. "Turns out I do a lot more digging than I do fighting!"

Marcus Didius, coming by with a long trunk of wood, settled to the ground nearby and began to chisel at the end of his post, sharpening it to a keen point. Didius was an *immunis*, one of the army's specialists, and as such was spared the rigors of routine labor such as digging, and digging, and digging.

"What's the stick for, anyway?" Titus asked, catching his breath between shovelfuls. He was already standing in a hole as deep as his shoulders, but he knew he'd be excavating a lot farther before he was done.

"Caesar has some new ideas about protecting the line, once you ditch diggers are done," Marcus said breezily. Titus had known the carpenter for most of his life—they came from the same town, along the Po River in northern Italy—and he took no offense at the remark.

Instead, he looked up at the formidable position of Alesia and shrugged. "I guess anything is better than trying to storm that place."

Marcus, following the direction of Titus's gaze, nodded in agreement.

Indeed, Alesia was an impressive redoubt, and no sane man

would welcome the prospect of a frontal attack. The city stood upon a rocky hilltop, with steep slopes dropping down in every direction from the walls. That stone and wooden barrier was a formidable obstacle in its own right, and it now protected some eighty thousand Gauls of the army of Vercingetorix, not to mention the full population of its own residents, members of the Mandubii tribe.

Many of those Gauls were camped outside of the city, in the shadow of the walls near the top of the hill. They had excavated a ditch to protect their camp, using the spare dirt to make an additional parapet as a deterrent to any Roman onslaught. But so far, Caesar had shown no inclination to launch an attack.

Away from the walls, the hill of Alesia descended to the north and the south into river valleys, as two separate watercourses flowed around the base of the elevation. To the east, the terrain was steep and rocky, while to the west the slope grew gentle until it leveled into a field some three miles long. Rising beyond the two rivers, a ring of hills surrounded Alesia and its plain, none of them higher than the city itself, and all of them too far away to provide any advantage in assaulting the stronghold.

Upon arriving below Alesia, Caesar had immediately put his legions into camp. The very next day, he'd ordered his soldiers to work, and now every legionary who wasn't foraging or actively serving on guard duty was working on the construction of a massive ring of fortifications. Day after day the soldiers labored, digging and building and preparing, creating a line of works that would eventually extend more than ten miles and completely surround the city. This line, called a circumvallation, was a daunting prospect, but not extraordinary to Caesar's men. Indeed, it was a standard siege tactic, for it provided the besieging army with the shelter of fortifications and walls against an enemy sortie, and also served to restrict access of even scouts and individual messengers who might try to enter or leave the besieged.

Once again, while the Romans worked, it was the cavalry that skirmished. Vercingetorix sent his horsemen out into the plain that lay before the city, a great swarm of riders charging with thunderous noise from the enemy camps below the city wall. The men, who had been working quickly like Titus, seized up their shields, helmets, and javelins, which they had kept nearby, and the cohorts assembled to meet the attack.

But it was the German horsemen, Caesar's faithful auxiliaries, that bore the brunt of the fighting. They rode against the Gauls with a fierce clash of barbarian howls and smashing steel. Despite the enemy's superior numbers, the Germans—with the legion infantry standing firm to guard their flanks—turned back the charging Gauls. When the defenders retreated up the hill, the Germans, urged on by the cheers of thousands of watching legionaries, pursued with a vengeance, hacking many of the enemy riders from their saddles. A great panic ensued as the Gauls tried to push their way into the city and camp, which were only accessible through a few narrow gates. The German riders wrought fearful butchery against these tightly packed and frightened Gauls. When the auxiliary cavalry finally rode back down the hill, they brought many of the Gauls' horses with them as prizes.

After that, the Gauls seemed content to sit on their height and watch the Romans work. The month of Sextilus ended and September, which in this year—since the calendar had not been adjusted for a number of years—was the middle of summer, began. As the sappers dug and the carpenters built, the extent of Caesar's fortification began to take shape, and it was impressive indeed. The initial barrier was a trench some twenty feet deep and twenty feet across. This barrier would eventually encircle the entire city, but even before it was completed the rest of the formidable line of circumvallation began to take shape.

Some four hundred feet outside of the first trench, and thus farther from the city than the initial ditch, the legionaries dug a second trench, equal in depth and width to the first. Immediately beyond the second trench they erected an earthen wall to a height of more than twelve feet in the air. The top of this wall was crowned with a wooden palisade, a series of wooden stakes woven into a tight barrier by the same type of posts and leather straps as were used to fasten together the stakes of the camp palisade. At frequent intervals—about eighty feet—along the high, flat wall top of the palisade the Romans erected tall turrets, wooden structures that Titus couldn't help thinking of as "birds' nests."

Each turret rested atop a square structure of sturdy posts, rising some twenty feet above the palisade. The support posts were braced with an X pattern of supports, and each turret was surrounded by woven branches, enough to form a barrier against arrows, spears, stones, and other weapons. (It was this network of branches that reminded Titus of a bird's nest.) Many of these turrets were topped with a second, even higher platform above. Each turret formed a secure fighting position for as many as twenty-five or thirty men.

Rising a little higher than the waist of a typical legionary, the branches surrounding the turret provided protection against attack from below, and still allowed the men manning the platform to throw javelins and other missiles down upon any enemy swarming into range. Furthermore, given their lofty vantage, the turrets allowed the legionaries to see a great distance across the field. The turrets were always manned by sentries, and as such, the Romans were able to keep a watchful eye upon the Gauls, and to report upon enemy movements long before they impacted the legions' defenses.

But even then, Caesar's circumvallation was not complete. Thousands of men went to work to make sure that the four-hundred-foot gap between the two trenches would be very deadly indeed for any Gaul who was attempting to cross it in a hurry. The base of the palisade on the earthen wall was lined with a thick tangle of sharpened stakes, all pointing outward as a stark deterrent to any foe climbing the steep slope of the earthen wall. More trenches extended across the interval between the two main depths, and these the Romans lined with sharpened stakes. They were not so deep as the massive gaps of the main barriers, but they were excavated in multiple rows, as many as five of them one after the other. The legionaries called these *cinni*, and they were steep-sided and treacherous enough that any man trying to cross from one to the next ran the risk of falling, which would almost certainly result in impalement on the sharpened stakes.

Even further, Caesar instructed his men to dig many cone-shaped pits across the space between the two great trenches. Into each of these, a stout stake with a fire-hardened, very sharp tip was emplaced, buried deeply into the ground so that it couldn't be easily moved or pulled up. The Romans piled loose brush around these stakes and then concealed the pits with a scattering of dirt and leaves, so that a careless or hasty Gaul could easily step on the false ground, thinking it was solid, only to fall down and meet the business end of the very sharp stake. These traps the legionaries called "lilies," because they saw a resemblance to that blossom in the deep cones with their central spikes.

As the fortifications neared completion, Caesar instructed his engineers to divert the streams into the forward trenches. This was accomplished over the course of a single day, so that both sides of the circumvallation, where the trenches followed the low, flat ground at the base of the hill, were quickly rendered into watery moats.

It was the night after that first moat was filled that the Romans were awakened by a loud commotion in the darkness. The men quickly armed and girded themselves, and marched out of the camp to form along the earthen rampart. In the darkness they could see little, but sounds of galloping horses and, occasionally, yells and clashing swords rang through the night.

Titus happened to have sentry duty in one of the turrets that night, so he had a better view than most. The city of Alesia was dark, but when the clouds parted to allow a wash of moonlight across the field, he saw a great swarm of horsemen moving across the sward, toward an opening where the line of circumvallation had not yet been completed. German cavalry rode in from the flank, and there was a confusing melee whirling across much of the ground. Gradually Titus perceived that the Gallic cavalry was fleeing the field—and not in the direction of the fortress.

"What can you see up there?" called a legionary from the cohort arrayed below him.

"It looks like the enemy horsemen are fleeing the siege," he shouted back. "Our Germans are giving them a few pokes to hurry them along the way!"

His guess was confirmed in the morning light, when they could see that the large cavalry camp, where the horses had been tethered below the earthen rampart outside of Alesia proper, was virtually empty. A great many rumors swirled through the ranks of the legions, as the men speculated about the departure of the enemy cavalry, and whether this was an act of cowardice or some new subterfuge intended to turn the tables on the implacable, determined Romans.

As usual, it was Caesar who would provide the answer.

* * *

"My bold legionaries!" proclaimed the army general, as he once again addressed the entire complement of his Roman army. "We are causing the enemy great consternation. We have learned, through prisoners and traitors, that rations grow short in Alesia, and that Vercingetorix still fears to come forward and face us, and our works."

This assertion, though not surprising, was greeted with a rousing cheer. Caesar, standing on the raised platform from which he typically addressed his troops, gestured to the great fortification around him, the wall that now extended some eleven miles, and completely encircled not just the city of Alesia, but the entire hill upon which that place resided.

"You all know that the enemy has sent his cavalry away, the horsemen escaping just before our circumvallation was concluded. We took prisoners from those fleeing riders, and from them we have learned of the enemy's newest intention."

The summer morning was still, the barest of breeze rustling through the grass, and even then this noise was louder than any sound made by one of the eagerly listening legionaries.

"Vercingetorix has sent his horsemen back to their homelands, and there he has ordered them to recruit many more warriors. He expects this great host to arrive in a matter of weeks, and when it arrives it will smite us upon the outside of our wall, while the enemy general leads his besieged troops against our works."

Titus couldn't help but feel a stab of fear at this announcement for he, like every other Roman in the great legion army, knew that their extensive ramparts, while virtually impermeable to attack from within the city, offered no protection from assault outside of the ring. Mutters of disquiet simmered through the ranks, and Caesar let the men absorb this knowledge for a moment, before he outlined the rest of his plan.

"Bold legionaries, valorous citizens of Rome!" he cried, his words carried thunderously through the assembly by the series of speakers who repeated the general's words. The approach was a clever appeal: all legionaries were required to be Roman citizens, and this was a point of great pride among them.

"Do they think we are fools? Do they think our works are completed? That we will await their relief army like a harlot awaits her lover in the dark of the night?"

The questions lingered in the air until, as with one voice, the sixty thousand legionaries shouted their response: "No!"

"No, of course not!" the great commander replied. "For I tell you now that we will begin a second ring of fortifications. This will be a line of contravallation, exactly the same in every respect to our siege works, except that it will face outward. And when the Gaul relief army comes, they will face a challenge every bit as daunting as that facing the poor, hungry garrison of Alesia. So I ask you, I beseech you, my children, my legionaries: will you build this line for me?"

This time the answer was "Yes!" and it was shouted so loudly that the roar of the Roman voices echoed and echoed from every one of the surrounding hills.

* * *

The line of contravallation was, as Caesar had declared, similar in every respect to the great circuit of the circumvallation, except that, by necessity since it had to encompass a larger area, it was even longer. Still, it was protected by the same barriers of trenches and an earthen wall, with a wooden palisade, stakes, and turrets guarding the outer wall as well. The space between the trenches was pocked with the *cinni* and lilies of the deadly man traps.

Four great infantry camps were placed around the periphery of the twin lines, between the two walls, so that many cohorts could be rushed in a matter of minutes to any threatened section. The legionaries felt a certain urgency as they worked on the outer ring of works, knowing that a large Gallic relief army was on the way, but this in no way provoked hasty construction or shortcuts. Instead, they labored with typical Roman efficiency, and as the month of September neared its end, the great line of contravallation, some fourteen miles in length, was completed.

Caesar's entire army was now protected by two rings of fortifications, one facing in toward Alesia, the other facing outward toward all the rest of Gaul. Many foraging parties had secured cattle, sheep, and even venison to feed the army, as well as great stocks of wheat and other grain. All these stockpiles were held in the safe space between the two massive walls.

In contrast to the well-supplied Romans, the Gauls within Alesia were obviously beginning to suffer greatly. Desertions became more common, with at least a few member of Vercingetorix's army slipping away every night. These were taken directly to Caesar, and they invariably reported that the people in the city were living on very short rations, and that Alesia would not be able to survive for long.

At the same time, cavalry scouts reported that a great host of Gauls, perhaps as many as a quarter million men, was gathering on the march, closing in upon the city. It was left to the Romans only to watch, and to wait.

* * *

"Look! The city gates open!" cried a lookout on one hot, sultry morning. The alarm came from a high turret and was audible all along the rampart below.

Titus Mocius happened to be among the cohort standing duty on the interior wall. He joined his comrades at the rampart, looking upward at the sturdy bulwark of Alesia on its hilltop. He saw a great throng of people emerging from the nearest gate, and more of them coming out of other gates. A strange, keening sound rode down from the heights, carried by the summer breeze.

It did not sound like a battle cry. When Titus looked closer, watching as the file of Gauls continued to stream out of the city, he began to realize that this was not a sortie, or any kind of attack. For one thing, he saw no sign of arms, shields, or helmets among the approaching crowd. As they descended closer, he saw that a great many of them were women, and that even children were mixed into the crowd, often being held by the hand. Other Gauls were clearly elderly, some tottering on canes or staves, others being helped along by their sturdier neighbors.

And as that keening sound grew louder, he realized that it was the noise made by many people weeping, crying in terror and despair. They advanced without spirit or urgency, but did continue down the hill, making their way toward the Roman works. They paused at the watery moat, following along their side of the diverted stream, right toward the section where Titus, his cohort, and the rest of *Legio VIII* stood watching.

It took a long time for the Gallic noncombatants to approach the wall. Some of them were halted by the deep ditch, for they carried no ladders or ropes, or other climbing tools. Eventually a few youths scrambled through the trench, extending cloaks and trousers as makeshift ties to pull several women and an elderly, though spry, man along behind them. This vanguard started across the open space between the two trenches, though the Gauls halted in consternation when a youth toppled into one of the lilies and was badly gored by the concealed stake in its conical pit.

The rest of them advanced with care then, probing the ground in front of them, slowly shuffling around the concealed pits so that no one else fell in. Finally they drew up before the second trench, barely a hundred feet from, and some distance below, the watchful legionaries on the high, sturdy rampart.

Titus felt a stab of pity as he looked at the weeping Gauls. Several of the women were not unattractive, save for the grief that twisted their features. One pulled her filthy robe aside to bare her breasts and shouted something in her guttural native tongue. The Roman soldiers watched silently, appraisingly.

It was the spry old man who at last stepped to the fore and called out to the Romans, speaking a decent Latin.

"Soldiers of Caesar!" he called. "We come to you and offer ourselves as slaves! Take us into your camp. Only feed us and give us shelter, and we will serve you faithfully through the end of our days."

"Why don't you serve Vercingetorix?" demanded a centurion. "Did he not shelter you in his own camp?"

"It is Vercingetorix who turned us out of our own city. We are the Mandubii, but we did not invite the army into our city. Now they have eaten every grain of corn we owned, and they have turned us out of our own homes! Please, admit us—take us as your slaves!"

There was a rumble of excitement among the legionaries, and Titus turned to see the great man, Caesar himself, climbing the ladder to the high rampart. He strode along, the sun brightening his red gold hair like a corona, his red cloak swirling smartly around his trim, fit physique. He came up to the palisade barely a dozen paces away from Titus, and for long moments he stared over the stake wall, studying the miserable Gauls below with an expression as cold as the glaciers that had flanked the army on its long winter march through the Alps.

"Go back to your city!" he ordered at last, his words snapping through the air like breaking sticks. "We have neither room nor food for you here! You speak sweet words of surrender—but you should have taken up these thoughts at the start of this season, when you were yet at peace with Rome.

"Now you have chosen the pathway of war! You Mandubii, like so many of the Gauls, turned steel and fire against the Romans who sought only trade and friendship with your people! Now you must reap the crop that you sowed. The harvest of blood and starvation is upon you! Go back to your city, or my soldiers will kill you where you stand!"

"But—great Caesar!" the old man implored. "Vercingetorix will not let us return!"

"Then go back to the field below your city. But know this: if you stand in the shadow of my walls, you will perish!" Caesar replied.

The elderly Gaul raised both hands, while behind him the women wept even more loudly, one of them falling to her knees, another pulling at her hair. Caesar said something to the legionary beside him, and that soldier hoisted his *pilum*—one of the short javelins capable of long, accurate flight, rather than the longer version most useful in close-order battle—and cast the weapon toward the miserable Gauls. Titus couldn't tell if the man was going for the kill or merely to warn, but the weapon stuck into the dirt a bare footstep in front of the old man.

Apparently convinced, the elder and his escort of women and children started a retreat across the field of traps and trenches, making their way only with great difficulty back to the great mob of refugees that had continued to gather on the far side of the first, deep trench. As word spread through that crowd, the sounds of wailing grew louder, until it seemed to Titus as if a great host of buzzing insects swarmed there. But the people turned from the Roman works and slowly made their way back toward Alesia.

The gates of the city remained closed, even as they drew near. Titus felt a burning contempt for the Gauls who would turn their own people out so cruelly, but he felt no regrets about denying them access to the Roman camp. Certainly the legions didn't have food to spare! Nor did they have need of new slaves, not now, in the midst of the campaign.

And even as he absorbed these truths, the campaign moved to its next step. He heard the alarms, shouts and cries and horns, blaring from the outer ramparts. When he looked over the field, and its three-mile sweep away from Alesia and the Roman works, he saw that the Gallic relief army was marching into view.

His first thought was that he had never seen so many human beings gathered together in one place. The Gauls swept over and around one of the large hills flanking the plain around Alesia. On top of the crest he saw hundreds of chieftains, each on horseback, distinguished by his own banner. Below them, spreading out like water spilling through a broken dam, the host of the Gallic army spilled forward and spread across the plain. Barely a mile from the outer Roman wall, the line of contravallation, they began to pitch their tents and to form their vast, city-sized camp.

"Looks like the waiting is over," mumbled a legionary next to Titus on the wall. Pushing his helmet down firmly onto his head, the young soldier could only agree.

* * *

The next day the whole of the Gallic relief force marched out of its camp and formed up on the wide plain, below the hill of Alesia and outside of the double line of Roman fortifications. The Gauls shouted and banged their weapons against their shields, while from within the besieged city a great shout went up. On this day Titus had been posted in one of the turret towers, a position far enough up the slope of the hill that, even though he was on the inner wall, he was afforded a good view in both directions.

The first thing he noticed was a force of many thousands of Gauls spilling down the hill from Alesia toward the first of the deep Roman trenches. These Gauls bore shovels and picks, and immediately set to work filling in the trench in several places, quickly creating wide earthen roadways over which a sallying force could move quickly and form up within three hundred feet of the line of circumvallation.

On the outside of the line, Caesar's German cavalry sallied from the series of forts on the low end of the line where they had bivouacked. Titus saw the bold horsemen, wholly and utterly outnumbered, advance toward the Gallic riders. The Gauls whooped and surged forward, and two great throngs of cavalry swept toward each other like waves churning across a sandy beach.

Before the clash, however, the Gauls broke formation, their riders sweeping away from the Germans. The maneuver revealed a great host of archers, men on foot who had been concealed by their allied cavalry. Even from a mile away Titus could see the cloud of arrows rising into the air, and he imagined the pain of those deadly missiles striking like a shower of rain among the Germans. Many a rider fell from his horse, and many of the horses bucked and shrieked, turning in pain and panic to bolt from this surprising threat.

Caesar's horsemen were not dismayed by the onslaught, however, and instead charged vigorously toward the veering Gallic cavalry. The enemy riders continued to sweep away, and in this maneuver they revealed another rank of infantry—this time disciplined men carrying long javelins, like pikes, which they braced against the ground to meet the onrushing Germans. Again many of the latter fell, while others were turned away, and now the whole of the Gaul relief army surged forward, striving to sweep around the German horsemen, to destroy this potent arm of the Roman force.

As the friendly cavalry fell back, escaping from the encircling wings of the Gallic army, Titus turned his attention back to the interior of the walls. Thousands of Gauls were visible there, still actively filling in the far trench, but thus far they had made no move to charge en masse across the intervening space. Several individuals ran forward, howling and jeering, and many of these fell into the concealed lily traps. Those who survived ran to within a hundred and fifty feet of the Roman palisade, where they taunted and jeered, but made no attempt to come closer.

Several burly legionaries threw their javelins at the venturesome Gauls, who quickly retreated, and Titus felt certain that, for now at least, the interior wall of the Roman fortification was spared from direct assault. The lethal *pila*, as usual, proved to be among the most effective weapons in the legionaries' arsenal. The javelins were made in two types, a lighter, shorter weapon that could be thrown for as much as two hundred feet with lethal force, and a heavier *pilum* that could puncture armor and shields with the weight of its punch. Each type included a bronze head, spade-shaped, on the tip of a long shaft of wood. They were designed so that the heads bent or broke free from the shaft on impact, so that an enemy could not simply pull a javelin out of the ground and turn it around to throw back at the Romans. When cast against venturesome Gauls, they either struck their targets with bloody force, or caused the enemy warriors to hastily back out of range.

The cavalry fight on the plain was a different matter, however, as the Gaul and German horsemen kept swirling around each other, darting and probing and charging and pulling back in an elaborate, and very deadly, dance. Abruptly, guided by some unseen, unheard command, the riders of Caesar's auxiliary formed together in a tight, compact mass, many thousand strong. Spinning like creatures of one mind, they charged directly toward the Gallic horsemen which, though still superior in number, couldn't stand against this lethal, concentrated assault.

As the enemy horsemen broke and fled, their flight revealed the vast body of archers, suddenly exposed by their cavalry's abrupt withdrawal. The archers had no time to ready their weapons before the Germans were upon them, and the big riders hacked about with great enthusiasm, butchering hundreds of the bowmen, exacting vengeance for their injured and slain comrades in a score of perhaps ten to one.

By then, the sun was setting across the valley and hilltop of Alesia. The weary Gauls retreated to their camp while the Germans, hooting and shouting victoriously, rode back into the enclosures of the cavalry camp.

And within the walls, the starving, weary garrison of Alesia could only return to the city, shoulders slumping, weary looks glancing with despair toward the vast host of their relief force . . . the great army that had come so near, but still remained out of reach.

* * *

"Get up—they're making a night attack!"

Titus heard the alarm and was instantly awake. Like his fellow legionaries, he'd been sleeping in his sandals and his cloak, so he had only to clap on his helmet, snatch up his shield and his weapons, and he was ready to charge to battle.

Once again his cohort was assigned the interior wall. He scrambled up the ladder to the rampart, holding two *pila* in his right hand, and quickly joined his comrades at the wooden palisade. No sooner had he stepped up to the barrier of posts than the man next to him grunted and fell to the ground. Kneeling beside him, Titus saw that he'd been pierced through the throat with an arrow. There was nothing to do for him; the young legionary could only stand at his post and listen to the gasping, gurgling sounds of his comrade's dying breath.

The sounds of battle at the outer wall rang through the night, a virtual storm of noise. Men screamed in pain and roared out challenges. Massive bangs and crashes echoed, indicating the force of heavy objects, perhaps rams, smashing into the sturdy palisade. Torches flared into light, and from his position Titus thought that the skirmish raged along more than a mile's length of the outer wall.

"Look sharp there, men—remember your duties!" snapped a centurion from nearby, and Titus quickly turned his attention to his own front.

Broken clouds scuttled across the face of a gibbous moon, and in the pale light he could see thousands of Gauls crowding the space beyond the innermost trench. They were filing across the earthen bridges that they had filled in during the previous sortie, and starting to move cautiously across the trap-filled field. Frequent shouts of alarm, and occasional screams of real pain, rang out from the besieged warriors as many of them slipped into the lilies. The lucky ones crawled out again; the unlucky were left to bleed to death, pierced by the deadly, fire-hardened tips of the concealed stakes.

Here and there the attackers, moving with a strange hesitancy, approached the final trench and the palisade wall. Titus saw a few of these Gauls carrying planks, and these they laid across the serrated lines of ditches protecting the approach to the final, deep trench. The attackers crossed these narrow bridges boldly, but even in the faint moonlight they made tempting targets, and the legionaries on the walls showered the makeshift crossings with *pila*. Many of the javelins found targets, and frequently the wounded attacker lost his balance and toppled, screaming, into the narrow ditch with its additional row of sharpened stakes at the bottom.

In one place, a dozen Gauls actually scrambled through the final trench, carrying ladders that they used to emerge from the side nearest the palisade. They struggled up the steep, earthen slope only to get tangled in the horizontal stakes lining the bottom of the palisade. Before they could extricate themselves, every one of these bold adversaries was pierced by a dozen or more javelins.

Whether it was hunger, weakness, or just the formidable defenses, Titus couldn't tell. In any event, it seemed clear that the Gauls who'd been besieged in Alesia lacked the strength and will to press home a vigorous attack. The Romans lining the wall took turns using the most venturesome enemy warriors for target practice, and within a half hour of the attack's commencement, not a single Gaul seemed willing to advance within range of the legionaries' weapons.

To judge from the sound, that was not the case on the outer wall, however. The sounds of battle there included the unmistakable clash of steel against steel, which could only mean that some of the Gauls had scaled the palisade and gotten close enough to use their swords. Titus, and many of his comrades, felt more and more isolated, knowing that the real battle was going on behind them.

As if sensing their desire, one of Caesar's legates, the tall, imposing captain called Mark Antony, shouted up to the men of Titus Mocius's cohort. "You men! March down here—and make haste! We're going to shore up the outer line!"

The legionaries responded with alacrity, several cohorts of

the Eighth Legion marching down from the wall. They hastened through the interior line, where slaves awaited them and handed out extra *pila* as quickly as the men moved past. Within a few minutes, they were climbing up the wall of contravallation where, true to Titus's guess, a violent skirmish raged. The young legionary found himself in the front rank as Mark Antony, grinning like a wild man, ordered the cohort forward.

"Charge!" he bellowed, in a voice like a trumpet. "Sweep the barbarians from the walls!"

The Romans advanced at a sprint. In the wild mixture of light from the moon and from hundreds of flaring torches, they could see that an entire section of the wall had been claimed by the Gauls. The enemy now charged en masse, whooping and howling, toward Titus and his cohort.

"Halt! Cast away!" cried Antony, and, as one man, the charging legionaries came to a stop. Titus cast his first *pilum*, sending the shaft along with a cloud of his comrades' missiles, right into the faces of the charging Gauls.

"Again!" cried the legate, and the Romans launched a second volley. Many of the deadly, bronze-tipped missiles stuck in the Gallic shields, their weight causing the enemy warriors to cast away their encumbered protection, while others pierced Gaul flesh, crippling and even killing many of the enemy soldiers.

"Now close! Put steel to them!" ordered Mark Antony.

Titus shouted fiercely, his voice blending with four hundred of his comrades' as the cohort, in tightly closed formation, rushed the mob of furious, but disorganized, Gauls. His *gladius* was in his hand, and he remembered his training, keeping the hilt low, even as he hacked and gouged and stabbed into the thronging mass of barbarians. The shock of the close-ordered cohort was too much for the attackers, and wounded Gauls fell from the interior of the wall, or were trampled under Roman sandals. A few survivors spilled out through the breach they had broken in the palisade, but within a few minutes the men of Antony's relief force met up with another cohort, coming at them from the opposite direction.

By the time dawn brightened the eastern horizon, the wall was free of Gauls, and a million crows came cawing into the valley, eager to feast on the thousands of barbarian bodies littering more than a mile of the battlefield.

* * *

Another day passed in peace, while the enemy licked his wounds, and the Romans rebuilt their line of contravallation where it had been damaged in the night attack. The legionaries were cautiously confident, for the enemy had been checked in every quarter.

Until the following day, when the third attack began, and almost immediately the enemy gained a startling, even shocking, advantage.

"There's a gap in the wall—the Gauls are coming through there!"

The cry echoed through the camp as the swarm of barbarians, more than a hundred thousand strong, hurled themselves at the outer wall. At the same time, the entire garrison of Alesia spilled out of the city, rushing through the trenches and traps and moats, desperation driving them into a frenzy as they fought to force their way into the line of circumvallation.

Titus paced along the wall, and looked across the moat, toward the northern sweep of the line of contravallation. He saw the weakness at once: a deep, steep-sided ravine marked the space between two hills. There the ground was simply too steep and rocky for the Romans to erect their defensive line, and, consequently, a narrow, thus far unseen gap had been left between the inner and outer lines.

Now, apparently, the enemy had discovered the gap and were taking advantage of the opening. Hundreds of bearded Gauls were already charging into the space between the two Roman walls, and legates and lieutenants were mustering two legions into position to block the sudden, unanticipated breakthrough.

At the same time, the Gauls under Vercingetorix smashed like a relentless ocean surge at the interior Roman wall. They assaulted in many places along the line, but clearly made their greatest effort against the place where the outer wall had already been breached. It was here that *Legio VIII* made its stand, and here where Titus hurled javelin after javelin, launching so many of the lethal missiles that his arm grew sore. In the teeming mob of Gauls below it seemed that every *pilum* found a target of flesh, but for every barbarian killed two more advanced to take his place.

After almost an hour, the attackers were beaten back from the near wall, but no sooner had the Romans of *Legio VIII* started to catch their breath than they were ordered to quick march to a new sector of the interior wall, where the Gauls had started to hack away the palisade and many of the original legionaries had been killed. Titus and his cohort once again swept in to the attack and cleared off the barbarians, though not before more than a dozen valiant Romans had been slain.

And even then there was no respite. When Titus looked to the interior space, the formerly protected gap between the two walls, he saw thousands of Gauls spilling through the gap, the tide of attackers barely held back by the flimsy dike formed by two battered, but still disciplined, legions.

"You there! *Legio VIII!* Follow me!"

The men turned as one to see that it was Caesar himself calling to them. The general sat astride a frothing horse and waved an imperious arm. Immediately Titus and his comrades followed the great man, forming into a column of cohorts on the run, jogging at double speed behind Caesar as he rode through the Roman camps. He summoned more and more men to him, until he had assembled some fifteen cohorts.

Only then did he lead them to one of the gates in the wall of contravallation. Without question the legionaries followed their general, moving *outside* of their massive fortification, forming into lines of battle on the open field. Caesar, his red cloak unmistakable, sat calmly astride his horse at the front of the formation and ordered the Romans into the attack.

With a roar, the fifteen cohorts advanced, marching in precise lines, their formation open enough to allow Caesar and a number of other officers to ride between the regular, tight blocks formed by the men of each cohort. From the walls of the fortifications, thousands more Romans saw their general make his bold sortie, and they added their voices to the roaring accolades that accompanied those fifteen cohorts into the attack.

Again Titus was in the front rank as his cohort smashed against the army of Gaul. It mattered not to him that he was one of less than ten thousand men attacking many times their number—what mattered was that his general had chosen him, and he would fight, and prevail, or die, for the glory of Rome.

Just as the flank attack ignited the passion of the hard-pressed defenders, it shocked and dismayed the Gauls. The great barbarian army had been on the brink of victory less than an hour before, but the sudden sally, the courageous attack, and the precisely lethal legionaries goring into their exposed flank all proved too much for the valorous, but shaken, Gauls.

The attackers broke and fled, the massive army scattering in every direction, many of the tribesmen fleeing the battle entirely, ignoring their camp as they hastened, in their panic, running directly toward their homelands. The German cavalry swept after them, and the slaughter was epic, and exhausting. Caesar would later remark that if not for the setting of the sun and the weariness of his men, every living Gaul might have perished on that bloody day.

At last the legionaries, flushed with victory and exhausted from the long pursuit, returned to their camps. It would be another day or two before Vercingetorix emerged from Alesia to offer himself in surrender to Gaius Julius Caesar, but already on the night following that bloody day the Romans understood the historic truth:

The Gallic rebellion was over, and the great nation of Rome had just gained its richest, and most important, province.

"All hail Caesar!" cried the legionaries, as their general finally accepted the armor and weapons of Vercingetorix. The enemy commander was placed in a cage and would be taken to Rome, where he would be executed at the grand triumph commemorating Caesar's victory.

And perhaps, a few of the more thoughtful legionaries perceived another truth. Caesar would return to resistance and civil war, and the legions' victory at Alesia would carry him to the ultimate victory, the victory that would signal the end of the Roman Republic.

For the time of the Roman Empire had arrived.

Knight of the
Third Crusade

With Richard in the Holy Land

BY KAREN DE WINTER

As the civilization that supported the legion faltered and failed, warfare changed. Armies grew smaller and the individual soldier more important. The introduction of the stirrup and metalworking also brought about the rise of armored cavalry. The Byzantine cataphract evolved into the knight. For more than five hundred years armored horsemen were the heart of any European army.

KAREN DE WINTER has worked on a number of British archaeological sites dating to the age of Chivalry and before. She is a full-time researcher.

[✳]

Third Crusade

God has conferred upon you above all other nations great
glory in arms. Accordingly, undertake this journey eagerly
for the remission of your sins, with the assurance of the
reward of imperishable glory in the kingdom of heaven.

—POPE URBAN II

When Pope Urban spoke these words at the Council of Clermont
in 1095, he had no way of knowing their impact. His pronounce-
ment launched the Crusades, one of the most volatile campaigns in
the history of warfare. Originally initiated as a rescue mission to
aid Byzantium and free the city of Jerusalem from the grip of the
Seljuk Turks, the Crusades would later become a war against two
opposing religious forces. These holy wars would last two hundred
years and would come to define the medieval knight, the Western
world's quintessential warrior.

The medieval knight embodied the perfect ideal of what a soldier should strive to be. Chivalry gave birth to a code of ethics and
honor still embraced by modern armed forces. Principles like in-
tegrity, virtue, valor, and bravery in battle have been permanently
etched into the soldier's psyche. But what was this standard bearer
of the medieval moral majority really like, and did he live his life
by the values set forth in the code of chivalry?

A Long Time Ago in a Land Far Away . . .

In July 1189 King Henry II dies, leaving the Holy City of Jerusalem in the hands of the infidels. The Angevin family feud that marked Henry II's reign delayed earlier attempts to recapture the holy city. The coronation of Richard I ushered in a new era of potential peace within the family and offered new hope to those seeking to recapture the jewel of the desert.

But to Richard, the new crown was simply a means to an end. His true obsession was to regain the Holy Land. He immediately took steps to quell his family's feud, lest it threaten his plans. Shortly after his coronation on September 3, he showed enormous generosity to his brother John, by giving him six English counties worth about £4,000, as well as the county of Mortain in Normandy. And, as if this weren't enough, Richard gave Isabel of Gloucester, his fourth cousin, to John in marriage. This made John very powerful, though not enough to attain the throne . . . just yet. Richard also arranged for his illegitimate half brother, Geoffrey, to be elected Archbishop of York, thus eliminating any possibility of him ever laying claim to the throne. With his political rear now covered in England, Richard set his sights on Jerusalem and his dream of liberating the holy city.

But this dream would be expensive—the most expensive campaign to date. Excesses during earlier Crusades led the Church to believe that the Holy Land was lost due to the extravagances and lasciviousness of the knights and nobles. As early as 1130, Bernard of Clairvaux wrote:

> "You drape your horses in silk, and plume your armor with I
> know not what sort of rags; you paint your shields and your
> saddles; you adorn your bits and saddles with gold and silver
> and precious stones, and then in all this pomp, with a shame-

ful wrath and fearless folly, you charge to your death. Are these the trappings of a warrior or are they not the trinkets of a woman?"

In addition to gaudy trappings, previous crusaders supplied themselves by relying on charity and the kindness of strangers. A marvelous Christian concept—on the surface. But these "donations" were rarely given willingly. Armed knights often took what they wanted from helpless peasants at sword point. To counter these excesses, a council established in Le Mans created a set of laws to govern the behavior of the crusading knights. As a result, any new campaign would be bound by the new laws, which meant they not only had to follow strict rules of conduct, they also had to pay for themselves. Richard knew, from his studies of previous crusades, that starvation and lack of proper equipment were a major cause of failure. Richard was determined to avoid those mistakes by ensuring that his troops were well armed, well fed, and well prepared. This made the venture even more costly. Fortunately, Richard the Lion Heart had one valuable commodity: England.

Richard ruled England, but he wasn't very fond of the land or its people. He considered the English uncouth and barbarous, not at all like the sophisticated Provincials from his beloved duchy of Aquitaine. So he used England as his personal bankroll, selling offices, lordships, earldoms, castles, towns, shires . . . everything. "I'd sell London itself if I could find anyone rich enough to buy it," he once quipped. As it turned out, he did not need to sell London, he could just raise taxes.

All over England, as well as the French provinces, he imposed the *Dime Saladin* or Ordinance of the Saladin Tithe. It was the highest levy ever inflicted on England, requiring that each man give one-tenth of his revenue and movable property to the church in order to help finance the crusade. Each man delivered his tithe to his local parish in the presence of the priest, a dean of the church, a clerk of the bishop, a servant of the local baron and the baron's clerk, a servant of the king and the king's clerk, one Knight Hospitaller and one Knight Templar.

Those who did not pay risked severe penalties. Anyone, including knights and lords, caught slacking, found themselves summoned before a jury of four to six lawful men from the parish. This jury's testimony decided the penalty to be paid, adding it to the amount already paid by the accused. If that wasn't bad enough, they usually faced excommunication as well. In a society where heaven and hell were quite real, damnation had to be avoided at all costs.

The tithe included some exceptions. A knight's horses, arms, garments, or other "tools of the trade" were exempt, lest his duties suffer. Clerical accoutrements used in divine service, such as vestments and books, remained equally untouched. But for the average person, these exceptions proved meaningless, and the "tax" became a heavy burden to bear.

But there was a way out. Anyone participating in the crusade did not have to tithe. As a result, many men took up the cross in order to avoid financial ruin. Of course, going on crusade had its own costs. Any man of means was expected to provide the bulk of his own expenses. Freemen all over Europe began selling off their assets in order to cover the cost of joining the crusade.

So how much was this?

Few sources of the time detail the expense. While a well-heeled noble might manage the cost without totally stripping his coffers, a less well-off noble had to generate four times his yearly income to meet two years of expenses while on crusade.

A Common Knight for an Uncommon Cause

Enter William Beaumont, an English knight of Norman descent of a small fief in Norfolk. His father, Hugh de Beaumont, had held the land as a *fief-rente* from Roger Deveraux, vassal to William de Blois, the fourth Earl of Warenne. Vassals were required to supply a certain number of knights (in Roger's case twenty-five) and foot soldiers to their lord during military campaigns. *Fief-rentes* were often paid to knights in lieu of money for their service, but the knight also had to swear an oath of homage and fealty to his lord. Thus, when King Richard decided to go to war, he summoned his nobles to provide knights and troops to go with him. This was "the draft" of its time. William inherited both the land and the obligation upon his father's death.

William owed fealty to Roger Deveraux's son, Charles, and to the current Earl of Warenne, Hamelin Plantagenet. Hamelin was the son of Geoffrey Plantagenet, which made him the illegitimate half brother of the late King Henry and the uncle of King Richard. He was known for his generosity and decided to ease the burden of many of his knights by donating funds to help subsidize the cost of their campaign. This contribution helped William Beaumont, but it was not enough. William sold many of his household items, his oxen, and his milk cows. He used the money to buy more weapons and three horses.

William needed at least three horses for himself so that two would always be rested and ready in reserve as remounts while he rode a third. He also needed horses for his squires. It took a special horse to bear a knight into battle, especially in harsh conditions. In William's time, horses were bred for specific tasks. William Beaumont probably chose a horse known as a *rouncy* for his campaigns. Unlike the larger, specialized *chargers* or *coursers* of the mid-thirteenth century, bred to carry knights in full-plate armor, the *rouncy* was a good all-purpose mount—the SUV of its day. These horses stood around fourteen to fifteen hands (four inches to a hand) high as opposed to the seventeen-hand *great horse* of later periods.

A knight such as William rode his horse using a basic practical style. Mounted in a saddle with a high cantle behind and a high pommel in front to hold him securely in position, he would place his feet in the stirrups, legs extended fully, and point his toes to lock himself in place. This was the original "lock and load." For protection he wore a kite-shaped shield on his left arm, leaving his right arm free to wield lance or sword. Thus anchored deep in his bucket seat he rode into battle at a brisk trot.

Each of William Beaumont's horses consumed two and a half kilograms of grain and seven kilograms of forage daily. The brutal conditions of the campaign made managing such large quantities of feed very difficult. King Richard contracted for some of the feed and supplies his men needed, but each noble bore responsibility for procuring the majority of his own provisions. As a result, many horses starved.

The English fleet departed from Dartmouth on Easter Sunday, 1190. William had been eager to get to the Holy Land ever since Jerusalem had been lost three years before to Salah al-Din Yusuf ibn Ayyub, better known as Saladin, the Kurdish king of the Saracens.

Saladin gained Jerusalem by defeating its newly crowned king, Guy de Lusignan, and his poorly provisioned troops on the hot desert sands of Hattin. Guy almost certainly could have withstood Saladin's attack, had he remained behind the thick stone walls of his city. But instead, he chose to face Saladin out in the open, in the blazing sun. Saladin easily defeated the ill prepared defenders, killing the bishop of Acre, capturing the True Cross, and taking Guy prisoner.

William believes that Guy's capture is the only good thing to have come out of the disaster.

Guy de Lusignan had been a player in the Angevin family feud in years before, and William Beaumont had the displeasure of crossing paths with him on several occasions. Guy was arrogant and untrustworthy. His word meant very little, and he would often change allegiances when it suited his ambition.

Guy sided with Richard in his war against Henry II. Henry's queen, Eleanor of Aquitaine, once exiled Guy from his home in Poitou after he attempted to take her hostage. Eleanor was greatly disappointed when Sybilla, Richard's cousin and the sister of Baldwin IV of Jerusalem, decided to take Guy as a husband, thus giving the rogue a claim to the throne of the holy city.

William often refers to Guy as "the buffoon." Well, the buffoon is on the loose, having spent the past two years after his release besieging Acre, locked in a stalemate with Saladin. William is anxious to arrive before the situation turns in Saladin's favor.

Be of Good Virtue

Before leaving Dartmouth, the soldiers and sailors are given strict rules of conduct. If one man kills another, he will be bound to the victim and thrown overboard. If they are not at sea, he will be buried with the dead man. If a man punches another without drawing blood, he will be keelhauled three times. If a man draws his knife against another, his hand will be cut off. Fines will be issued for abusive or blasphemous language, and thieves will be tarred, feathered, and dropped off at the next port. William is not only responsible for his own conduct, he has to make sure his squires and servants obey the rules as well.

William is traveling with the main flotilla of sixty-three ships under the command of Robert de Sable. They safely reach the Tagus River in Portugal but must then wait for the remaining thirty ships under the command of William de Fors. The crew is restless. William decides to join the other knights in going ashore to see Lisbon. He and his two squires, Tom and Roger, disembark. William and his companions make their way through the narrow streets and crowded market, teeming with people unlike themselves, speaking in strange tongues. Smells of spices and incense permeate the air, mixed with the unpleasant, smothering aroma from the slaughter-houses. William looks around the square. Merchandise from all over the known world is for sale: everything from silk, to spices, rugs, garments, wine, and food. The vendors shout in many languages, in perfect accompaniment to the exotic music being played by the street performers. Lisbon has no established religion. It is home to Jews, Muslims, and Christians alike. It is also a center for lawlessness.

William tries his hand at haggling with a local merchant over the price of a rug, with lots of gestures and shouting. Across the square, an English knight slaps a Jewish merchant across the face with the back of his hand. The knight then begins to wreck the market stall. The knight's companions begin wreaking havoc throughout the square, stamping out anyone in their path.

"No! Don't!" shouts William, as he tries to push his way through the stampeding mob to reach the knights. "This is not what God wants!" he shouts, as his fellow knights loot and plunder the square. They take their swords to Jews and Moslems, making no distinction between men, women, and children. They also make sport of raping the local women.

William manages to flee the square, bludgeoning a knight in the back of his head when he tries to kill William's squire, Tom. The other squire, Roger, is nowhere to be seen. Before the night is over, the king of Portugal has the gates to Lisbon closed, trapping hundreds of drunken crusaders inside. He then has them thrown in jail, to keep his subjects safe until the fleet is ready to leave. The remaining thirty ships finally arrive, but the matter of the locked-up crusaders must be settled before the fleet can continue on its journey. The delay keeps the fleet from sailing until July. When they reach Marseille they find that Richard has already left and they must meet him in Messina.

Richard arrives in Messina with great pomp and ceremony in late September. The sound of trumpets and clarions ring throughout the city as the gargantuan fleet drops anchor in the harbor. The sight is magnificent, much to the chagrin of King Philip of France, who arrived one week earlier, virtually unnoticed. Ironically, it is Philip who stays in the royal palace, while Richard camps with his army along the shore. When the rest of the fleet arrives from Marseille, they find they must wait.

Waiting causes unrest among the troops. They have seen very little action apart from the street brawl in Lisbon and they are spoiling for a fight. For the knight on crusade, the deal is simple: go to the Holy Land, meet interesting infidels, and kill them. But for King Richard, the trip also means settling family business in far-off places, this time with the "ugly little bastard," Tancred of Lecce, who just succeeded William II as king of Sicily. Tancred will not release Richard's sister, the recently widowed Queen Joan, or her dowry. A settlement is eventually reached with him, gaining Joan's release, and a million *tari,* plus forty thousand ounces of gold. Richard grudgingly shares one-third of the gold with Philip.

The delay may have been necessary for Richard, but for his men it was costly. Extra time spent dallying meant extra expenses. The knights for hire are not bothered, they still receive their pay. But the vassals and their men are becoming disgruntled. Richard decides to ease their dwindling pocketbooks with great monetary gifts. He also keeps them occupied building heavy siege equipment.

Meanwhile, the Christian armies in Acre are hemmed in by Saladin and are dangerously close to running out of supplies. Reports trickle back that the men are out of their minds with hunger. They throw themselves on the ground and eat the grass. When a horse is killed in the fighting, men descend upon the animal in a frenzy, leaving nothing of the carcass behind. While Richard and Philip spend Christmas in the lap of extreme luxury, the crusading forces besieging Acre are starving to death.

Mediterranean "Vacation" Ends

Early in 1191, Eleanor of Aquitaine arrives with Richard's betrothed, Berengaria of Navarre. It is Lent, so a wedding cannot take place. However, with the arrival of his mother and future bride, Richard sees no reason why he can't set sail. This is the moment William and the other soldiers have been waiting for. Everything is loaded onto the ships, including the siege equipment, horses, treasure, food, and wine. Even Richard's temporary wooden castle of *Mategriffon*, meaning "Kill the Greeks," is dismantled and stowed on the ships. On April 10, 1191, the highly anticipated departure takes place. At long last, the fleet of 219 vessels carrying 17,000 soldiers and sailors sets sail, leaving the Sicilian coast behind. The Sicilians are relieved.

William is traveling on one of the thirty-nine galleys. The conditions are anything but pleasant. The men lie on the passenger deck, practically on top of one another. The ship is perfumed with the sloshing stench of rotten bilgewater. A few fortunate men have hay to rest on, but most have only their cloaks. For drink, there is hot wine. For food, William gets a half bowl of beans and something like a cracker, known in the day as "twice baked bread." Seasickness robs William of his appetite. Many of the other men are also sick and find it too grueling a task to relieve their stomachs overboard. Vomit, bile, and urine now mix their odors with that of the stinky bilgewater.

Come Good Friday, the fleet marks its third day at sea. "This must be what Hell is like," William mutters to himself, trying to cope stoically. "Just as Christ suffered for salvation, I must suffer, too." William is launching into another theological discussion, which his brother in arms, François de Gies, is not eager to hear . . . again.. They have known each other since childhood, and both lived in the castle of Hamelin Plantagenet while undergoing training for knighthood. François looks at William and diverts this tired thread of conversation. "Remember when we were training to be knights?" he asks. And the two men begin to reminisce . . .

As the eldest sons of knights, William and François began their training as pages upon turning eight. They learned how to fight hand-to-hand combat and with spear and sword. They also became proficient at riding horses. "Remember the first time we practiced with the quintain?" François recalls with a chuckle. William laughs a bit, the seasickness still dampening his sprits. The quintain was a heavy sack hung from a pole and shaped like a person holding a shield. The trainee had to hit the shield and move out of the way quickly before the quintain turned full circle and hit him. "Yes, I hit that thing with all my might, only to have it swing around and floor me," William says. "It knocked the wind out of me." François laughs along. "Yes, you lost your first combat to a dummy!"

At the age of fifteen, William and François became squires, acting as valets to their knights—serving them at mealtime, dressing them, and caring for their horses. They assisted their knights at tournaments and on the battlefield. But squires were not servants. They had to continue training with sword and lance, and were expected to wield their weaponry while wearing sixty pounds of armor—on horseback. After these skills were mastered and the squire proved himself worthy, he would be eligible for knighthood. For William, this happened when he twenty years of age. William reflects upon the day with a sense of nostalgia. "That was a proud day," he says.

First, candidates for knighthood were bathed, to symbolize the washing away of their sins. Then they were clothed in white robes, which represented their strength in defending God's laws. A white, narrow belt was tied around their waists to remind them to rebuke the sins of the flesh. The candidates were then given the accoutrements of the knight: the golden spur, to give them courage to serve God, and the sword, to fight the enemy and "protect the poor from the rich."

Finally, their lord, Charles Deveraux, delivered the *colée* to William and François. The lord took his hand and smacked each of them across the side of the head. "This is so you remember *He* who ordained you and dubbed you a knight," Deveraux told them. (It should be noted that *He* refers not to the person performing the knighting ritual, but to God.)

William takes his oath as a knight very seriously. He is pious and is well liked by most. In a time when loyalty is fragile at best and shifts with the death of kings, this is unusual. William is no stranger to these wavering loyalties. During the Angevin family feuds, he served under King Henry II. Now his fealty lies with King Richard. Fortunately for William, Richard doesn't hold a grudge. He rewarded many of the men who fought against him on the side of his father.

Right now, William is wishing Richard would reward him by exempting him from this campaign. This is not what he signed up for. He never expected to be spending this much time in a leaky old tub. The galley begins to rock violently as a storm begins to blow. The crew is running about like madmen, doing everything they can to keep the ship afloat. William sees two galleys collide about two hundred meters off the port bow. Chaos is the order of the day. People jump overboard as the pair of stricken ships sink quickly. They die the lonely death of those lost at sea. William prays for deliverance from the storm.

Come daylight, William and François realize that their ship, along with two others, is on its own. The galleys sail for Cyprus, turning toward Limassol on April 24. Before reaching shore, the ships run aground and break up. William awakens on the beach to see the locals swarming about the wreckage, plundering the supplies. He looks around for other survivors. "François!" he yells. "François!"

"Over here!" François is lying on his back among the strewn-out wreckage. William runs over to him, stumbling as he approaches. He still has his sea legs. William barely has time to assess the situation before he and François are snatched up, bound, and tied to the back of a cart. They are forced to walk for miles and are thrown into a prison fort along with the other survivors. The locals, however, prove no match for well-trained knights and the men are able to escape after only one week in captivity. They eventually make it back to the landing party where they join the other men onboard the remaining ships.

Back in Rhodes, Richard learns that the ship bearing his sister, Joan, and his beloved Berengaria has been spotted near Limassol. The tyrant of Cyprus, Ducas Comnenus has denied them fresh water and permission to disembark. Richard also discovers that supplies have been looted from his wrecked ships. He is furious. He meets up with his ships at Limassol and sends an envoy to Comnenus demanding the return of the looted supplies. The tyrant is less than accommodating. He tells Richard in no uncertain terms to "get stuffed." Richard had not intended to invade Cyprus, but Comnenus has left him little choice.

Richard orders his men to prepare for battle. This is just what William and François have been waiting for, a chance to get even with the Greeks. The men row to shore in small boats. Strategically they are at a disadvantage. The Greeks are waiting for them on the beach. So, Richard's forces will have to disembark and wade through shallow water in order to confront them. There is no time for retreat. Greek archers open fire on them and pepper the oncoming flotilla with arrows. In what seems like an act of God, the arrows fling past Richard, leaving him completely unscathed. Richard's men, on the other hand, are in great danger.

William and François endure a great deal of onslaught from the incoming missiles. Although none of the arrows are able to penetrate their mail coats, their outer surcoats are pocked with arrows. Despite looking like a couple of hedgehogs, they are essentially unharmed. The men on the outside of the flotilla are not so fortunate. Several of them are wounded and three are dead. Richard orders them to divert. The main flotilla finally reaches the shoreline and the men disembark. Richard wades through the water with his sword held high, and leads the assault. He orders crossbowmen to the front of the line. It's payback time.

The crossbow is Richard's secret weapon. It required little training to use and was accurate up to two hundred yards. It was also quite deadly. A crossbow bolt could punch through a shield and penetrate mail armor. Crossbowmen did not need to stand and could fire from undercover using a *pavise*. These oversized shields were propped up on a type of kickstand, allowing the shooter to pick off targets through a notch in the top. The crossbow was considered so deadly that Pope Innocent II outlawed its use against Christians in 1139. This does not stop Richard from using them against non-Catholic Christians in 1191. The crossbowmen easily take out the enemy front line. Richard and his men charge the Greeks, setting them to flight. Then they occupy the town and "liberate" much needed supplies.

Richard discovers that Isaac Comnenus has set up camp miles away and decides to launch a night raid. Hugo de la Mare, a clerk, reminds Richard that they are greatly outnumbered. Richard turns to Hugo and bellows, "Sir, clerk, you stick to your writing and leave chivalry to us." The raid goes better than planned. Richard's men easily overtake the enemy, sending Isaac Comnenus running without his clothes. The looted supplies are recaptured along with Comnenus's royal standard, which Richard donates to the abbey in Bury St. Edmunds. Local land owners submit to Richard and his forces, leaving Comnenus no choice but to see for peace.

* * *

Richard's troubles are not yet over. Guy de Lusignan and his brother Geoffrey have come to Cyprus with a special request. Guy informs Richard that Philip of France has been plotting ever since his arrival in Acre to give the throne of Jerusalem to Conrad de Montferrat. Philip believes that Guy's claim to the throne became null and void with the death of Queen Sybilla and their two daughters in autumn the previous year. Conrad de Montferrat, on the other hand, recently married Sybilla's sister, Isabelle, giving him a stronger claim. He is also the new golden boy in the Holy Land, successfully defending Tyre while Guy was in prison. After Guy's release, Conrad refused to hand over Tyre. Guy was without a kingdom. Now he wants Richard to support him as the rightful king of Jerusalem.

Richard contemplates this carefully. He likes Conrad and believes him to be a worthy knight, while Guy is rash and often makes poor decisions. Richard has always had a tumultuous relationship with the Lusignans, and there is no love lost between him and Guy's brother Geoffrey. As the duke of Aquitaine, he is Richard's overlord and he owes him his allegiance. With this in mind, Richard decides to support Guy as it may prove politically advantageous.

William is sorely disappointed to hear that Richard will still be supporting Guy. He had hoped that some good would come out of the unfortunate death of Queen Sybilla, and that a truly noble king would sit upon the throne of Jerusalem once the city is regained. Now it looks as if "the buffoon" will be back in power. Surely, this is not God's plan.

Richard is anxious to leave Cyprus, but there are still matters of state to be settled. First, he takes Comnenus prisoner, having him bound in silver chains in order to avoid breaking an earlier promise not to have him clapped in irons. Then on May 12, he marries Berengaria and has her crowned Queen of England. As a final parting gift to the Greeks, he imposes a 50 percent capital levy on each citizen and orders the men to shave their beards.

Richard and his fleet finally depart on June 5, and the Cypriots are relieved. After making a brief pit stop in Margat to drop off Ducas Comnenus, they continue on to Tyre. They are not received with open arms. The garrison under orders of Conrad de Montferrat refuses to let them in. Conrad has obviously heard of the pact between Richard and Guy. Richard and his army spend the night camped outside the city walls. The next morning they set sail for Acre.

Acre Besieged

William is sailing in a ship just aft of Richard's own ship, the *Trenchmere*. William has spent much of the campaign at sea and is not fond of it, although he is no longer comparing the experience with hell. The crew is good-humored, despite not being allowed into Tyre. François is especially jovial, singing the "Chanson de Roland" while accompanying himself with a lyre. The "Song of Roland" tells a heroic tale of a knight in Charlemagne's service, glorifying knightly virtues, loyalty, honor, and courage in battle. The crew is mesmerized. William, on the other hand, is on the verge of vomiting. He hangs his head over the starboard side of the ship, giving up his breakfast to the sea. He then sights something far off in the distance—it becomes apparent that it is a ship of mammoth proportions. "A sail!" he shouts, pointing wildly.

The crew of the *Trenchmere* also spots the man-made leviathan. Richard orders the fleet to pursue. Normally, galleys would never be able to catch up with a ship that big, but, as Baha al-Din would write later, "providence ordained that the wind should fail." The *Trenchmere* pulls up alongside. A barrage of darts, arrows, and the deadly Greek fire begin pummeling the crusader ships. Richard yells to his crew from the top of the *Trenchmere*'s forward castle, "You are all cowards! You have become lazy from defeating easy foes and the whole world knows you are in the service of the cross."

On Richard's signal, the commander of William's ship orders his crew to close in on the enemy ship and ram it with the galley's iron prow. The jolt sends many of the men tumbling on both vessels. Three other galleys take turns ramming the infidel ship, and its deck suddenly catches fire. Another strike sends one of its masts plummeting into the sea. Water rushes in through the penetrated hull and the mammoth craft sinks, leaving no trace of its existence but bits of debris and the fallen mast.

The sunken ship was heavily laden with supplies for the garrison of the besieged city. So, even before setting foot on Acre, Richard manages to shift the odds in favor of the crusaders. This buoys Richard's arrival at Acre, adding the flourish of reputation to the pomp and ceremony of the occasion.

Richard rides up on a Spanish charger donning the silver scabbard, golden spurs, and the scarlet cap that he wore on his wedding day.

Richard's extravagant entrance could prove to be an embarrassing one considering the bad blood between himself and the French king. Fortunately, Philip chooses diplomacy rather than animosity and greets Richard with open arms. It is a commendable move and William for one is glad to see common sense prevail. Camp loyalties are already divided between supporters of Philip and Conrad and those who support Richard and Guy. If they are to make any progress in Acre, both sides must cooperate.

The stubborn Saracens have defended Acre for two years, despite the crusaders using every siege tool and tactic known to man. Trebuchets, catapults, and battering rams have not yet breached the walls. Miners have dug tunnels but failed to undermine Acre's ramparts. At least the outward-facing trenches give Saladin pause in launching an attack to relieve his garrison. The pointless stalemate shifted in favor of the crusaders after Richard sank the supply ship that was the garrison's last hope. The Saracen supplies had been running low. Now was the time to press harder.

Richard orders his siege equipment assembled. The most popular of these war machines is the trebuchet. Unlike the smaller catapult, which relied on torsion, the trebuchet sometimes exceeded three stories and used counterweights in order to swing the hurling arm. They had a range of one hundred fifty to three hundred yards and were used to launch projectiles weighing up to three hundred pounds at enemy strongholds. In a primitive form of biological warfare, they were also used to fling rotten corpses into rival camps. Two A-frame structures attached to a platform held the mechanism together. This was advantageous as the pieces could be built in advance and assembled when needed. Richard perfected the manufacturing of prefabricated siege equipment; all this eight hundred years before IKEA. The trebuchet was not the only weapon of mass medieval destruction. Crusading armies also used battering rams and siege towers to infiltrate enemy strongholds. William and the other men spend the next few weeks reassembling the siege engines and placing them outside the walls of Acre. Soon the English siege engines add their weight to the French effort.

Some of the most successful strikes come from *Malvoisine*, or "Bad Neighbor," which Philip's men use to try to take out one of the Saracen's own trebuchets, *Mal Cousin*, or "Bad Relation." William and François help to set up one of the English trebuchets while Philip's men rebuild "Bad Neighbor" after it has once again been damaged by "Bad Relation." They soon have their revenge.

"God's Stone Thrower," one of the biggest and most expensive trebuchets used by the crusaders, pounds Acre's walls. A priest stands near the giant apparatus, enduring the deafening thunder and praying with each earth-shattering jolt that the machine makes its mark. His prayers are obviously being answered.

Inside Acre, the Saracen defenders are being worn down by

constant bombardment and slow starvation. But the crusaders are not without their own trouble. They are not only losing men in the siege, they are also being worn down by chronic fatigue and disease. Weeks of continual noise and little sleep have taken their toll on William. At least, that is the excuse he is giving François for his illness. François has been worried about William ever since he left Tyre.

"Come on, William, you have to eat something," François says as he pushes a bowl of beans under William's nose.

William turns his head in disgust and lies back on his bedding. "I never want to see another bean as long as I live," he moans.

François's concern is growing. "William, you've been in this tent for weeks and you've barely eaten a thing."

The words fall on deaf ears. William is asleep. François notices the purple sores that have formed on his friend's feet and ankles. He lifts up the side of William's shirt and sees bruises that have also cropped up. He turns William's head to face him. He then pries William's mouth open and examines his teeth. François pokes the swollen tissue around William's gums. William groans. The odor from William's mouth is so offensive that François flinches back at the smell of it. When he removes his hands from William's head, François is shocked at the amount of coarse, matted hair that is stuck to them. François recognizes the symptoms all too well. William is suffering from scurvy. François hurries from the tent to go and get help.

A few hours later François waits outside the tent. He hears muffled screams coming from inside. He goes in to check on his friend and is affronted by a scene of horror. Arthur Goodwich is standing over William with a scalpel, his hands covered with blood. Arthur is a barber? Yes, that's right, a barber. They cut hair. They shave beards. They do surgery.

Medicine is not an elitist skill practiced only by the well-educated. Although surgeons went to prestigious schools to learn their trade, there were a great number of people who performed medical procedures without any formal training whatsoever. Virtually anyone could practice medicine, and it was not a skill limited to men. Women often worked alongside men as surgeons in field hospitals. William's ailment is not considered severe enough to be treated at the field hospital, although it is quite gruesome. Arthur proceeds to cut away the infected tissue surrounding William's gum-line—all this without painkillers. Those are reserved for more serious injuries. He then extracts the tissue and plops it into a pail. William eventually passes out from the pain.

He wakes up to see Heloise, one of the camp laundry women, fussing over him. She is checking for head lice. After this, she practically force-feeds him a concoction of chicken and asparagus soup, the ingredients of which she secured from Richard's fleet. Heloise is one of the few women allowed to participate in this campaign. Normal camp followers and hangers-on are banned. The matronly Heloise and the other laundry women, however, perform grooming tasks and generally keep the camp clean. Camps without these women are rife with disease.

As William lies in his sickbed recovering from his "mild illness," François visits. "King Philip and King Richard are just as sick as you," he says. "But Philip stays in his tent. Our Richard is also bedridden, but he had men carry his bed to the trebuchets. Right now our king is directing fire and taking potshots at the infidel with his crossbow. He is even offering a reward of four gold pieces to anyone who can bring back a chunk of Acre's walls."

This image gives William newfound resolve. Within days he feels much better. Emerging from his tent, William finds the siege is . . . over. With no relief imminent, Baha al-Din Qaraqush, the eunuch commander of the Acre garrison, wants to discuss terms for surrender. Jubilation spreads throughout the crusader camp. All that can be done now is to wait.

The next day, William learns the terms of the surrender. The garrison will be allowed to leave, unharmed, in exchange for two hundred thousand pieces of gold. In addition to this, fifteen hundred Christian prisoners will be released and the True Cross will be returned. There is one slight problem with the terms. Saladin was not included in the negotiations. He tries to send word to Baha al-Din Qaraqush, the eunuch commander of the garrison, ordering him not to agree to the terms but it is too late. Saladin sees the Christian banners hanging from Acre's city walls.

The banners cause quite a controversy. Duke Leopold of Austria, who was at the siege for two years, is angry that he and his troops will not be getting a share of the booty, leaving them with no compensation for the financial sacrifice of crusade. Duke Leopold orders his flag to be flown next to Richard's lions and Philip's fleur-de-lis. This is not a protest, but a claim. English soldiers remove the banner and throw it into the moat. Whether or not Richard ordered the removal is a matter of debate, but the act has dire consequences.

While the Germans complain, William and François make the best of life inside Acre. They visit one of the bath houses established by Saladin, emerging refreshed and clean after living in the same unchanged clothes for weeks. Later, they walk down the rue de la boucherie, the main street, which runs from the outer city wall to the harbor. The streets are lined with cookshops, tanneries, slaughterhouses, and taverns. The pungent odor from the pigs, which have been reintroduced to the city, fills the streets. The brothels that were outlawed under the Saracen occupancy are restored at a remarkable rate.

And miraculously, as if out of nowhere, the town is teaming with prostitutes. "Tinted and painted, desirable and appetising, bold and appetizing, with nasal voices and fleshy thighs . . . these girls offered their wares for enjoyment," writes Imad ed-Din, secretary to Saladin. Like many of the other knights, François indulges. William does not.

Occupying a city is not all fun and games.

William and François have been putting in their share of guard duty. The dungeons in Acre are horrific. Bloodcurdling screams from tortured prisoners pierce through William's flesh, turning his blood to ice. Many of the knights and sergeants seem to take pleasure tormenting the prisoners. One man, who is simply referred to as "the knife," cuts off the ears and noses of his victims. To William, this is unconscionable.

He is compelled to be kind to his captives, even if they are not Christians.

He has gotten to know some of them, though François is not keen to do the same. He becomes conversant with Salah al-Bashil, and is fascinated by his accounts of life in Jerusalem when it was occupied by the crusaders. William wishes to see the Holy City, and is eager to hear all about it from one who was there. He is fascinated by their talks. The two have a mutual esteem for each other, but this is all about to come to a halt.

Richard has been locked in negotiations with Saladin for weeks and very little progress has been made. In the meantime, nearly three thousand prisoners that comprised the garrison are supposed to be ransomed, but are using up valuable resources instead. The cost of feeding them and the manpower needed to maintain the guard is taking its toll. There is no way to continue on to Jerusalem without first relieving this heavy burden. Richard believes that Saladin is stalling. He decides to make a move, the effects of which will echo through history for the next eight hundred years.

Richard orders his men to start taking the prisoners outside the city walls. William and François join the other knights in herding the Saracens through the streets and out the gates. They line the men up against the wall, and within full view of Saladin, begin to drive their swords through the men. Then they cut open their stomachs to search for any jewels they may have swallowed. William is frozen. He has never killed a man who did not directly threaten his life.

Bertrand de Bois, a Templar knight, throws a man at William's feet for execution. It is Salah al-Bashil. De Bois snarls at William. "Kill him, Beaumont. Your king commands it."

"I will not," William replies.

"William, we are sworn to obey our lord. Put the blade to the Saracen. He's not a Christian. It is no sin to kill an infidel," says François, trying to reason with his comrade.

"No. This is not God's work." William stands his ground.

"All right, then," says François. And with all the indifference of one shoveling out a stable, he plunges his blade into Salah al-Bashil's stomach, cutting it open. Blood pours forth in a torrent. The pain widens the man's eyes. He looks at William, as if imploring for help, and dies staring at his Christian "friend." François takes his blade and cuts a bigger gash into al-Bashil's body.

The slaughter continues for most of the day. William stands and stares in shock at the massacre, unable to stop the horror. He feels a mailed hand smack him on the side of the head. It is De Bois who snarls at him sarcastically: "This is so you remember *He* who ordained you and dubbed you a knight. Do you think we came here to be friends with the infidels? We are here to take back the Holy Land and keep it for Christendom. Don't forget that, sir knight! Killing the Saracen *is* God's work."

The bodies are burned (a sacrilege, as Moslems believe it proper to bury a body). Then the ashes are raked to see if any precious stones survived the flames. None are found. The only prisoner allowed to go free is Baha al-Din Qaraqush. In a futile attempt at retaliation, Saladin sends the True Cross back to Damascus.

Onward Christian Soldiers,
Marching as to War . . .

Next, Richard settles the dispute over Jerusalem between Guy de Lusignan and Conrad de Montferrat. Guy will remain king for the rest of his life and will be succeeded by Conrad. In the meantime, they will share the tax revenues. There is a serious flaw with this arrangement—Jerusalem was not Richard's to give.

The French King Philip now makes ready to quit the crusade. Relations with Richard remain tainted by suspicion. Philip embarks for France at the end of July, leaving his army in the command of Hugh, the duke of Burgundy. But Philip does not leave enough treasure to pay the French knights, and Richard's funds are exhausted. Hugh at first refuses to serve under Richard. Conrad won't join, preferring to sulk in Tyre. The alliances are falling apart.

Despite these setbacks, Richard decides to continue onward. He has the men prepare for departure. William has been thinking heavily on the matter of the hostages. It is not normal to kill prisoners. They are supposed to be ransomed. He comes to the conclusion that this is a matter for kings and philosophers, and above his station as a knight. He turns his attention to his work. The word has been given that they will make ready for Jaffa within the hour. Jaffa is a port city, and if captured would allow the crusaders direct access to Jerusalem.

William's squire Tom finishes readying the supply cart and now must help William dress for battle. First, Tom puts on William's *haubergeon*, a quilted, leather shirt stuffed with animal hair, which acts as a cushion against blows but is also very hot to wear. Then goes on the *hauberk*, or coat of mail, which extends down to William's knees and covers his arms past his wrists.

Tom uses a leather thong to lace the mail mittens at the wrists to prevent them from bunching up. He then attaches mail *chausses*, or leggings, to William's waist belt. The *chausses* are generally worn over hose. Tom holds up the green surcoat for William to put his arms through, and it goes on over the mail coat. Then William dons a padded cap, before putting on a chain-mail coif. His choice of headgear is a cone-shaped helmet with a face shield attached. Tom then adds the finishing touches, tying spurs to William's feet and the sword around his waist.

The sword was the knight's most valued possession and could cost the equivalent of up to twelve oxen. It was made of forge-welded steel that was folded for added strength. The typical sword used by the crusaders had a thirty-five-inch blade, a *quillon* or crossbar, and a pummel. Unlike the earlier swords used in the Norman Conquest, swords used in the Crusades did not have a heavy blade, and were good for thrusting as well as slashing.

The only commoners allowed to carry swords were sergeants. They had the same outfits as knights, but lacked squires and valets. Sergeants were normally hired soldiers, and were looked down upon by the knightly class because they did not go through the same training and dubbing rituals.

The port of Jaffa lies sixteen miles south of Acre. The crusaders will be marching in open view of Saladin and his men. William, François, and the other knights are riding under the protection of the infantry. These crossbowmen and spearmen march in a square around the knights and baggage train. They keep the shore on their right, so one flank is always protected. Men on the right exchange places with those on the left of the square, so that no one has to endure Saracen arrows for the entire march. Occasionally, the men at the rear are forced to march backward in order to stave off attacks by the Saracens.

One of the favorite Saracen tactics is to launch quick attacks wherever the square appears weakest. Richard orders the men not to break ranks, but the blistering heat begins to take its toll.

Men, overcome with exhaustion and fatigue, begin falling out of the march. Even William is feeling the heat. His sweat cannot cool him, instead dampening his *haubergeon*, making it warm and itchy. William tries to scratch the itch through his chain mail and feels nothing. He draws a deep breath to release the agonizing weight he feels in his chest, but breathing the hot air only makes things worse. William looks ahead in the distance at Richard, who appears unmoved by the intense heat. It is the encouragement he needs to push forward.

The reluctant Hugh of Burgundy is leading the French rear guard, which lags behind the main formation. They start drawing fire from Saracen horse archers. William hears the commotion and turns his horse. Upon seeing the onslaught of enemy horsemen, he lowers his lance and charges. Many other knights follow suit. Richard rides down to join the skirmish and relieves Hugh and his men. One swift charge drives the Saracens away, so Richard halts the charge. Hugh and his men are relieved. Putting them in a rear guard was a mistake Richard will not make again.

He orders the Templars and the Hospitaller knights to maintain the rear guard. They take turns in performing the task. These two orders are made of disciplined warrior-clerics who answer to the pope. They dedicate their lives to protecting the Holy Land while other knights go home. The Templars and Hospitallers are the closest thing to professional soldiers that exist at this time. Their discipline is just what the rear guard needs. Throughout the march they are bombarded with volleys of arrows, and yet they never break ranks. At one point, William counts as many as twelve arrows protruding from the mail of one of the Hospitallers. The Saracen missiles generally do not penetrate the mail; nonetheless, it is an amazing sight. Richard's decision to put the Hospitallers on rear guard is paying off so far.

Richard is determined not to make the same mistakes Guy de Lusignan made at Hattin. His army only marches early in the morning and late in the afternoon. Although the conditions are still exceedingly uncomfortable, they are not unbearable. Richard's fleet sails offshore, supplying Richard's host and taking the wounded, which would otherwise be left for dead. The rest stops take place by water sources to refresh the men and the horses.

That night the men make camp. Many spend this time in prayer. William believes that the constant attacks by the Turks are a direct result of the sinful behavior of the knights in Acre. More time was spent in the brothels than on prayer and vigil. The knights spend a bug-ridden night trying to sleep, but getting little.

Facing another day's march, William is feeling worn. He is starting to dose in the saddle. The rhythmic movement of his horse sends him into a trance. He slips into a pseudo-slumber; however, he is soon struck sober when an arrow hits his mailed arm. The Turkish horse archers launch another wearisome assault on the knights. At one point the rain of arrows is so thick that William cannot see the sun.

Meanwhile, the Hospitallers in the rear guard are tired of being a subject to constant raids and are losing faith. Garnier de Nablus, master of the order, asks for Richard's permission to attack. Richard denies his request and tells him to wait until the signal is given. After a day spent losing horses to the Turkish archers and undergoing constant harassment, de Nablus breaks. He, along with another Hospitaller, Baldwin Carew, charges toward their tormentors. The rest of the Hospitallers follow, as do the French. Richard has seconds to make a decision. He commands the remaining knights to follow him. He must add the weight of his charge to the Hospitaller and the French knights or he will be cut off and mowed down by the Saracens.

William and François join the charge, attacking Saladin's left flank. William uses his sword to hack at the Turkish infantry, while François prefers to cleave Saracen heads in two with his battle-axe. In the melee, one enemy archer puts an arrow into François's horse. The stricken beast throws François. He feels his shield arm crack as he hits the ground. William dismounts and cuts the archer down as François rolls over to recover his battle-axe. But he can't bring his shield into the fight—he can't lift his arm. William tries to block a nearby Turk, who is trying to slash at François with his scimitar. But William does not have eyes in the back of his head. A Saracen knight delivers a mighty blow to the back of William's right shoulder, and he drops his sword. The Saracen knight swings his sword high above William's head to deliver the killing blow. Alas, the Saracen knight does not have eyes in the back of his head, either. Geoffrey de Lusignan runs his sword through him, saving William.

Saladin's army is soon driven away.

Though the victory is not purchased cheaply. About seven hundred crusaders lost their lives in the impromptu battle. Many more are wounded. Richard's surgeons attend to their needs once the army reaches Jaffa. They tie William's upper arm to his torso to give his broken shoulder a chance to heal. François's shield arm is now in a sling. Their squires are definitely going to have their work cut out for them.

Rush to Victory or Defeat?

Weeks go by and the men sit idle once again while Richard decides his next move. Jerusalem has never been an easy nut to crack. It sits deep in the Judean hill country, where every piece of high ground is its own natural fortress that will overlook any army marching on the valley floor. Most of the men believe he should give the order to march; instead, he chooses to wait.

Richard launches a diplomatic campaign to try and regain the Holy City through persuasion. He writes Saladin a letter, pleading for the return of Jerusalem to the Christians, explaining the spiritual significance of the sacred sites. Saladin responds in writing that Jerusalem is also sacred to members of his faith.

Saladin dispatches his diplomatically talented brother al-Adil to deliver the reply. Al-Adil spends a great deal of time with Richard and the two develop a genuine liking for each other. Richard then tries another ploy—offering the hand of his sister Joan to al-Adil, suggesting the two would rule together as joint monarchs. But Richard forgot one thing—he never consulted Joan, who flies into a rage upon hearing of Richard's plan. She says she will never marry an infidel. Richard jests to al-Adil that he should consider converting to Christianity—a nonstarter for a devout Moslem. Nothing ever comes of Richard's plan.

Richard's army grows restless. They want to take Jerusalem by force; they do not want to negotiate. William is grateful for the delay as it has given him time to heal. He was not looking forward to fighting without the use of his sword arm. The rest of the men are not as understanding. They constantly harass Richard about postponing the departure and even accuse him of showing favoritism to the infidels, which the Pope says should be exterminated. Richard has no choice but to give in to their demands.

The march toward the holy city is not an easy one. In many ways, William and his fellow knights have truly taken up the cross. It is winter. The rain is relentless. Hail storms are constant. Their chain mail begins to rust. The food is growing soggy and moldy. The knights are marching in the mud. François is traveling on foot after having lost his horse in the last fight. He and William take turns riding their shared *rouncy*. Despite these hardships, the crusaders are in good spirits. They thank God for bringing them this far. They are anxious to lay siege to the city, but the army comes to a halt six miles outside of Jerusalem.

Richard confers with some of the local knights. Many are Hospitallers and Templars who have made the Holy Land their home. Together they ponder the challenge of taking Jerusalem. With the army now marching inland, a supply line would have to be set up to bring provisions from the fleet. That line would have to be protected by detachments from the shrinking army, lest Saladin cut it off. Even if Jerusalem could be taken quickly, many of the European knights would still go home, their pilgrimage completed. The Hospitallers and Templars would stay, of course, but even they knew they would be too few to hold the city. The smart thing to do, they argued, was to head back to the coast. Rather than suffer a pyrrhic victory taking Jerusalem, Richard gives the order to march back to Jaffa. Most of the knights are outraged. François is extremely upset. "I haven't come all this way just to turn back now! The holy city is within reach. Just take it!"

"But our king is right. We must gather more strength to keep the holy city," William says, approaching heartsickness.

"Our king is a coward!" yells François.

William strikes François across the face with his mailed hand. "Richard is no coward!"

François looks at him in shock. "I thought you were my friend." William feels too ashamed to respond, but cannot bring himself to apologize. The two knights do not speak to each other for the rest of the retreat. François walks rather than share the *rouncy* with William.

Many of the men lose heart. Some succumb to the elements and lay dying on the other side of the road. Thousands of others desert altogether. François is among them. William watches him take a detour into the forest with six other knights and several footmen. François turns and takes one last look at William, then disappears into the woods.

The Faults of the Few

Rumors fly around the camp about discord back home in England. Richard's brother John has been trying to seize power. As if this weren't enough, Philip of France is threatening Richard's lands in Normandy. Richard is forced to make a choice. If he stays, he could return home to find his domains seized. If he returns home, this has all been in vain. Richard speaks with his chaplain, who reminds him that God has preserved him in battle. He continues by telling Richard that the souls of the men are reliant upon taking back God's holy city for the remission of their sins. In addition to the constant moral attacks from his chaplain, Richard must also endure being called a coward by his men, This proves too much. He leads his men on another march toward Jerusalem.

This time Richard gets close enough to see the city. But, once again, he orders a retreat. He has no way of knowing that Saladin is close to defeat. When William hears they are to retreat, his heart sinks. He starts to doubt Richard's sanity. This time, they do not return to Jaffa. They travel to Acre instead. William knows what this means. Richard is planning on going home. Jerusalem is to be left to the infidels.

Saladin learns of Richard's march to Acre and seizes the opportunity to take Jaffa. The town is virtually defenseless and Saladin's army storms through the gates. Saladin orders his men not to plunder it, but his men grow tired of his indulgent treatment of the crusaders and ignore his command. They lay waste to the town, killing the wounded crusaders.

Richard learns of Saladin's attack on Jaffa and musters his men. He sends his galleys down the coast and arrives before the final siege can be implemented by Saladin's unruly army. Richard orders a handful of his knights and crossbowmen to the shore. William prepares himself. He is exhausted, but is in better shape than others. Charles Deveraux orders William into the same boat as Richard.

The time has come. They reach the shore and Richard orders his men out of the vessels. It is just like the raid on Cyprus except Richard hasn't had time to put on all of his armor. He wades through the water in his sea boots with his sword in hand. Richard's crossbowmen take out the first line of Saracens. Richard charges the Saracens like an enraged lion. William and his fellow knights follow their king's lead, tearing into the Saracen horde with no thought but Attack! Attack! Attack! The enemy is powerless against the charging English, led by a madman seized by the full frenzy of battle, eager to blood his sword with their bodies. William takes some blows from the panicked infidels, but does not succumb. He sees Richard in his glorious rage, leading and fighting, by example asking of others no more than he would do himself. Any doubts William had about Richard vanish with each stroke of the king's sword. The Saracens flee for five miles before regrouping, not even sure of what hit them. "By God's legs, we have won," exclaims Richard. "And I am only half-armed."

Final Order of Business

It is the last charge William ever sees of King Richard, *Couer de Lion*—the Lion Heart. In the end, Richard and Saladin sign a three-year truce. The cities of Acre and Jaffa and the coastline in between will remain in Christian hands. Saladin will keep Jerusalem, and allow Christian pilgrims to visit the holy city.

The war is over. They can all go home. Richard leaves without ever stepping foot inside Jerusalem.

William returns home, disheartened by the ideals of "Christian valor." He regrets his fight with François and hopes to reconcile with him once he gets back to England. He does not receive a hero's welcome upon arrival. Most people blame Richard and his crusaders for bankrupting the country, and their financial problems are about to get worse. King Richard has been taken prisoner by Duke Leopold of Austria and held for ransom. This is payback for the insult Leopold suffered at Acre. Money must be raised to pay the massive ransom. At least that is the excuse Prince John gives for increasing the taxes again.

William is feeling the weight of being an outcast. He travels to Yorkshire to visit François and beg for his forgiveness. He arrives to find François's lands given over to the local parish. François never returned from the crusade, having been killed by Saracens shortly after leaving Richard's army.

William tries to go on with his life as though the crusade never happened, but he is haunted by night terrors. He wakes up with fright every time he sees the face of Salah al-Bashil in his dreams—no, his nightmares. It is always the same Salah, staring at him again, asking to be spared the blade that plunged into his gut, killing him again, just as it did the night before, and the night before that. William cannot get the faces of the executed Saracens out of his head. No penance will make up for what he failed to do.

In the end, William sells his lands to the church and joins an order of Cistercian monks in the north of England. He spends the rest of his life seeking God's forgiveness.

A Soldier of the Emperor Napoleon

France Against Europe

BY TODD FISHER

The widespread use of gunpowder weapons, first cannon then muskets, brought about another change in the way war was waged and the lot of the infantry. The effectiveness of musket or rifle fire meant that infantry once more was the backbone of any army, though the artillerists would have argued this. While easily learned, the smooth-bore muskets of the early nineteenth century were surprisingly inaccurate. To do significant damage to your opponent's massed fire, shoulder to shoulder formations were required. Napoleon became the unquestioned master of such warfare, and France dominated Europe for more than two decades. But by 1813 his enemies had learned a lot, and France was on the defensive.

TODD FISHER is a Napoleonic historian and collector who has published several books on the emperor and his wars. He is also the executive director of the highly respected Napoleonic Historical Society and often leads tours of the wars' battlefields.

[★]

FRANCE, 1813

Jean Laurent, a Breton born in the middle of the Wars of the Revolution, grew up hearing glorious tales of his noble ancestors who had ridden in the service of the king. Indeed, some of his cousins and uncles, royalists to the end, had fought in the civil war against the Revolution, for the Whites against the Blues. They had told him of the terrible atrocities committed by the Jacobins, of mass drowning and beheadings, and other nearly unimaginable massacres, things that had taken place in Brittany just before Jean was born. Jean's father had not fought, and had quietly mourned the death of his brother killed in the Vendée; wine or brandy fueled an occasional outburst of anger against both sides for the brutal fanaticism they had spread throughout the region, one killing in the name of liberty, the other in the name of God and King. Although they were members of the *petite* nobility, the absence of wealth proved a boon to Jean and his family during the days of terror, and had saved the modest household from any confiscations, or worse, imprisonment and a possible appointment with the guillotine.

It was only the rise of Napoleon that had brought some stability back to the region, and restored the Church to France. Indeed, Jean had lived all his conscious life under Napoleon, but he would not come to love the emperor as many in the army did. He had in fact always planned on entering the priesthood and had just started his studies when his father's heart gave out in the summer of 1813. Jean was suddenly left to support his mother and two sisters. Economically, it was a bad time with much hardship; militarily, it was worse. The disaster in Russia left the enemy closing in on the Rhine. With his lineage still imparting a feeling of martial pride, Jean decided to join the army.

After a trying scene of departure from his mother and sisters, Jean had no broad illusions of glory when he set off from his home in Vitré, a fortified town on the border of Brittany. It was November 1813, and the rumors in France of the great battle around Leipzig and its terrible results made the overcast weather and clinging cold inordinately depressing and bleak. To Jean, a palpable sense of doom seemed to hover above the people as he passed through the many small villages on the way to Rennes, where he hoped to enlist at the primary depot of the Sixth Regiment of Artillery. Jean hoped his solid mathematical skills would allow him to advance quickly up the ranks. Besides, the artillerymen tended to survive much better than the infantry.

The rumors of defeat proved all too true. Napoleon would again have to raise an army to replace the one destroyed in Saxony. All new recruits were welcome (while many young men instead hid in the woods to escape conscription). Jean began his training under Sergeant Martel, a wounded veteran of Austerlitz too infirm for active duty, and almost too gruff for the younger recruits, who shook with fear at his rebuke. Barracks life proved austere, and Jean spent his first homesick nights wondering what sort of fool he had been to volunteer, but, seeing no other choice, he soon applied himself to learning the manuals and studying the many treatises and schematics on the art of gunnery. Sergeant Martel took great delight in making fun of Jean's religious education and monastic habits, and told him that he had best find a willing young lady while there was still time and forget what the foolish priests had told him of life. "One great battle," the sergeant laughed, "beats the lessons of a thousand schoolbooks."

Even during the winter months training proved rigorous. Unlike in the past, it seemed certain that the Allies would be invading France. In anticipation, Napoleon ordered the depot transferred to Douai, to bring it closer to the front. Five of the Sixth Regiment's companies or batteries were distributed along the western coast, in case the British attempted to come in the back door with a naval invasion. But Jean stayed with the main depot and spent the cold December trying to keep warm and learn his trade. The urgent pace of training would prove particularly useful when the Allies made a winter crossing of the Rhine and invaded three months earlier than had been expected.

The Sixth was pressed into the campaign. Jean saw three months of miserable marches, at first leading to glorious victories and hope-filled pursuits, and then, increasingly, to soul-searching defeats. Against almost hopeless odds, Napoleon dazzled the world with an improbable series of victories in March before the gates of Paris, and nearly captured the main Prussian army, but the enemy kept bringing more men to bear. During these battles, Jean saw many unspeakable things, the sights of men and horses killed, some cut in half by round shot, others blown to bits by howitzer shells, and some hit by the desultory musket fire of the skirmish troops sent to snipe against the artillerists. Jean did not understand what lessons could be learned here beyond a sharpening of his military skills, and the hardening of his soul to the horrors of war. He often thought of Sergeant Martel and looked forward to seeing him again someday, so that he could show him what sort of fellow he had become now.

His skills and obvious intelligence had earned him a promotion to corporal. His duties in firing the cannon thereby changed. It was now his responsibility to "lay the gun," which is to say, to aim the gun at the target designated by his lieutenant. Jean took pride in this achievement, but that pride he kept checked by the greater humility gained by his experiences. The Campaign of 1814 ended with the first abdication of Napoleon at Fontainebleau in April, and Jean mustered out of the army.

Jean returned to Brittany and looked for work to provide for his family. All he could find was a farm laborer's job, and with the high cost of bread and wine, the remainder of 1814 proved tough. Jean welcomed the return of the Bourbon kings, and Louis was initially popular in Brittany. This area had been a hotbed of Royalist sympathy during the Revolution, and despite Napoleon's great and successful efforts to improve the local economy, old ties of loyalty to the Bourbons remained. But as the year wore on and the economy worsened, rumblings of discontent were heard. Jean thought, "If even here people wish for Napoleon's return, I can only imagine how they long for him in Paris." Jean himself began to spend time with the other veterans at the local café. There they could talk of what they had done, and Jean had a great appreciation for the stories of the older veterans, those who had marched to such far-off places as Vienna, Warsaw, even Egypt or Moscow. He found a peace among these men, as they understood what his mother and sisters never could know about him. Nothing was the same at home now, and he grew impatient and irritable at times among the women and their complaints about money and the lack of goods.

The spring of 1815 indeed was a season of rejuvenation. Napoleon had returned from Elba! Jean was shocked by his own reaction to the news, by finding that a suppressed pride was suddenly unleashed into joy, at a chance to escape the dreariness of his life in Vitré. He would soon be marching again, along with his newfound friends from the café and his old comrades-in-arms from the Sixth

Artillery. Everywhere the country seemed gripped by energy, and, one would dare to say, hope. While Jean had not forgotten the horrors and privations of the last campaign, peace had grown stale, and the Bourbons seemed inept and weak.

* * *

Despite making a concerted effort to make peace with the Allies, Napoleon very soon came to realize that he would have to fight to retain his throne. Calls were made to join the army, and Jean, along with most of his veteran colleagues, returned to the colors. Jean once more left his home and walked to Douai to rejoin the Sixth Artillery Regiment.

The activity at the depot was familiar to Jean, but now most everyone in the main roles was a veteran and knew his jobs. The new recruits would start in the jobs requiring little or no knowledge.

For the upcoming campaign, Jean was assigned to one of Napoleon's "Beautiful Daughters," a twelve-pounder cannon. This piece was the heaviest of the army's field pieces and was used to pummel the opposing forces into submission. Its primary load was a solid shot weighing twelve French pounds (almost thirteen pounds in modern weight). When fired, this round usually traveled not more than ten feet above the ground, as far as eight hundred yards, until it struck the ground and, under good ground conditions, bounced along at a height of less than six feet, churning up the ground and spraying rocks and soil at each bound. The round could plow through enemy formations tearing limbs or smashing down the unfortunate victims, and inflicted terror on even the most experienced infantry.

The French twelve-pounder gun was the best of all at delivering the killing blow. The kinetic energy created by its round, the powerful charge, and the French gunners' skill were unequaled in the world. Men such as Jean took great pride in their abilities. The trick, however, was not how to use the gun once in position, but how to get it there in the first place. While Napoleon had gone to great lengths to improve metallurgy to allow for a lighter gun, these guns still weighed nearly one-and-a-half tons, and it took six horses to move each piece around, under ideal circumstances. If the horses were less than ideal, the weather poor, or the roads bad, men and additional horses would have to be used to have any chance to get the guns to where they could do their assigned job. Often the heavier pieces would never get into position before the attack of the French would rob them of their best targets. This meant that it was often critical that orders were given in a timely matter, so as to allow the additional time to position the guns and anticipate possible difficulties. The guns almost never advanced to the attack with the infantry, but stayed in position to soften the enemy or to cover any retreat.

Jean was the immediate commander of his gun and had to teach all the men under him to do their jobs in handling their "Beautiful Daughter." The process of firing the cannon was an orchestrated ballet. Timing and the ability of every gunner to do his role were needed to achieve maximum effect. The service of one cannon took nine men when fully crewed. There were the seven men firing the gun and at least two men running ammunition back and forth from the supporting caisson. Additional men could be conscripted to aid in dragging the gun into position and to run ammunition. While the runners and support staff could exchange roles easily enough, to replace a gunner could hamper the performance of the cannon. It was inevitable that losses would occur in battle, so training a replacement out of the support staff was part of Jean's job. At the same time he needed the best performance out of the initial team. The weight of the cannon and its importance in battle meant that hopefully the very best personnel out of an artillery regiment would be assigned to service these twelve-pounder guns.

In the nine-man crew servicing Jean's gun, each had his assigned job during the firing process. They were divided into four groups of servants, with only the third group having three men assigned to it, the others having two.

The first servants' job was to clean the barrel of the cannon between firings and load the next round. The second servants made sure the touchhole of the cannon was covered during loading, and then primed and fired the gun when ordered. The third servants, including Jean, the gun commander, aimed the gun and gave the order to fire. And the fourth servants ran the ammunition to the gun from either the caisson or ammunition box (*coffret*).

Once a cannon was pulled into position on the battlefield by its limber, the men would pull the tampion out of the mouth of the barrel of the cannon. This was a plug whose purpose was to keep rain and other foreign substances out until it was time to fire. The tampion was hooked to the gun carriage and the cannon was swabbed out to prepare for its first firing of the day. The loader would take the cartouche, a bag containing the cannonball and powder, and present it to the rammer to be shoved down the barrel. Once the ball was placed, the two men would use the ramrod to tamp the round hard into the rear of the barrel, to ensure that the gunpowder in the rear of the charge was properly packed and in a position to be ignited by the firer. While the two men were ramming the round home, one of the two men in the second servant group, called the ventsman, would cover the touchhole with a leather pad, called a thumb-stall, to ensure that no air could ignite any embers that had not been cleaned from the barrel. For if this was not done, the powder being rammed into the cannon could ignite and discharge the gun, with possibly disastrous results. Once the round was in place, the firer would stick a metal pricker, a type of long pin, down the touchhole to puncture the powder bag seated behind the cannonball. This exposed the powder to a fuse that was now put down the touchhole and into place.

Jean now sighted his target and ordered the two other men in the third servant group to use handspikes to swing the cannon into the proper aim. These handspikes acted as levers and could easily swing the gun into position. The gun could also have its elevation adjusted by turning an elevation screw located under the rear of the barrel, though this needed to be done much less frequently.

Then the cannon was ready to fire. In times of normal combat, Jean, the corporal, would look to the section two gun commander for the order to fire. The order would come and Jean would give the word to the firer. The soldier would take a long pole, called the *porte-feu*, with a piece of cloth match at its end that was smoldering like a cigar, and touch it to the top of the touchhole. This would ignite the fuse and in turn fire the gun.

The runners coming from the ammunition reserve would approach with a new round, the gun would be swabbed with a sponge soaked in water, and then a brush would be shoved down the barrel to scrub away partially burned pieces of cloth and powder, to prevent premature ignition. Then the process could start all over again.

Jean practiced this over and over again, though often only pretending to put in a real charge, for target practice was a luxury that was only done on a limited basis. He got his crew to be able to fire two shots per minute and could even get off three rounds for a short burst.

Jean had reflected on the fact that his battery had been unable to attend the ceremonies in Paris prior to the start of the campaign. While it would have been nice to have seen the pomp and majesty of the ceremonies, he did not regret missing them, since it would have involved a long march to Paris and, as it turned out, an about-face and a march toward Belgium, which was closer to where they trained than Paris. The weather was hot, and the journey would have gone a long way toward tiring them out even before the first shot was fired. Jean's battery fell into position with the First Corps on the road to Charleroi. He knew of his corps commander Drouet, the count d'Erlon, and had heard that he had proved a steady soldier. Jean's battery was assigned to the corps reserve and would move in the rear of the columns.

Normally a regiment of artillery would be broken up through the army. Batteries or companies would be assigned to either divisions or a corps reserve. In general, the lighter guns received the divisional roles.

A corps was the largest field formation in the army. This was subdivided into divisions, and again into brigades, and those were made up of regiments, which had one to six battalions each, in this campaign well below their book strength, at five to six hundred men. Even battalions were further subdivided into companies, but as a rule, these only operated independently when skirmishing.

Jean's battery would move in the First Corps' artillery reserve for the first days of the campaign. On June 15, 16, and 17, Jean could hear the firing and often see the smoke of a battle, without ever being asked to pull into line. He and the rest of the First Corps went through a very frustrating day on June 16. Their columns were made to reverse course twice during the day as orders conflicted. The first came from the Battle of Ligny, where Napoleon thrashed his familiar foe Blücher. At the same time, orders came from the Quatre Bras, where Marshal Ney, the bravest of the brave, engaged in a slugfest with Wellington, who held his ground.

Of course, Jean and the rest of the men had no idea why they were told to turn about face, only that they were being marched around needlessly on a stiflingly hot day without firing a shot. Each time the column turned about, the artillery would have to pull off the road so as to allow the infantry to move to the front. The foot soldiers trudged by slinging their Charleville muskets over their shoulders, walking with heads downcast, weighed down by eighty-plus pounds of kit. If they had been in battle, much of this weight would have been left in the rear with a provost guard, but for now they had no idea where the battle even was. They all yearned to pour their devastating fire of one-ounce, .69-caliber balls into whatever enemy, British or Prussian, first presented himself.

As the artillery waited, the infantry passing by would cause the expected delay. That was in addition to the usual rests that the artillery would take after a march of eleven kilometers. Just the maneuvering of so many horses and men caused traffic congestion that would make even the most organized man weep. To do this twice exceeded in frustration anything that anyone could remember. The natural grumbling of the veteran French soldier was perfected in that afternoon.

The corps marched through much of the night and was treated to a downpour that first cooled their overheated bodies, but then soaked everyone to the bone and caused the wool uniforms to chafe. Through much of June 17 the corps sat stacked up on the Brussels Road waiting for the lead cavalry to push aside the British rear guard. The rain continued and men found little shelter from it.

By sunset, the men had taken whatever shelter they could against the continuous rain. Jean and his crew found partial shelter in a copse of trees, one hundred meters from the main road. Tents were never taken on campaign for the men. They were expected to sleep on the ground wrapped in a blanket. They huddled together, but as the night wore on, the rain turned into a deluge and the men had a miserable time of it. The sky erupted in a tremendous lightning show that many felt was surely a precursor to a titanic struggle the following day. It was small solace that the British a few kilometers away were faring little better.

* * *

Therefore it troubled Jean and his men little when reveille was sounded at four in the morning and the men went to the fire to get their morning soup. Each man used his own bowl or ate directly from the communal pot (*gamel*). In addition, each had a loaf of wheat bread. The rain had slackened to a drizzle, and the men squatted in the mud to eat their breakfast. Thinned wine was also drunk, and the alcohol helped to ward off the damp. After breakfast, the men went down to a nearby stream and filled their canteens. Sergeant Thomas, who was in charge of Jean and his comrades, took a teaspoonful of vinegar from a second canteen he owned and poured it into each of the men's. (This acted as a disinfectant, killing the bacteria in tainted water sources, but no one knew why it worked at the time.)

With nothing to do after, the men settled down by the fire and talked of girls and their latest conquests. All hoped to find good food, drink, and a willing doxie in Brussels. Around the fire the men began to sing one of their favorite songs, *"J'ai du Bon Tabac."*

The rain was a major concern to Jean and even more so to the high command and the artillery officers. Anywhere that men moved off the Roman-built Brussels Road quickly turned into a quagmire of mud. Horse teams would have to be assisted by men pulling ropes attached to the trunnions of the cannon. This would quickly tire the men and on top of a sleepless night would compromise Jean's gun crew's efficiency. In the meantime the men just waited.

Napoleon anticipated the problems of Jean and his companions, and waited to have the ground as dry as possible. In addition to moving the guns, there was the problem of the cannonballs burying themselves in the soft ground rather than ricocheting along through the enemy ranks. Muddy ground would mean only a direct hit could have any effect, and would make the opening bombardment much less effective. The emperor would rather wait.

* * *

Napoleon wanted to mass his reserve artillery in the center and use it to bludgeon the Anglo-Allied line. He sent orders for most of the artillery reserve batteries, assigned to each corps, to be put under the command of General Count Desvaux St. Maurice, who would then position the batteries opposite the Allied center. The rain had been constant, and though it had slowed to a drizzle, it continued to make deployment off the main road difficult. Horses had to be moved from one limber to the next to "double team" the guns just to pull them out.

Jean stood in the early morning mist and waited his turn to move. Anticipating that horses to double-team his gun would be in short supply, he attached ropes (*bricoles*) to the axles and prepared to have his men act as the additional muscle to move the gun.

Unfortunately for Jean and his battery, his assigned position was on the left of the Grand Battery, meaning that he would have to wait the longest to move into position. This meant that the ground would be all the worse.

As the morning wore on, the sun began to burn off the mist, and made brief appearances as it approached nine o'clock.

* * *

Jean was chatting to one of the men from his corps as D'Erlon's men began to assemble.

"It looks like you're going to send the *Rosbifs* packing," Jean joked. "That is after we have opened some nice canals for you to sail down."

A sergeant from General Donzelot's division smiled. "Perhaps, but hopefully they will be hurrying to Brussels to prepare our bivouacs before we even reach the ridge. I know a good 'lottery of Venus,' where you have a good chance to avoid the *gros lot* [the clap]."

Both men sat on a stone wall and lit up their clay pipes. There was nothing to do but wait. As the smoke formed halos about their heads, a great deal of commotion was created as the emperor and his staff came riding down the road. The emperor dismounted and stepped into a field to get an overview of the enemy position in front of his army. While he chatted with several of his marshals and General St. Maurice, Jean recognized one of Napoleon's staff as a friend from Vitré. Pulling himself up from his seat, he trotted over to his friend and hailed him. "Claude-Marie!" he called. "A dirty day for a dirty business. How have you been?" Claude-Marie was a few years older and had been a close friend of Jean's cousin, but everyone knew everyone in Vitré.

"The emperor has been riding around for hours," he said, "but I can tell you the high command knows little more than we staff. We have nothing from Grouchy, and the emperor was up all night throwing up blood. I am surprised that he has even gotten out of bed, if what his doctor tells me is true." Claude-Marie adjusted his shako and turned to be sure that he was not needed by General Soult, Napoleon's chief of staff.

"Well, I guess he's just like us," Jean mused. "We common soldiers have to be almost dead before our sergeant will let us fall out. In the emperor's case, I guess his sergeant is God and has told him no slacking today!"

Both men saw that the emperor and his immediate servants had returned to their horses and were mounting to continue their tour of the front. "*Bonne chance!*" said Claude-Marie, and he moved quickly to his horse and mounted. Just as quickly, he and the imperial staff were gone. Jean returned to his stone wall and relit his pipe.

* * *

About ten, Captain Charlet, the battery commander, told Sergeant Thomas and Jean that it was their turn to move their guns into position.

The men assembled, and each was assigned to his *bricole* to help pull the cannon along. Leather harnesses were worn, to which the ropes could be attached, and others pulled on the ropes in a tug-of-war fashion. The limber was brought to the rear of the twelve-pound, and the ring at its rear was placed over the spike on the limber. Two riders mounted up on two of the six horses in the horse team and on the signal urged their mounts forward. They had not gone more than thirty meters when the gun sank into the mud. Men strained against the suction that the thick clay soil created and had trouble keeping their footing, often falling face-first into the muck. The second gun of the section, moving just to their right, was having no better time of it. One of that crew called to Sergeant Thomas to wait as he had lost his shoe when it was pulled from his foot by the mud's suction.

"If you need to remove your shoes until we get into position, do so, but we need to get these guns up there today!" Thomas shouted, and cursed. The day was getting hotter, and the mud and the heat combined to make the men miserable. No sooner had they pulled from one hole than another would draw them in. One man pushing against a wheel pitched forward face-first in the mud when the cannon finally was pulled forward. The straps and harnesses chafed against men and horses, and sores appeared where the sweat and heat combined to rub the flesh raw. There was nothing to do but adjust the straps to begin the process all over again on another spot on the body. The sweat saturated their blue wool, red-cuffed and -collared uniforms, causing the dye to leach and stain their underclothes and exposed skin. The riders often had to dismount to take some of the weight off their horses when the gun bogged down. They then pulled the horses by their bits to lead them to a more promising path. One of the riders bruised his leg badly when the limber trail banged into him after one of the horses stumbled. If it had not been for the leather leggings he wore on the outside of his pants, his flesh would have been ripped from the bone. He now could no longer walk, and this only worsened the slow advance. It took a hideously long time for the men to roll the cannon to its assigned position one hundred yards to the east of the

Brussels Road. The limber was then swung around facing to the rear, and the gun was lifted off the limber spike now that it was facing the Allied line.

About three hundred meters to their rear and left of Jean's cannon was the inn of La Belle Alliance, and it was there that Jean could see the activity that indicated the location of the imperial headquarters. For now, Jean took the *coffret* off the limber and made sure that the caisson was positioned optimally for action. There was nothing more for his men to do but sit and wait. They sat on the wet ground, or used their pack as a seat to keep the mud from oozing into their pants.

Jean relit his pipe and looked across the field at the enemy.

Five hundred meters to his front he could see the men of Bylandt's Brigade, in blue or green uniforms, deployed to the right and across the road from the small white farmhouse of La Haye Saint. He had no idea which of the enemy troops these were, for at this point their regimental flags were cased. He could see that these men would present a very tempting target. All other activity seemed to be up on the opposite ridge, with most of the enemy movement occurring out of sight.

Napoleon, who had been ill throughout the night, was trying to catch a nap. He slept as his men struggled to place the guns. Awaking at noon, he observed that cannon fire was going on to the far right of the field, and he called St. Maurice over to ask his opinion on if it was time to begin the bombardment. "Another hour, sire. Those guns you hear are just the supporting artillery of General Reille." Satisfied, Napoleon went to sleep for another half hour. He arose and assembled a few of his staff. He mounted his horse, Désirée, and rode up and down his line. As he approached, the crowd of men began to cheer wildly. They took their shakos off and hoisted them on the points of their bayonets, waving them as flags of salute. Jean saw the emperor ride by. "How the men worship him, and how silly is that? He's just a man like any other, yet they've made him a god. But then again, he is a remarkable man, for now he can stir himself to show great energy when I know he is ill. So if one is to follow a man to death, best it to be a remarkable one." The entourage moved by and the cheers could be heard in the distance long after they were out of sight.

* * *

Jean saw the activity of the other batteries as the day approached one o'clock, and knew that his men would soon be pressed into service. Taking a swig from his canteen, he told the boys to start getting ready.

"It's going to be warm work, boys, and I suggest you get a drink and take a piss, for there will be little time for either, until 'the goddams' are routed." Men took a break and some a quick bite from any food they had in their packs, before taking their positions and preparing for their day of battle. The tampion was removed from the barrel and the first shot was loaded.

A battery of six guns was most often commanded by a captain. He would direct the fire of his battery and would give the order for each of the guns to fire in turn. It was important to time the fire of each gun so as to observe the effect of every shot on the target. Many times this was impossible, as the smoke of the battle would soon obscure all but what was immediately to the front, but even a slight breeze would allow the commander to take better aim at the enemy. Captain Charlet was assigned the target of the troops to the right of the Brussels Road. Bylandt's men, though, had been withdrawn, as it had soon become clear that they would be the target and suffer to no good purpose. This meant that, with the exception of the troops occupying La Haye Sainte and the grounds around it, all the Anglo-Allied army was in position behind the ridge.

Not being able to fire directly at the enemy meant that the rounds had to be "skipped" or "grazed" up and over the ridge. This was far less effective and was made even worse by the mud, which would eat up every other round. But there was little chance that Wellington could be coaxed to expose his men needlessly, so this was the only option.

At one o'clock, the order was given to commence firing. Eighty guns opened up, each cannon belching gray white smoke from its fiery mouth. The ground in front of the ridge was plowed by deep furrows, but many rounds bounded over the ridge and into the Allied troops behind. Jean's men worked feverishly to fire off as many shots as possible in the heat. As he happened to look behind him to check on his men bringing additional ammunition from the reserve caisson, Jean saw the First Corps lining up to prepare an assault upon the troops that Jean and the remainder of the Grand Battery were targeting.

The first of these men were moving to his left, toward La Haye Sainte. Two more divisions were on the low rise to his rear, with the fourth division out of sight.

To the front, the smoke now had blotted out everything, and it stung the soldiers' eyes. The sergeant was shouting orders, but no one could hear him. Jean was laying the gun, ensuring it was aimed and ranged properly, but at this point that really meant nothing more than making sure the gun was the same as before, as nothing of the enemy or even the ridge was still visible. As the twelve-pounder fired, it dug deep ruts in the wet ground and Jean's men had to shift it every half dozen shots to keep it from sinking up to the trunnions. This slowed the rate of fire and wore the men out more quickly. Yet there was only going to be a limited time before they would cease fire, and they all wanted to get the most out of the guns while they could do their job.

At some point, the Allies began to return fire. Enemy cannonballs would bounce along the ground doing for the most part little harm, but still making the men keep an eye out for shots coming their way. Even a slow-rolling ball could shatter a leg or worse. Getting to a surgeon in the quickest time possible was critical to having any chance of survival. Napoleon's army had the best surgeons in the world, but as the battle went on, even they could get overwhelmed. Amputation would soon follow, with a coin flip's odds for survival, so men would keep a wary eye on the smoke to their front when they were not hard at their work. Streams of sweat rolled down the muddy faces of the men, who were trying to gain their breath in the acrid smoke. So it was with relief that the order was heard to cease fire. As the men bent over panting, they glanced up to see a huge mass of blue-coated men marching in their rear. The units moved through the batteries, breaking ranks and quickly forming up again once the guns were cleared.

"Who you with?" Jean asked a sergeant leading his *peleton, a small platoon,* past his guns.

"Schmitz's Brigade, Donzelot's Division," came the reply. "Get your guns ready to move. We're going to chase these shopkeepers like rabbits. You'll have to keep up so you don't miss the boat to England."

"Always wanted to see London," laughed Jean.

The division cleared the line of guns and began to re-form into massive phalanxes, gigantic formations that bore no resemblance to the battles Jean had seen before. The light infantry companies were sent to the front to form a thick skirmish line. Riding right past the guns and to their front came General D'Erlon and Marshal Ney along with their staffs. All looked resplendent in their gold braid and fine uniforms. Taking a position near the front, they gave the signal and the advance resumed. Men shouted, "*Vive l'empereur!*" and the bands struck up the familiar slow march from the "Triumph of Trajan." The marching pace kept time with the music. There was nothing to do but watch the show. The wind coming from their left started to slowly clear the smoke. Jean knew that while the enemy to their front would be a major concern soon enough, for the moment what was on the minds of most of the men was to keep pace and watch their step crossing the broken, muddy fields. Soldiers could do nothing about oncoming bullets, but if one fell and disrupted the formation, there was a very real sergeant that would have to be answered to as well as the jeers from comrades.

As the soldiers advanced through the high grass, Jean could see the enemy batteries opening fire and watched as huge swaths were carved through the French files. Orders were then given to send rounds over the heads of the French column in hopes of landing in the British ranks on the ridgeline. At close range, this was usually a very bad idea as the wood sabot that made up part of the gun charge would send splinters out among your own men. But at this point the French infantry formations were more than two hundred meters away, so sabot splinters no longer posed a threat. D'Erlon's men had advanced into the valley between the French gun position and the enemy-held ridge. For ten minutes, they would be below the trajectory of the rounds. Even so, the artillerists needed to elevate their fire enough to avoid hitting their fellow soldiers, and that caused most of the rounds to overshoot. This played hell in the British rear but had no effect on the troops on the ridge. "Why are we shooting like this, Corporal?" asked one of Jean's men. "I thought you told us that these shots never did any good."

"Against the enemy, no, but it stiffens the backs of the younger boys in our ranks," Jean said with a smile.

Each time the enemy artillery thinned them, D'Erlon's men dressed their ranks, as they began to climb the low ridge. The order was given to cease fire along the Grand Battery. With the cessation of the barrage, the smoke once more began to dissipate. It was magnificent to watch the men. Jean thought he had never been able to see so many men at one point in his life. To the left smoke rolled out from the orchard in front of La Haye Sainte. Colonel Charlet's men (of the Fifty-fourth *Ligne*; no connection with Jean's battery commander) were driving the riflemen of the king's German legion out of the garden and were at the walls of the farmhouse. Even the smoke from musketry made it hard if not impossible to see what was happening. As the First Corps reached the crest of the hill, a barrier of smoke arose from the front as both sides opened fire. Soon all that could be seen was the billowing smoke around the firefight and the file closers in the rear of the formations chasing any stragglers back into line.

"It's only a matter of time; they'll break soon," Claude-Marie, one of the fourth servants on Jean's gun, stated with certainty.

He was right, but not in the way he thought. The gunners could see, coming out of the smoke, French soldiers running back in their direction. Confusion seemed to have broken out to the front, and Jean thought that he had never seen French rout like this. Not even the young boys of the 1814 campaign, the "Marie Louises," ever broke like this. It did not take long before the cause of the panic became evident, for out of the smoke came the British heavy cavalry of the Union Brigade, its troopers mounted on imposing horses and brandishing big swords. They had been hidden from sight and had launched a charge upon the flank of D'Erlon's men. Cutting their way through the ranks of the French columns, they continued on toward the Grand Battery. Jean saw what was happening before most others and shouted for his men to load canister. (This was a round made up of a tube filled with small balls and used like a giant shotgun shell.) Jean called out to Sergeant Thomas to let him know of the danger and screamed at his men to hurry, for it was nothing less than their survival at stake. The Union Brigade was coming on quickly now and heading right toward them. The French infantry was scattering in every direction, and it was clear that there was nowhere to run for cover. It would have to be "Stand by your guns and kill or be killed." The twelve-pounder cannon was swung into position, and as the British heavies closed upon them, Jean ordered the gun to fire. The enemy had not gotten within optimal canister distance, about two hundred yards, but the round cut a swath through the men directly to the front. Several of the horses and riders were shredded, and a spray of blood, bone, and viscera filled the air. Several fleeing French infantrymen were also splattered, an unfortunate price to pay for the gun's survival.

Firing on the charging cavalry only cleared the men directly in front of Jean's gun. The remaining redcoats plowed ahead into the guns to their front. Jean's men dove under their guns or used their implements to swing at the remaining horsemen moving past them. To his right, Jean saw one of the soldiers manning the sister gun of his section have his head split almost in two by a sword stroke swung from the giant rider moving past him. Several men to the left and right were simply ridden over and trampled. At the next battery over, in an effort to hurry their shot, the rammer shoved home the charge before the vent was properly sealed, and an early discharge tore his finger off and sent the ram flying out of the barrel along with the cannon ball. While creating a bloody mess, he was fortunate that he had properly rammed with the open hand position, or it would have been likely that his entire hand or even his arm below the elbow would have been blown away.

Some gunners tried to run, and many were cut down within a dozen paces. While some riders pulled up their mounts and chopped at the nearly helpless artillerymen, many of the red-coated Inniskilling Dragoons swept over the position like a huge wave and continued on toward the French rear.

Jean was ducking and weaving around his gun, never knowing from which direction a deathblow might come. Shouts and cries of the wounded and dying made giving orders impossible, but then there was little his men could do. It was at that moment that Jean heard a happy sound, a French bugle sounding a cavalry charge. Jean had taken a position under the wheels of the gun and looked in the direction of the bugle call. There he saw French cuirassiers, under General Farine, crest the rise behind them and plow into the disorganized formations of the victorious British horsemen.

A fierce but short fight occurred before the spent British cavalry broke and headed to their lines. One of the enemy cavalrymen was shot dead by a pistol fired from one of the Sixth's captains. As the French horsemen pulled up from their pursuit and fell in again behind the artillery position, Jean got up and looked around. His cannon crew had only suffered one wounded man, but around him on either side lay the dead and dying from the other guns of the Sixth. Many had suffered slash wounds from the British sabers, while even the untouched but stunned survivors would need some time to return to action. Men helped the wounded to the rear, and those who were not the bravest would often join in to help so as to take them as well out of action. Noise was deafening, with the whine of cannonballs flying by and the high-pitched screaming of wounded and dying horses and men. Disorder reigned.

Jean called his men together, and all brushed themselves off and took the opportunity to catch their breath. The air had become stifling. The heat of the June day was near its height and the trauma of the last few minutes had left the men temporarily spent. Lieutenant Roger, who was in charge of the six guns, was up and moving around the battery trying to gather the men and assess how many guns had been put out of action. While Jean's crew was soon ready to resume fire, one-third of the gunners of the battery were wounded or missing. Lieutenant Roger combined the remaining gunners to man four of the six cannons, but was fortunate that only two of the guns needed new crews.

Napoleon now appeared and was urging his officers to get the guns back into action as soon as possible. Batteries that had taken a beating were being pulled out to his right. Smaller guns were being shuttled in to replace them.

* * *

General St. Maurice was riding back and forth, trying to reorganize the units and determine what he had left to renew the bombardment. He had dismounted and had just left the emperor's side when a cannonball cut him in two. It happened not more than fifty feet from Jean's gun, and the shock of seeing their commander killed in such a way stunned and dismayed the men. One of the younger soldiers began to cry uncontrollably. Sergeant Thomas came over and put his arm around the boy. "He was a good man, Charles, but he is beyond our help and we've got a job to do."

It was now clear that with the death of St Maurice, it would take even longer to reorganize. Jean told his men to have another canister round at the ready to load, but beyond that they could all relax for a bit.

Just then Jean and his men were treated to an unusual sight. A British rocket battery had been set up and was firing toward the French line The rockets of the British battery streaked through the air and suddenly made sharp turns in an unpredictable pattern. Some of them actually reached the French line, but did little damage, while several boomeranged into friendly formations and more than once almost started a panic. In the end, it was a wash, but it gave the survivors of Waterloo another lurid story to tell.

Much more important events were occurring off to the left. As they sat on the ground, they could look over to La Haye Sainte and see it covered with smoke. The French were swarming around it, and fires could be seen on parts of the roof. Heavy fire was still coming from the building, and it was obvious that the king's German legion were in no mood to yield gracefully. If these men had looked over to their left they would also have noticed that fresh French batteries had been swung into line. They extended over the Brussels Road, and the howitzers were pouring in supporting fire to aid in the effort to take the heavily contested farmhouse. Rounds exploded above the buildings and more fires broke out. Men shooting down from the rooftop were peppered with chunks of iron from the exploding rounds.

After a thirty-minute rest, General Henri Lallemand, the new commander of the Grand Battery, rode over to Lieutenant Roger and instructed him to renew fire and concentrate on the troops beyond the Brussels Road.

Orders were given, and Jean's men began a steady but slow fire upon the enemy on the ridge above and beyond La Haye Sainte. Their rounds would fly out of sight and their effect was a mystery. Unknown to them, their rounds were doing good work in finding their mark. Wellington had his main British force deployed just behind the ridge, and the rounds from Jean's section of the Grand Battery were careening through their formations. Men were torn limb from limb, and there was little option but to stay in place and risk being obliterated at any second. From the target's viewpoint, it was well that the French had no idea how effective their cannonade was. It was now a bit past four in the afternoon, and orders were given to change targets. The effort was once more redirected to their front. The reason soon became obvious. Through the smoke to their left, thousands of French cavalry were advancing up the ridge. The first to advance was the cuirassiers, followed soon by the Dragoons and still more cuirassiers. Double lines of cavalry moved forward in their regiments, one stacked upon another. They swept to the west of La Haye Sainte and out of sight. Some time later two more massive waves of cavalry went thundering by and followed their comrades up the ridge. As for Jean and his men, they continued their one-round-a-minute pace of lobbing over the ridge to their front.

"That'll keep the boys in front of us heads-down. They won't hurry to help those fellows that are dancing with our cavalry So what's everyone want for supper in Brussels?" Jean said. While there was little doubt that the battle was still to their front, it was only an act of faith that had them keep up their fire. The smoke and noise had obscured all in front, and Jean's men increasingly had to stop for a moment a take a drink or catch their breath. The acrid smoke choked them and stung their eyes. Their muscles ached and their heads pounded. The concussion of each cannon discharging left a physical effect on them and made their motions like those of a nonthinking automaton. At one point an enemy round carried over their position and hit a caisson, causing it to explode. The rush of wind from the explosion swept over them, but the sound of the massive blast was lost in the general din. "How can they still be standing?" wondered the men. For another hour the steady bombardment wore down the allies to the front, while the cavalry ordered forward by Marshal Ney assaulted the British squares. Occasionally, a brief glimpse could be caught of returning French cavalry, but Jean and his men had no idea that Wellington's center had held. What could be detected was that the farm of La Haye Sainte was near collapse. A fresh assault was made, and now the French soldiers were over the wall in several places. Men were fighting hand to hand and were seen clubbing one another with their muskets. The roofs were all ablaze and the German prisoners were being escorted to the rear. Then it was over; the remaining defenders either broke and ran, if able, or threw up their hands. The taking of this strongpoint opened a way to the heart of Wellington's army and his line of retreat. But inexplicably, after the building had fallen, activity seemed to come to a halt.

"Now's the time that we should deliver the coup de grâce," thought Jean.

It was only now that Jean heard the sounds of heavy fighting coming from his right and rear. As he strained to make out what was happening, he slowly realized that the French were under attack from an unknown force. Had Wellington launched an attack around their right flank, he wondered, or had the Prussians somehow managed to sneak up on them? Jean shouted out to Sergeant Thomas to ask if he knew what the fighting was. "It looks like Blücher's back for another bloody nose. But he's too late."

From Jean's vantage point, it appeared the British had been

defeated. But before the victory could be exploited, Napoleon had to deal with Blücher and stabilize his right.

Jean was partly right. Napoleon had been forced to divert one-third of his army to defend against the Prussians. Napoleon had taken to his sickbed during the battle, and roused himself only to find that Ney had used up the cavalry against the British squares. Ney was ordering the Guard to follow up the assault when Napoleon stopped it to assess the situation first. The Prussians had taken and lost Plancenoit twice, and it was not clear that the troops in the area could sustain another attack. The Young Guard had been sent there and had reviewed the situation, but more and more Prussians were arriving every moment.

For Napoleon to send his last major reserve against the British seemed dangerous while so much was unknown. A half hour later, he would know that the risk needed to be taken, for time was working against him and there were no other reserves. It is very possible that this delay lost the last chance for a French victory. That Ney had squandered the resources available was undoubtedly true, yet the bravery of the French Army had put the Allies on the point of breaking. If the Guard had been sent in when Ney had ordered it, it would have found the British reserves out of position and might have proved decisive. If Napoleon's plan had been followed throughout the day, the victory would have been won in a much more elegant style. But the fateful combination of going back and forth between Ney's and the emperor's orders would prove disastrous.

The advance and rout of the Guard was soon to occur, but it would matter little for Jean and his men. The Guard had reached the British line and was engaged in a fierce firefight, when a cry went up that enemy cavalry was upon them and the every man should run for his life. (Sauve qui peut.) Prussian cavalry had worked their way around the flank of the men defending Plancenoit and had ridden into the right flank and rear of the Grand Battery. A wave of panicked men were heading in Jean's direction, and while he could not yet make out the cause of the panic, he turned to his men and told them that they had better make their way to the rear, for they were out in the open and had no cover for hundreds of meters. Picking up the personal belongings that they could easily carry, the men began to move at a trot in the direction of the small inn of La Belle Alliance about three hundred meters away. The mud stuck to their shoes and men fell easily. Casting an eye over their shoulders, they eventually made out the enemy cavalry coming toward them. Prussian lancers were swirling among the frightened artillerists and were thrusting and stabbing them even if they tried to surrender. Jean and his men escaped this fate for now, as the impetus of the Prussian attack had stopped and the cavalry was turning about and returning to from where they came.

As the Prussian lancers retreated, many leaned over their saddles and stabbed at the men trying to escape under guns and caissons, as well as spearing men wounded upon the ground. The sight enraged Jean, but there was little he could do. He and his crew were separated from the remainder of the battery, and he wondered about what he should do next. As far as he knew, he was expected to return to his gun and either resume fire or limber up to relocate. There was so much smoke and noise that it was hard even to try to find his way back to his gun. Not far in the distance, he could see limbers waiting behind the far left of where the Grand Battery was, and he sent over a runner to find out if they knew what to do next. As they stood near La Belle Alliance waiting for instructions, several men went running past them. What began as a trickle soon became a steady stream of soldiers fleeing down the Brussels Road toward France.

"I don't like the look of this," Jean mumbled.

Right then his runner returned and told him that nobody knew what to do and that it appeared to be total confusion. Looking around him, Jean called his men together and began to tell them that they were going to get a limber and try to get their gun out. The number of men running past them continued, and just as Jean was going to begin to return to his position and work on saving his gun, he saw several Imperial Grenadiers among the routed men.

"Boys, that's it! Forget about the gun! We had better get out of here—the day is lost! If the Guard has given up, there is little that we can do."

Jean and his men started to walk south down the side of the road. He kept up a steady pace, but told the men that unless they saw an immediate danger, running would only increase the chance of having something terrible happen to them. At least for now, they knew the way home. It was at this time that the setting sun broke through the clouds, illuminating the cloud cover in a deep red. Jean thought of how it reflected both the day and perhaps the fortune of France.

To the right and left, he could see men in utter despair. A small drummer boy was crying on the side of the road, appearing to be totally abandoned. Jean grabbed him and told him that he should come along with them and they would find his regiment soon. The mud had remained thick on the ground. The Brussels Road was the best road for miles around, but despite its improved nature, it had become impassable to most wheeled traffic. The sounds of fire were slackening to the rear, and as evening began to diminish the light on the long day, the thoughts of the men were to get as far as they could from the battlefield. Jean knew enough from the stories about the retreat after Leipzig to be on the lookout for deserters shooting and taking anything they wanted from those who looked vulnerable. Discipline was breaking down, and it would take heroic efforts to restore it. For now everyone must be on his guard. Many of the soldiers on both sides thought that looting was the right of all who survived a battle. Even cutting the throats of one's own countrymen was not unheard of once a retreat began.

It was to prove a terrible night for those left wounded on the field. Some would be found days later, barely alive but stripped to their underclothes. If you had to be worried about your own side, the enemy was even more of a threat. Kindness was not uncommon, but neither was brutality. One of the best chances for survival was to be come upon by a fellow Mason. A secret sign could and did make all the difference on many occasions. But it often was luck of the draw. Apart from these dangers, medical help was hard to find this night, as the surgeons were overwhelmed and no good organized effort had been made to recover the wounded. Then again, even if one did get to medical help, the results were indifferent. Amputation was the best solution for serious wounds because the alternative was gangrene. Many would die from shock on the spot. The knowledge of the consequences of a serious wound meant that Jean and his men felt fortunate that their crew had come out of the battle in such good shape.

The men walked until well after midnight, retracing their steps of two days ago.

As they trudged along, their way was blocked by various wagons clogging the road. They found a spot several hundred meters off the road to bivouac for a rest near a campfire left from some supply unit that had bugged out not long before. Some firewood was taken from the local farmhouse to add to the fire, and they warmed themselves around it and fried up two onions and a potato that one of the men had in his knapsack. Always looking for imminent signs of the enemy, they thought it a good idea to rest before resuming their retreat the following morning at first light. The loaves of bread that a few still had on them were passed around, and they all shared in the meager meal fortified by a swig of brandy from Jean's flask. Two other soldiers wandered over to their fire and asked to join them and cook their own provisions. Jean recognized one as wearing the uniform of a cuirassier, but he no longer wore the metal cuirass from which that cavalry got its name. Another was an infantry soldier. As they sat in the gloom, each told his stories of the day and of the friends that he had lost.

"I was part of the attack on the *Hommard* squares," the cavalry trooper explained. "We made attack after attack and would shoot our pistols point-blank into their mass, but they held firm. At one point, I was able to follow my captain into the mass when one of the charging mounts tumbled into the ranks and opened a hole. We hacked and slashed many of them down, but my horse was mortally wounded and I pulled away. My horse only lasted a couple hundred paces before he pitched forward in death, throwing me onto the ground. It hurt like hell, but after a minute or two, I pulled myself up and started to walk to the rear. I was sure that I would get an easy remount, as many of our friends had been shot down, but catching a riderless horse in the noise and battle was impossible. After the Guard broke, I pitched my cuirass into a ditch and made my way with the others. I will tell you this, those *Anglais* are great soldiers. I have never seen such courage in an enemy to such a determined attack."

"Well at least you got to catch them in the open," grumbled the infantryman. "I was over on the far left and General Reille threw us against a fortress farm without competent artillery support. We made thirty or forty attacks against the walls and buildings but could never get a proper foothold. What a waste of life!"

"Perhaps, your men just didn't have the stomach for it," said one of Jean's men to gibe him.

"*Va tu faire enculé!*" ["Go play with yourself!"] shot back the man with an angry glare.

Jean admonished all. "Men, it has been a terrible day and many of our dear friends and comrades lie dead. We have little to be ashamed of."

Another soldier strolled up to the fire and told them that there was a bunch of abandoned food just down the hill and that they should go take full advantage of same. Jean pulled himself up and told his men that if there were good biscuits and drink, they should get what they could, for it might be some time before they ate again. They found what had been the camp of the supply train and filled their knapsacks with whatever they could stuff into them.

"Come back to the fire and cook a little of this up," said the soldier that had clued them in about the cache.

"It is best to get down the road, as we will not be able to keep up as fast a pace. Best to leave the fire for others to use." And with that Jean started his men once more down the highway toward France.

As they marched, nearly all the men around Jean were bemoaning the fate of the emperor and France. All were disconsolate. Everywhere there were wagons, limbers, and guns sitting abandoned. Many men were wounded, and little by little many of their belongings were discarded to lighten their loads. Even *Charlevilles* muskets had been cast aside, and while the enemy was not in sight, it was clear that panic had set in on many of the army's units. As for Jean, he was more concerned about how he would earn his money now, and while he felt sorry for his fellow army men, he was alive and that was not so bad.

With the Union at Gettysburg

The Experience of Combat
in the Civil War

BY WILLIAM R. FORSTCHEN, PhD

Fought only four decades after the Napoleonic Wars, the American Civil War was in many ways the beginning of modern warfare. The increased firepower and range of all the weapons used meant that battles had to be fought in an entirely new way. By 1865 railroads, breach-loading muskets, and highly accurate rifled artillery, not to mention the Henry and Spencer repeating rifles, both introduced in 1863, had changed the battlefield experience of a soldier entirely. The war began with massed formation at Manassas Creek and ended in the trenches around Richmond.

DR. WILLIAM R. FORSTCHEN is the *New York Times* bestselling author of numerous novels, alternate history novels, and nonfiction books on the American Civil War and other military topics. He is a published and noted scholar on the war and a history professor at Montreat College in North Carolina. Many of his experiences on the lot and life of an American Civil War soldier came firsthand from years as a member of a historical re-creation Maine infantry regiment.

[*]

It was the bloodiest, most costly war in American history.

There is a romance to the Civil War that overlays the reality of it. Artists make a lively business of painting romantic farewell scenes of young cavaliers and their ladies fair, perhaps with an indulgent father like Robert E. Lee looking on. Gettysburg on a Fourth of July weekend is almost like a fairground.

Perhaps it is the distance of time that separates us from the harsher reality. Long gone are the last of the veterans, what few memories we have of them preserved on fading black-and-white newsreels, as very old men, recalling a time of youth that was indeed "touched by fire." But though "touched by fire," words penned by Oliver Wendell Holmes Jr. and immortalized in Ken Burn's epic documentary series, sounds romantic, anyone who has truly been burned in the fire of combat knows the pain and the memory of that pain, which is universal regardless of time or place.

Who Were These Men of 1861–1865?

The demographics: Average age, figures range from twenty-one to twenty-four years of age from the North, slightly older from the South because of a near universal and draconian draft. Single largest age group, nineteen to twenty. In reality slightly older than the mass levies of World War II, especially when it came to combat infantrymen.

Average education? Hard to compare to modern standards. From the North, literacy was close on to 100 percent, the South about two-thirds that number. Both armies were extremely conversant when it came to the complex political issues of the day, of states' rights, slavery, and a concept called "The Union." Political debate, in that pre-media age, was almost a form of public entertainment, and participation in those debates the mark of an educated young man who could engage intelligently.

Motivation to fight: The South had the edge on this point. There is a story most likely replicated a thousand times or more, of a Union soldier challenging a captured rebel in a debate as he led him to the rear. "What you fighting for, reb? You don't own any slaves." Back and forth the debate raged, until finally the reb snapped, "Because you're on my land, damn it."

For the South, the political issues of states' rights, the defense of slavery, would take a backseat to the simple and universal point across so many conflicts . . . "I fight because you are on my land, damn it."

For the North there was perhaps a higher ideal, the concept of a Union that must be preserved. Slavery was, at the start, an issue for only a few radicals. After the Emancipation Proclamation, many veterans all but rebelled, saying that this was not their issue and even threatening to desert. But by 1864 more and more saw the "crusade" aspect of that issue, especially when by the end of the war nearly one out of every four Union soldiers in the field was of African descent.

Joining Up

When the movie *Saving Private Ryan* was released, it hit public consciousness with an electric shock. For the first time, a major motion picture about war truly captured the supreme shock of battle, sparing nothing in terms of the ghastly nature of death and wounding on the battlefield. It set a standard that has not been re-treated from since. Many still wait for a Civil War movie with that equal reality. And yet sit with any veteran and watch the movie, and he might nod in agreement but then quietly exclaim that yes, visually it "almost" got it, but it lacked the gut-wrenching fear, the smells, the sensations of being freezing or staggering in jungle heat. A movie will, of course, never be fully real.

At least, though, the youth of today contemplating volunteering for the military have some vague idea of what they might encounter on the battlefield.

If ever there was a generation that went forth to war as utter virgins when it came to the reality of violent death, it was the boys of 1861. The photographic images of Matthew Brady and others, shot amid the carnage of Antietam battlefield, had yet to be taken. Visual images of war were heroic paintings usually focused on a gallant leader such as Wolfe at Quebec, Warren dying at Breeds Hill, Mercer at Princeton, perhaps a thimble's worth of blood staining their otherwise spotless uniforms.

The last major conflict fought on American soil in the east was nearly fifty years past. The dozen or so aging venerated heroes of 1776 still alive in 1861 were indeed iconic heroes. War was glory. In a nation of 30 million, perhaps little more than thirty thousand had been exposed to combat, in Mexico or along the frontier. There were still some survivors of the War of 1812, and from the Revolution half a dozen still lived.

The education of a generation of boys in the 1850s as to war was one of romantic ideals from the poetry of Hawthorne, the wild penny press stories of Crockett and Bowie at the Alamo, and history texts that at best had a few woodcut prints of our gallant lads driving away the cowardly redcoats. War was a fantasy of glory and the prospect of romantic adventure.

The majority of the boys of 1861 had been born and raised on farms, this percentage was nearly 100 in the South; in the North there were a fair percentage from cities. In the South nearly all were native-born, but a fair percentage of Northern regiments, particularly from the East Coast, were Irish, German, or, if from the old Northwest, German and Scandinavian.

Among the farm boys of the North and the South, few had ever traveled beyond the county of their birth. A visit to the "big town" was a trip to the county seat of perhaps a couple of thousand. Very few had even been aboard "the cars," the new high-tech wonder machine of the railroad, which by 1861 had more than thirty thousand miles of trackage, three-quarters of it in the North.

When the news of Fort Sumter echoed across the land on April 12, 1861, excitement was already at a fever pitch. Lincoln called for 75,000 volunteers for ninety days to suppress the rebellion, the seven states of the Confederacy soon expanded to eleven, and mobilization was on.

* * *

Consider the alternatives in that spring of 1861 if you were a boy of nineteen years. You could look forward to the prospect of continuing with the spring planting, staring at the butt end of the old horse dragging the plow, awaking to the timeless drudgery of milking before dawn, mucking out the stalls, plowing, planting, and hoeing, and each day would drag on into the next. Or . . . with laughing friends by your side, you could go to the county seat. A band might be playing, a crowd gathered; a local bigwig, perhaps the mayor, a judge, or even a congressman, would extol the crowd to rally to The Cause. If you stepped up with your friends, cheers would erupt, strangers would slap you on the back, admiring girls would gaze at you coyly, and at that moment you would indeed be a hero as you raised your hand and took the oath.

* * *

The recruiting of armies for the Civil War had a certain practicality to it that would disappear, perhaps with good reason, in the twentieth century. The old British tradition of mistrusting a standing national army had been transferred wholesale into the American psyche when the republic was formed. A standing army might be necessary in time of actual war, but in peacetime, it could be a tool of suppression. Though forgotten today, Oliver Cromwell, after winning the English Civil War of the 1640s, had turned "his" army on the Parliament they had fought for and established a dictatorship.

The standing army of the United States in 1861 numbered around twenty thousand, scattered in small outposts across an entire continent. Mobilization would be based upon a state system of quotas (though early in 1862 the South would go to a universal draft). Each congressional district was given a quota of X amount of men to be organized as infantry, artillery, or cavalry. In turn the governor of the state would assign to his adjutant general the task of organizing and mobilizing for the quota assigned to the districts within his state.

Well into 1862 it was an easy enough task to fulfill; in fact in the first months for every man "lucky enough" to get in, a dozen stood waiting anxiously for the chance. The governor held the right to appoint a colonel for each of the regiments. Some chose wisely, looking for experienced veterans, but most chose political cronies, often with little or no experience. In some cases, a personage of wealth would announce he was forming his own regiment and would even outfit everyone who joined (of course with an eye toward political office after the ninety-day war was over).

In turn, the assigned colonel would dole out positions of company captains, and the recruiting was on within that congressional district. At times a local hero would show up with enough men behind him to equal company strength, already declaring himself to be a captain. In some cases, particularly among the frontier states, militia units already existed and were instantly ready for mobilization.

From urban areas various organizations sprang to the call. Entire fire departments volunteered and insisted that their uniforms would be their red fireman shirts. In some cases student bodies of colleges would join en masse, led by a favorite professor or even the college president.

In short, it was chaos. Once into the actual army, many of the officers would quietly be convinced to step aside; a few had to be shoved out, a few ran away, but not too surprisingly, many actually rose to the occasion, learned their jobs, and led with valor. The body of men that made up a regiment or a battery in nearly all cases was local boys banded together. Neighbors, childhood friends, brothers, fathers and sons, students and teachers formed the ranks of a regiment. It created a unit cohesion that would never be seen again in an American war. It also was the setting of tragedies. It was the potential of a Private Ryan or Sullivan brothers scenario. Throughout the bloody war to come, one scathing volley or blast of a double canister could, in an instant, annihilate an entire village or bring an end to the future of a family.

* * *

What was the experience like for one of the boys of 1861 or early in the spring of 1862, when more calls went out for yet hundreds of thousands of additional volunteers? It was basically the same for both North and South, at the start at least.

It is easy enough to create a "composite" of the estimated three and a half, North and South, who donned either blue, gray, or butternut.

We could profile him out as being single, nineteen years old, raised on a farm and still living with his parents on that farm, with about six years of formal education (worth at least twelve today when you compare the expected ability level), having never been out of the county of his birth, except when quite young and his parents picked up and moved several hundred miles farther westward, where new land was opening up. He has never taken a ride "on the cars" or a steamboat, the realm still of only the wealthy or urban dwellers. His experience "with the girls" might have been several church socials, perhaps a stolen kiss behind that same church, though there is a "sweetheart" in his life. He is a regular churchgoer, has maybe had a few experiences with demon rum or the local moonshine, and took a licking for it when he staggered home. He has been warned that tobacco, rum, loose women, and drink are most certainly the paths to damnation, and has a very literal belief in the rewards of heaven and the punishments of hell.

In short, by the definitions of the twenty-first century, he would be seen as painfully naïve, innocent, idealistic, and narrow in his views. He was also the quality of a man that would stand in a volley line in ninety-degree heat at Gettysburg and slug it out to the end.

* * *

Our typical soldier, we'll call him William since Billy is seen today as a diminutive meant for a small boy. Let's assume he is from a regiment out of Ohio, which was nearly the demographic center of the United States in 1861 and a state with an interesting social and cultural cross-section: rich agriculturally, but harboring as well the beginnings of the great Industrial Revolution to come along in the urban centers of Lake Erie, and crisscrossed with a web of railroads that in 1860, for the first time, fed more goods back and forth between the Midwest and the East than did the river traffic of but ten years earlier. Even the state's politics were mixed. Some cells of strong abolitionist feeling existed, especially in the northern part and areas settled by Quakers. Along the southern shore bordering the Ohio, more than a few would be defined as Copperheads, meaning Northerners with pro-South leanings, with some even crossing over into Kentucky to join their Southern cousins. The state would even have an antiwar governor who would eventually go head-to-head against the president.

* * *

William, along with most of his friends, missed out on the first great rush of enlistment in the days after Fort Sumter, as the few regiments from Ohio quickly filled out. In fact thousands of potential recruits swarmed the recruiting officer (before he could bolt with some of his friends to the county seat), only to return at day's end filled with shame but greeted at least by a mother, father, and sisters, who were relieved.

For the next ninety days he followed every scrap of war news, filled with anticipation for Union victory but also with an inner dread that a stunning single victory would mean he'd miss out on the action and forever after lower his head in shame when old classmates, proudly wearing their uniforms, returned home to glory, cheering crowds, and a shower of kisses from the girls, perhaps even the one he secretly pined for.

And then the debacle along Bull Run creek, the demobilizing of the ninety-day regiments upon completion of their enlistments, and now the call for hundreds of thousands of volunteers . . . room enough at last for William to join in the fray and prove he was a man. He might be delayed for a few months with parents demanding that he stay for the bringing in of the autumn harvest (thus hoping to buy time, with the prayer that the war would be over before winter), but finally no further arguments could dissuade him from his patriotic duty.

* * *

At last his chance finally comes with the announcement that his congressional district will form yet another regiment for the glorious cause of the Union. There would be a fairlike atmosphere yet again in front of the county courthouse, perhaps a veteran of one of the ninety-day regiments extolling, "You young men of virtue, strength, and courage, come forward now for your country needs you. And you ladies, perhaps you will give your sweetheart the kiss he deserves!"

So young William signs the roster. There might even be a perfunctory medical, a quick thump to the chest and minutes later he signs the muster roll, takes the oath, and steps back out into the village square to cheers, and yes, that treasured kiss from a girl he will leave behind . . . who with tears in her eyes will pledge her love and to write every day . . . and for any nineteen-year-old of that time, that alone is worth all.

A few days later he is ordered to report back to the center of town with the other hundred recruits of his company. And then, perhaps as exciting to him as the offer of a space shuttle ride today, a train pulls in, a car reserved for the young heroes, his first train ride, which will bear him all the way to the state capital. Amid cheers and tears, he is ready to depart. As proper to that time, his father will tell him to behave like a man. Don't push too far to the front line, but never run. His minister will extol him to carry his Bible in his breast pocket as a shield and with lowered voice urge him to avoid the temptations of sin that await him in the wicked world of the army. His mother will tell him to avoid sinful men, and of course there might even be another kiss from the beloved young lady who is all but saying that upon his return they will marry.

The hero departs. And in every depot along the way, more recruits pile aboard, all of them laughing, cheerful comrades . . . And thus did a million or more in that autumn and winter of 1861–62 set off for war.

* * *

Civil War regiments were first sworn into service to their state governments, with allegiance to their governor, a ceremony usually performed at the state capital. Often they would then be immediately "federalized," meaning transferred to federal authority under the President and those officers appointed by him. Outside of nearly every state capital, campgrounds were established. Here William would first be introduced to military drill and discipline.

The parade-ground maneuvers that are the dread of every recruit even today, had a basis in battlefield reality that existed well into the nineteenth century.

The foundation of it all was the .58-caliber Springfield rifle or the .577 Enfield rifled musket. Linear warfare, the type of combat where troops, arrayed in standing lines, blaze away at one another, seems like madness today, but in the nineteenth century it had a foundation in logic and combat reality. A typical Civil War regiment, arrayed two ranks deep, standing shoulder to shoulder, covered a front of approximately a hundred yards. With each man eventually trained to load and fire three rounds a minute, a regiment could thus put out the firepower of a couple of modern machine guns, sweeping all before it.

Linear warfare was based upon the premise of massing troops at the point of attack, overwhelming with firepower at fairly close range, and then delivering the coup with a charge to break the opponent's line.

The rifled muskets of the era had an effective "aimed range" of two hundred and fifty yards and could easily kill at four hundred yards, the instrument of death a one-ounce conical soft-lead bullet, the infamous minié ball. Drawn up in linear formation, with an enemy approaching at the rate of a hundred yards a minute, a well-drilled regiment could slash out with half a dozen rounds or more per man in just a few minutes. The tendency was to force an enemy charge to "go to ground," meaning grinding to a halt and returning fire in an attempt to break the "firepower superiority" of the defenders. Thus would start a bitter fight on the line until the courage and will of one side or the other broke.

Standing? The rifled musket could be loaded while lying on the ground, but loaded two to three times faster when standing. Thus disciplined, aimed volleys were considered the best method of breaking an enemy charge, or breaking the will of a defender before closing in with the bayonet. As to the bayonet, it was later found to be rarely used in the mid-nineteenth century, one side or the other breaking back and fleeing before that final onset of hand-to-hand combat so often talked about but actually rarely seen in Civil War combat.

The timing and math of moving a linear formation of hundreds of men in a dual line, however, was complex. Men had to be trained to shift from a marching column of four abreast into a battle formation of two lines shoulder to shoulder, and to do so instantly. Once in line, if an enemy should appear on a flank, men had to be trained to rapidly shift direction, to wheel, turn, come about, advance, to maintain formation, to charge at the double, to maneuver first as a company of a hundred men, a regiment of a thousand, and then up to the line of a brigade of five regiments, and from there a division of three brigades.

To gain an enemy flank was always a sought-after goal, a position where a formation of a thousand or more men could pour fire into an enemy caught off guard, with only a few dozen able to return fire in reply. Flank an opponent and the day was won, thus yet more drilling in rapid maneuvers and movements to gain a flank, how to turn to repel such a maneuver, or when and where to form into a column like a battering ram to crush a way through an enemy line.

It was a formula for casualties on a horrific scale.

It was one thing to do it on the parade ground, it would be another thing to do it in the smoke, noise, confusion, and terror of the battlefield, no longer on a parade ground, trampled flat and smooth, but across rolling farmland, woodlots, dense forests, swamps, and mountains.

The math starts becoming more complex when moving an army from marching to battle order is considered. A marching column of five thousand men, moving on a typical dirt road of the period, would occupy at least a mile of roadage, more likely a mile and a half. To shift that column into a battle formation, say with three regiments deployed forward across a front of a quarter mile, two regiments in reserve a hundred yards back, could take a half hour or more. With two columns approaching and stumbling into each other, he who deployed first could easily roll up the other . . . thus the ever-incessant drill, and drill and more drill, from company level on up.

As William's regiment prepared at the state capital to go to the front, casualties would begin to add up, in fact more casualties in that first month than might ever be sustained on the battlefield. For every man who died in combat, two would die of disease and accidents, and it started almost literally on day one.

Medical technology was on the edge of a revolution in 1861. Anesthesia, thank God, had been in use for nearly twenty years. Ironically, a Dr. Simmelweiss, in Budapest, had discovered how infection was transmitted and how sterilization of medical equipment and proper washing of hands could radically cut infection rates, but his work was not yet known in the States and, due to a poorly written report of his discoveries, was known only by a few in Europe. The first antiseptic would be developed in England just as the war ended, and Pasteur's near-miraculous discoveries and development of inoculations for a host of diseases would take place ten years after the war.

In short, other than for anesthesia, the mass armies of the Civil War were little better off than the armies of Caesar. In fact worst off, because Caesar's legion were far better trained in field sanitation.

Within days after gathering, the boys would begin to fall ill. An irony was almost immediately noted, the somewhat scorned "pasty faced shopkeepers," as more than one wag described them, seemed to weather the epidemics of chickenpox, scarlet fever, whooping cough, and measles far better than the husky farm boys who'd grown up in relative isolation. Within a few weeks, the vast majority would be hit by a variety of gastrointestinal ailments due to poorly prepared food and the by-now-tainted water supply. A hundred or more of the initial thousand enlistees for the regiment might die, or become so sick as to be discharged and sent home. Given the cursory physicals, another hundred or more would simply break down. Our fantasy image of Civil War soldiers being tough, lean young men stood true for those that survived the first months, but many never should have been allowed into the recruiting hall: boys with bad teeth that could not handle the hardtack rations, with bad hearts, flat feet, asthma. And finally, more than a few, with the romance beginning to wear off, turned for home and slipped off on a dark night. Thus the numbers of the regiment rapidly dropped.

* * *

Being from Ohio, William's regiment could anticipate posting nearly anywhere from the Mississippi to in front of Washington, and orders would finally arrive.

There would be a farewell send-off yet again. A grand ceremony would be held, featuring patriotic speeches, with the governor and perhaps the local congressman in attendance, ready to cheer the boys on and press the flesh for votes as well, and presentation of the flags, usually by a delegation of fair ladies.

Union regiments tended to carry two flags into battle. The national colors, with the name of the regiment emblazoned on it, and beside it the state flag . . . for this was definitely a war between the states, and in both North and South identity was defined by a soldier's home state.

Regimental flags took on a highly symbolic nature for the men of the regiment. It was their totem, their symbol of pride and what they fought for. In the smoke of battle, flags were posted to the center of the battle line, the men told that above all else, they should keep an eye toward the colors: If the flag advances, go with it, stand with it, and defend it with your life. The greatest glory would go to a man who captured an enemy flag; the greatest disgrace a regiment could endure would be to lose their flag in battle. Carrying the flag was the highest of honors for an enlisted man, and the term color guard was literally true, the men of that guard the toughest of the regiment and the bravest. Few flag bearers and color guards survived more than one or two battles.

Again loading aboard a train, with spirits high, the regiment headed to the front to join an army in the field. In those early days of the war they would be feted and cheered along the way . . . Boys ardent for some desperate glory, fearful even that it might be over before they arrived, boasting as well that once they were into the fight, things would be quickly settled, joyfully went to the killing grounds in Virginia, Tennessee, and along the Mississippi.

* * *

Few regiments ever had the time to learn their business properly before being sent to the front; few grasped what they were about to get into and the reception they would receive.

If they were assigned to the eastern theater of war, there would be a final honor of parading through Washington, D.C., and, with luck, perhaps even catching a glimpse of Old Abe himself and given a day of leave to tour the sites, including the beginnings of the pillar dedicated to Washington and a trip to the Capitol to gape at the half-completed dome. And by the time they formed up to march on, or take a short boat ride down the Potomac to where the main army was camped, more than a few would be dying and not yet know it.

The Victorian ideal of the men in blue being "straight arrows," was as absurd then as it would be in any war. Free of the constraints of home, other than perhaps the watchful eye of the regimental parson or maybe the hometown mayor or schoolmaster, more than a few slipped off for "a frolic" as some called it, and there were more than enough "soiled doves," as they were so delicately called, ready and waiting. It is estimated that upward of 10 percent of the Union Army serving in the D.C. area would return home with a venereal disease, which in the 1860s would eventually prove to be fatal, ten to twenty years later.

As the new regiment finally marched into the vast encampment area, the reception they received would be far different than their boyish fantasies. The first thing that would assail them would be the smells, squalor, and confusion. High command usually tried to slot a new regiment in with a brigade of four or five regiments from the same state or region. The reception, however, would be far from a welcoming one. If the brigade had seen battle, and gained a reputation as hard fighters, the reception was downright icy. Enlisted men of the veteran regiments would taunt the new arrivals, even the officers, as "fresh fish," who had not yet "seen the elephant." It was made clear that they were not part of the fraternity until they had proven themselves in a fight, and by God, if they failed, they would be hounded from the army as cowards.

The amateur officers would suddenly be confronted by the professionals. Nearly all high command slots, both North and South, finally gravitated to West Pointers and, in the South, graduates as well of VMI and the Citadel. They were a no-nonsense lot, and in general throughout the war there would be a divide between the professionals and the volunteers, and all chafed right away under the tougher discipline now imposed. Boys so proud of their ability to march and even change formation would be drilled, cussed out, drilled, cussed out again, and drilled and drilled yet again.

Food was usually the same, a perfectly balanced diet of hardtack, salted pork or beef, black coffee, and maybe on occasion some fresh meat if you were lucky. Scurvy was not unknown, as well as larger epidemics of typhoid and dysentery, and especially in rainy weather and winter the army sounded like a smokers' ward with the respiratory infections running rampant . . . and still more men would die or be discharged as no longer fit for service.

It was not at all unusual for a regiment that was a thousand strong to have six hundred or fewer fit for duty when the army finally began a campaign.

* * *

Weeks, perhaps months, might now pass, of tedious drilling, of learning how to fight on a brigade and division scale . . . and finally rumors spread that the army was "going up." An evening would come when the men would be paraded and ordered to draw several days' marching rations and sixty rounds of ammunition. A sleepless night of anticipation would follow, and long before dawn tents would be struck, extra gear sorted out to be left behind, the men mustered, roll called (and several more would be found missing), and then the remaining men would fall in and set out on what the fresh fish of William's regiment believed was the greatest adventure of their lives.

A typical day's march might be fifteen miles or so. With rifled musket, sixty rounds of ammunition (forty in a cartridge box, twenty tucked into a pocket), three days' ration, blanket roll, rubberized ground cloth, half a tent (which was known as a pup tent, to be buttoned together with a comrade's at the end of the day), perhaps some extra socks and a shirt, William would be ladened down with thirty to forty pounds of equipment. The uniform was all wool, and regardless of the claims that wool can breathe and stay cool, it was ill designed for a summer campaign in the south with ninety-degree heat.

In a few short miles, especially along the trail of a green regiment, the roadside would be littered with castoffs: books other than the precious Bible and, after a dozen miles, tents, anything that could lighten the burden, with veterans usually marching with little more than a blanket roll covered by the useful rubberized blanket, a haversack filled with rations, and a cartridge box carrying forty rounds—and of course the eight-pound musket on the shoulder.

March discipline was tight, a unit that did not keep a compact column would be unmercifully harangued by brigade and division staff; otherwise a column could "accordion" out to twice the accepted length and thus take twice as long to go into battle formation, and delay even more the units behind them. Standard drill for march was a pace of two miles an hour, being fifty minutes of march and a ten-minute break by the side of the road before falling back in again. The famed and feared "foot cavalry" of Stonewall Jackson would at times push that pace to three and even four miles in the hour. During the Gettysburg campaign, John Sedgwick's Sixth Corps would march nearly forty miles, in sixteen hours, in ninety-degree heat.

The army might maneuver for days, with only the highest levels of command understanding the meaning of the intricate minuet being played out with their opponents, of march and countermarch, maneuver, probing, and looking for an opening. An army of 1862 could only see as far as its forward line of cavalry pickets, who were tasked to discover the positions, strength, and disposition of their opponents while denying that information as well.

On several occasions William and his comrades might be rousted out of line by the long roll of the drums, shouted commands from an officer galloping by, and with beating hearts form up, only to wait and perhaps in the distance hear what sounded like popcorn popping, an occasional low growl of thunder, and then silence. Forming back into column, they would move on, a half hour later passing a spot where half a dozen dead were sprawled by the side of the road, the men of the veteran regiments shouting taunts to the "fresh fish" to take a good, careful look.

And then finally the test would at last come.

* * *

It could still be a cool, gentle morning, or a hot afternoon with sullen clouds promising a storm on the horizon. It would often be felt before actually heard; more than a few described it as sounding like someone beating a carpet off in the distance, an occasional thump, almost like the echoing of a storm on a summer evening far over the horizon.

The pace of the march would pick up, muttered comments drifting back from the veteran regiments that there was "mischief ahead." Interestingly, the side of the road would start to be littered with a different breed of castoffs. This was still an age of literal interpretation about good and evil and carrying the tools of Satan on your person when facing eternity. Boys who might have drifted toward sinful ways would now be casting aside the devil's instruments of playing cards, dice, whiskey bottles, the new rage of "French postcards" (the pinup photos of the nineteenth century). No one wanted to meet his Maker with such items in his haversack, or just as bad have the regimental parson discover them on his body as he was laid out after the fight.

An officer would come galloping by, shouting hurried orders to the regimental colonel to uncase the colors and close up the ranks. Protective covers would be removed from the flags, the silken folds shaken out. Drummer boys would be ordered to pick up the beat, the regiment would surge on, the new recruits filled with excitement but also the first knots of real fear.

This was a war where courage and cowardice, honor and dishonor were played out on an open stage for all to see. An officer was expected to literally lead from the front, saber in hand. A soldier stood on a volley line, with childhood friends, cousins, neighbors, perhaps the brother of his sweetheart standing to either side . . . and only the dullest or most supremely foolish did not wonder, going in, if he could stand it or not.

The thumping would grow in intensity. Where an hour before it was only a point of sound on the horizon, it began now to spread out, broaden, and grow in intensity and volume. A regimental volley in the distance would often be described as sounding like a sheet being torn in half. Mingled in was the deeper, throatier thump of artillery. A pall of yellowish gray smoke would now be visible cloaking the next ridgeline ahead, pierced by flashes of light . . . and they would enter the rear area of the spreading battle.

Grant, along with many another veteran, would later write that the first impression of the rear area of battle was one of defeat. Wounded would be staggering back, wide-eyed, some hysterical. Provost guards would be deployed, demanding to "see blood" before letting a man pass, and if not, trying to turn the panic-stricken about with the flat of a sword or the threat of a drawn revolver. Units, broken up in the fight, would be pulling back to reorganize, rest for a few minutes, clean out their muskets, draw more ammunition, and be readied to go back in.

There were no neat, orderly vistas of parade-like lines, gallant officers astride prancing mounts leading the way . . . All would seem to be confusion, chaos, overwhelmed with the noise and confusion.

The regiment would be ordered to move at the double, wheel to the right or left off the road and form line. Many would later write that at that moment they felt like nothing more than a herd of sheep being driven toward a slaughter pen with no escape. When they had drawn into battle line, the order would be passed to load.

On a parade ground William might have done the routine a thousand times, though in more than a few cases entire regiments went into their first fight with only a day or two of drill, some having never even fired their weapons once.

The ritual seemed simple enough. A cartridge would be drawn from the cartridge box and placed between the teeth. When it had been torn open, the powder was poured down the barrel, a grease-covered bullet was thumbed into the muzzle, the ramrod drawn, the bullet slammed down the length of the barrel, the ramrod then withdrawn and reset (and more than one green recruit would forget to pull out the ramrod and fire it downrange on his first shot). A percussion cap would then be taken from a small pouch attached to the belt near the right hip. Quite often the cap would be fumbled and dropped, or once put on the nipple under the hammer, it would fall off. The hammer would be half-cocked, and to signal that the soldier was loaded and ready, the weapon would be returned to the shoulder.

And then came the wait. It might be only a few minutes, it might even be hours under a blazing sun, not yet sure if you were to go in, wait in reserve, or suddenly face an enemy onslaught. Officers would nervously pace, sergeants keeping a watchful eye on those whom they suspected might try and bolt, men perhaps given permission to stand at ease in place.

One grim reality that few would talk or write about was the simple fact that a fair percentage of the men were usually sick, perhaps just a case of what was known as the "two steps," from bad water and food. Nerves made it worse, and if overwhelmed, a man would only be allowed to step back a few paces to relieve himself, so that in short order a fetid stench hung over the ranks. Some would begin to vomit because of the fear as well, a few might even break down, crying out that they were sick, and beg to go to the rear. Calmer men would try to encourage, and given the religious values of that time, nearly all would have a Bible out, seeking solace, many reading passages aloud.

At last the order would be given to go in.

With weapons shouldered again, the tradition of an officer giving a speech would be played out, the usual extolling the soldiers to remember their cause, an appeal to the honor of the regiment, usually a quick prayer and blessing by the parson, and with the long roll of the drums the regiment would step off.

They might pass through the artillery line as they advanced. The vast majority of field guns of the war fired either ten-pound rifled shot with an accurate range of upward of a mile, or round shot ranging out to just over a thousand yards. As the battle line swept through their ranks, gunners would cease fire and shout encouragement, more than a few of the infantry undoubtedly wondering to themselves why the hell they had gone for the infantry rather than the artillery.

The advance toward the enemy position would begin.

* * *

Linear warfare, the fighting of battles with rigid line formations, had evolved out of the gunpowder revolution of the seventeenth century, when reliable enough shoulder firearms became the standard weapon for the armies of Europe (and also Japan during its civil wars). Though strange, even foolish to the modern eye, there was a well-thought-out logic to the methods.

Standing and arrayed in lines, well-trained men, especially after the transition from matchlock to flintlock, could fire three, even four to five volleys a minute. Effective range was at most eighty yards, but once into that range, the idea was to sweep the field ahead, turning it into a killing zone. There was also a simple logic to maintaining the lines. Black-powder weapons generate a tremendous amount of smoke. For a line formation ordered to open fire, anything ahead of it was fair game, and with visibility often down to ten to twenty yards after a few minutes, anyone foolish enough to wander was dead.

European armies tended to fight in three-line formations; American armies by the middle of the Revolution tended to engage in a two-line front. Standard battle formation was for a brigade of five regiments to advance, with three regiments forward and two in reserve fifty to a hundred yards back. These two reserve regiments were ready for a number of potentials that might evolve. The vulnerability of a linear formation was always the flank. If a flank was being threatened, the reserve regiments could form to block that effort. If one of the forward regiments sustained heavy casualties, the reserve would be pushed in . . . or, ideally, at the right moment be ordered to sprint forward to charge and close with the enemy.

The obvious drawback to linear battles of the nineteenth century . . . the incredible level of carnage that was readily accepted, even by the victorious side. With the advent of the rifled musket, killing range had of course been extended. It was not unusual for a regiment, if in the forward line, to sustain 50 percent casualties even in a successful attack. As the war progressed, tactics changed, and by the last year or so, the standup rigid formations had been all but abandoned, though a "battering ram" type technique was still used. A division of fifteen or so regiments would form up on a front only one or two regiments wide, with the rest in column behind. Under the cover of darkness or early dawn the entire column would move forward at the run, a technique often employed against fortified positions. Needless to say the first few regiments were usually slaughtered in the attack, such as the famed Fifty-fourth Mass., in the assault on Battery Wagner.

* * *

As William's regiment advanced into the open field, the enemy position might be only several hundred yards away, or in some cases, such as Pickett's Charge, nearly a mile off. The advancing troops would immediately come under artillery fire—which was not very effective at ranges much beyond six hundred yards, but still as unnerving as solid shot—or explosive case shot would hit the advancing lines of soldiers. The impact of a well-aimed solid shot of twelve pounds would pulp the two men in the line that it hit; if it smashed into an advancing column, it could kill a dozen or more.

At less than six hundred yards, gunners had a far clearer chance of placing well-aimed shot into the advancing line and a battery of six guns could drop dozens as the regiment surged forward.

When the range reached about two hundred and fifty yards, the defending infantry would open up, and now the death match truly began. Their Revolutionary grandfathers had not had to face this gauntlet until the range was down to eighty yards or less, but with rifled muskets, the killing ground now reached out to more than two hundred and fifty yards or more. By war's end, troops would usually open fire at a quarter of a mile or more. Officers would urge the men to keep pressing forward, to keep an eye on the flag to mark the advance, and at this point order the men to begin advancing at the double.

It is at this moment that any true student of the Civil War cringes when watching movies supposedly set at that time. Most of the footage used involves reenactors as doubles. Well-meaning men, but one must remember their average age is in the thirties to forties (it is an expensive endeavor that costs a couple of thousand dollars to get into), and very few indeed are like their tough sinewy great-grandfathers raised on farms or working as laborers in factories. There was no surging mob who advanced at little better than a walk or, far worse, kept their lines but moved in a wooden lockstep of only forty to fifty yards a minute, acting as little better than targets.

A Civil War attack at this stage would attempt to surge forward at a couple of hundred yards a minute, sweeping over the deadly ground, but still maintaining some form of disciplined lines. Witnesses often described the advances as looking like inverted V-formations, at the point of which would be the flag and commanding officer.

At some point, hard to describe, the attack would tend to stall.

It was a strange, mysterious point, impossible for any observer who has never truly experienced it to understand. Perhaps the best descriptions of it come from the writings of Ambrose Bierce, who described an action where his attacking line just stalled. To advance further into the blazing guns of the enemy now seemed impossible, as if a line of death had been drawn in front of them. The few that did try to cross those last few yards instantly dropped. If facing artillery, the tendency was for the charge to stall at extreme canister range . . . a couple of hundred yards out. The only response . . . fire back, and especially against artillery, to drop the gunners before closing in.

Canister was a terrifying weapon, nothing more than an oversized tin can, filled with thirty to seventy iron balls, which turned the weapon into a giant sawed-off shotgun. Double canister, fired from a battery at a range of fifty yards, could shred an entire regiment. No wonder the tendency was to hesitate before closing the last few yards, even though to remain in the open for any period of time could be just as deadly.

Thus a deadly firefight would begin. Often the first few rounds would be delivered as hammering volleys, but then the next would break down into independent fire at will. Smoke would obscure both sides, especially on a warm, humid day with little or no wind. Men would soon be reduced to trying to pick out flashes of light from the other side and aiming at that. Though the weapons were deadly accurate, usually, after the first few rounds, hundreds of shots might be fired to inflict only a few casualties.

After a dozen rounds or so, loading became slower, as the black powder formed a thick glue-like substance inside the barrel, making it harder to load. A typical regiment, firing two rounds a minute, could be "fought out" in little more than a half hour, having to be temporarily pulled from the line to clean muskets, replenish ammunition supplies, form ranks, and go back in. In addition thirst was a constant problem. Civil War canteens carried only a quart; a hard march before a battle would often result in the canteens being drained. The thick, choking smoke, combined with adrenaline-pumped fear, would usually leave men on the edge of collapse. In the famed standoff between the Twentieth Maine and half a dozen Confederate regiments on the flank of Little Round Top, the Confederate survivors of that fight swore, with good reason and not just injured pride, that if they had only been given a few minutes to refill canteens before going in, they would have taken the hill. Hundreds of them were felled by heat exhaustion and thirst, and the victorious Mainers noted that the first thing their prisoners begged for was a sip of water. The Mainers, hunkered down behind the rocks of the slope, had not force-marched a dozen miles before going into the fight, but their canteens were empty as well.

The firefight between William's regiment and the rebs standing before him might last but a few minutes; in some cases fights could actually go on for hours, men finally "hunkering down," behind cover, digging in even as they fought, calling for more ammunition to be brought up, and hanging on. Often though one side or the other would wither and break under the sustained hammering. If a charge was to be successful, the usual tactic was to have a fresh reserve ready to go in.

The standard advance of a brigade, as mentioned, was usually three regiments forward and two in reserve. A division-level advance would usually be two such brigades side by side, with the third brigade a couple of hundred yards to the rear. An experienced commander did not usually expect his "first wave" to break the enemy position. Their task was to "fix the enemy in their position," meaning pinning them down, and then "develop them," which meant tearing into them. As well, the task of the lead regiments was to absorb the body blows inflicted just getting across the fields to within close combat range.

Now came the supreme moment. Judging the timing to be

right, brigade, division, or even corps command would order the reserves to sweep in. Having suffered few casualties in the advance, with muskets clean and spirits high, the secondary line would be ordered to surge forward, charging through the first wave of attackers. This was the attack meant to slam things home and finish the opponent. This was the moment of the supreme test of nerves. Could the fresh troops cover those last few hundred yards, or would they collapse under a withering fire?

Of course the other side, led by comrades trained at West Point so many years before, knew the game as well, and would push their reserves, if they had them, into the forward line, poised and ready to deliver a killing volley at fifty yards or less. If artillery crews still survived (often they were told to hunker down and wait for the enemy to get into canister range before resuming the fight), they would leap to their guns and slam in the deadly loads.

What ensued was, to any modern eyes, a bloodbath. If one wishes to conjure an image of what the final moments of a Civil War charge looked like, ignore such films as *Gettysburg* or even *Glory* . . . turn instead to the opening scenes of *Saving Private Ryan*, for the level of firepower was nearly the same, and the damage sustained just as ghastly.

William and his comrades would, more often than not, leap forward into that final charge regardless of exhaustion. Regimental pride was a powerful thing to Civil War soldiers and especially a green regiment would never let it be said after the fight that they had not gone into the storm with the other regiments of their brigade.

The final moments of such a charge were wild confusion. Units mingled together, all obscured with smoke except for the flashes of musketry and the flaming bursts from the muzzles of cannon. Men would be swept down by the score. Veterans would later recall such moments to have been surreal, like nightmares. The term "slow motion" was not introduced into our lexicon until the advent of moving pictures, but read the description of Joshua Chamberlain's charge at Petersburg, and he will exactly describe such an adrenaline-fed moment, of looking back at his troops who seemed to be moving in a dreamlike state, mouths open, shouting but not heard, of men drifting past him, of the sudden numbing impact of the bullet that cut through his body.

Such descriptions are eternal, whether recorded by a veteran with Caesar or Patton.

Far too many movies of the Civil War portray that final moment of a charge as hand-to-hand, with bayonets flashing in a gristly brawl. It almost never happened. Statistics gathered during and after the war by the medical corps showed that only a fraction of a percent of all wounds were ever inflicted by sword, bayonet, or clubbed musket. Some argue that this was true because most injuries inflicted by that stage were fatal. But more than a few veterans stated that throughout the entire war they never once used a bayonet, a far better function for that legendary weapon being its use as a candlestick holder in camp. Many finally just tossed them away as deadweight. There was something about crossing those last few feet to close that made men hesitate. They might stand and fire at one another from a dozen paces away, scream and curse at each other, or in some cases even shout for the other side just to "get the hell out of here, you damn rebels!" which might prompt the enemy to turn about and flee and end it. At least during the Civil War, in infantry combat, men recoiled from the final act of Neanderthal-like slaughter.

* * *

Tragically for all involved, Civil War battles were defined by the terrifying power of defensive fire. Well-dug-in troops, armed with rifled muskets and backed up by artillery, could repel odds of even six or more to one. In an open firefight, what the veterans came to call "a cornfield meet," such as at Antietam or in the first day's fighting at Gettysburg, it came down to which side had the most nerve and the willingness to sustain 50 percent casualties or higher to hold or take a position.

Perhaps William's regiment succeeds and actually dislodges the rebels from their position, driving them back, maybe even taking a flag and several field pieces, which cannot be pulled out since all the horses have been shot and the guns overrun. Then what?

The battle was rarely over. The length of time of a battle is a function of logistics and simple human strength. In ancient warfare, even the toughest of men could not be expected to sustain the relentless swinging of swords while wearing sixty or more pounds of armor for more than a few hours at most before one side or the other broke and fled. Well into the eighteenth century, rare was the battle that lasted for even half a day, except of course for sieges.

Even in the age of Napoleon, most battles were day-long affairs. Borodino going for two days was the exception rather than the rule.

But by 1863 modern logistics had changed that paradigm. Supported by railheads within a day's wagon ride of the front line, an army could resupply every shot fired and every ration consumed overnight and resume action in the morning. By 1864, though Grant was losing thousands of men a day in the Overland Campaign, fresh troops, moved by steamship and rail, flooded in from across the nation to continue to support the fight. The age of logistical attrition was at hand. It was most definitely a foreshadowing of what was to come in France and Belgium in 1914.

For young William this might mean a brief moment of glory. Perhaps the old vets of the other regiments coming through the ranks of his, would slap newly made "comrades" on the back, telling them they were no longer "fresh fish" now that they had "seen the elephant" and proved themselves to be "bully good lads." They were part of "our brigade" and pride would swell with that acknowledgment.

Weapons would be hurriedly cleaned, watering parties sent out to fill canteens (usually from creeks already befouled with corpses), and perhaps the soldiers would even be sent into reserve for a few hours of nervous, exhausted rest and the serving out of rations.

In those few hours the reality of what they had endured would begin to set in. After the exaltation of the moment, as his company formed up, William would see how the ranks had been tragically thinned. Where once fifty had stood, now there might only be twenty or twenty-five. Where was Jim, his childhood buddy, or the old schoolmaster, or the younger brother of his girl whom he'd promised to keep an eye on?

There was no time for that now, and the men had been reassured that orderlies and the surgeons would look after the fallen.

A lie.

Not even to the end of the war was either army even remotely capable of dealing with the level of casualties sustained. But more on that later.

Waiting in reserve, William might see another division advancing forward yet again, perhaps to come fleeing back an hour later. Or as was so typical for Union forces in the eastern theater, all might seem well, and then suddenly would come a distant rumble, not from their front, but instead now from a flank or even behind them, and worried whispers would sweep through the ranks. "My God, they're behind us again! That damn Stonewall's doing it again!"

The typical private of any war rarely has a sense of exactly where he is. Long after the war, if he survives, he might be able to trace a line on a map and exclaim, "That was me," but at the moment it was just another field, a hill, a woodlot, a tangled swamp, like a hundred other such places he had fought over. But in a tactical sense, the typical soldier of the Civil War had a fairly good grasp of the immediate situation and could tell which way the tide was flowing by the sound of battle, what kind of position his men held, and the obvious behavior of officers, often far too officious and self-important, rushing back and forth.

An officer who could keep his nerve and look unperturbed was worth his weight in gold. Old "Pap" Thomas at Chickamauga, when dealt a losing hand and ordered to be the blocking force while the rest of the army fled in panic, won the undying admiration of his men for pacing the line, offering reassurance and defiance, even as gunfire swept into the ranks from nearly a 360-degree circle. Eighty years later his example lived again when with one defiant word in response to the Nazi demand to surrender, the reply "Nuts," the "battling bastards of Bastogne" drew inspiration and threw back attack after attack.

* * *

The fight for the day might not yet be over for William. Perhaps indeed the flank or rear had been turned by Stonewall, and now their job was not to attack but defend as wave after wave of Confederates swarmed in until finally darkness settled.

It was very rare for a Civil War battle to continue after nightfall, if for no other reason than that after a day of such combat, both sides were fought to exhaustion.

Now at last William and some of his comrades might be relieved from the line to go back over the path of their attack to try and find wounded comrades.

Yes, there was a hospital service, and as the war progressed more effort was placed into evacuating wounded from the field of action, but right up until the last day of the war, the best bet for any help at all usually came from comrades of the regiment, detailed off once the fighting had settled down, to go back and seek out their fallen friends. If front lines were fairly stable, informal truces would be offered by both sides, and it was not unusual for former foes to mingle together on the stricken field during the night, looking for their brothers and friends, calling out regimental numbers and names.

In an age where we are used to the promise that our brave wounded are never more than ten to fifteen minutes from the best medical care in the world, it is hard to imagine that not so far in our past, in the bloodiest war in our nation's history, men might lie in the field for hours, even days, without help.

* * *

The plight of the wounded was ghastly indeed. Survivability was a studied subject during and after the war and listed in detail in the medical history of the conflict. Wounds to the limbs dominated. If no bone was broken, amputation might be avoided. There is a mythology that the typical Civil War surgeon was a butcher. It is hardly the case, though without doubt there were more than a few who were quacks and deserved to be shot . . . and who were usually driven out of the service in short order. But the grim statistics speak for themselves. A good regiment, properly manned, would have assigned to it a surgeon and assistant surgeon. Few field surgeons in 1863 actually had more than a year or two of formal medical training at a major university. Many had simply apprenticed with their town doctor, studied, learned common sense, eventually hung out a shingle, and then gone into the army with their friends and neighbors.

If a regiment of five hundred sustained 25 percent casualties, typically one out of four was dead on the field or within a few hours. That meant approximately 110 to 120 would still be alive. Of that number, upward of half might be ambulatory, meaning they could get themselves off the field, or help one another back to the rear. The first flood of wounded coming into the hospital area would be men with arm, head, and even chest wounds. In a major action, surgeons for a brigade would combine efforts. Triage existed then as now. If a man was lucky and had a flesh wound, without severing of artery or breaking of bone, an assistant would bandage him up, and if enough opium or morphine was on hand, he'd be given a dose and sent further back to clear the way for the more serious cases.

The non-ambulatory wounds were usually those to the legs

with broken bones, stomach wounds, major head wounds, and most chest wounds, and the soldiers with these wounds were usually carried in by distraught comrades.

Now came the difficult choices. If faced with getting shot, this author, if given a choice, would without hesitation choose a 7.62 jacketed round over a .58 minié ball any day. Even with today's medical technology, a femur, shattered by a minié ball fired at close range, or slammed by a three-ounce canister round, might be beyond any treatment other than amputation.

Beyond that was the sheer number of casualties flooding in. If a regiment sustained 110 wounded, and a surgeon devoted but fifteen minutes to each man, it would be close on to thirty hours straight before he had seen the last of them. A primitive nineteenth-century "procedure" of an hour or more to try and reconstruct a shattered bone and tie off bleeding arteries might save a man's arm, but in the interim, four or five others might bleed to death. The grim statistic was this: ten minutes to amputate or an hour to try and save while others died. It was a horrid choice, made more gut-wrenching because in so many cases, the surgeon was not some unfeeling butcher, but instead the town doctor who had joined with "his boys" and knew each of them and their families by name. The psychological casualties among the surgeons of the Civil War must have been horrific.

For men hit in the stomach, the chance of survival was far less than 1 percent. They were triaged off to a dying area, given opiates to ease their agony, and left to the attention of a couple of harried orderlies until at last they died. Hospital areas were usually nearby homes, churches, and yes, barns. The post-wound and surgery infection rate was near on to 100 percent.

The terrible statistics broke down to this: Roughly one out of four would lie dead on the field at day's end; these were the lucky ones taking a bullet to the brain, heart, or femoral artery. Most, though, had lingered on for a few minutes or hours, men who by today's standards could have been saved if treated fast enough. Of the remaining three out of four, one faced radical surgery, meaning amputation. Fatality after surgery ranged from as low as 5 percent up to nearly 90 percent if it was a radical removal of more than one limb or amputation of the leg at the hip. Of the other two, most recovered, though a small percentage would later succumb to infection anyhow.

The impact on morale must have been shattering. By World War II, army psychologists knew and taught that frontline troops should be kept removed from the fate of their wounded comrades as much as possible. Keep the healthy ones moving forward, but reassure them that their wounded buddies were in good hands. In general there was a truth to that with a medic assigned to each platoon and battalion aid often set up only a few hundred yards to the rear. Civil War soldiers had no such luxury or psychological balm as they wandered the battlefield at night, searching for lost comrades and, ironically, at times helping an enemy from the daytime carry a dying friend to the nearest barn for treatment.

This intermingling of troops before and after a battle was commonplace throughout the war. The famed scene from *The Red Badge of Courage* where Henry Fleming is warned by a friendly "reb" not to stand in the moonlight while on picket duty else wise he might have to shoot him was common fare. They might kill without hesitation in the heat of battle, but in general sniping was seen as little better than murder. After a battle, enemy combatants might meet between the lines to talk about the day's "fracas" or "tussle," boast a bit, and then shake heads about how damn insane the entire thing was. A canteen with a bit of corn liquor in it might be shared for a tin of condensed milk or plug of tobacco. To the dismay of the professional officers corps throughout the war, both sides would talk openly about which regiment they were with, what they had seen, whom they had fought, and heartbreakingly, even pray together before going back to their separate sides.

For young William, this was his first taste of battle, his first drink of liquor from a rebel canteen in disobedience to his mother, shared with a frightened boy from South Carolina, then both of them saying the Twenty-third Psalm together before parting. This was not the enemy he had been led to believe he would face. This was not the enemy he had shot at and exulted over earlier that day when he had seen one of his shots strike home, killing the comrade of the friend he now shared a drink with, wept with, and prayed with. This was the experience of the common soldier in the Civil War.

* * *

The miracle of it all, the tragedy of it all. If William had any idealism about war, if he had been, as a later poet would write, a youth "ardent for some desperate glory," he would have been disabused of it on that first shocking day of battle . . . be it at Manassas, Shiloh, the Peninsula, or Fort Henry. And yet they endured. We should abandon all idealism in one sense, for yes, hundreds of thousands turned and fled and cried "Let others face it." By the middle of the war, tens of thousands made a living out of collecting bounties that in today's currency would be worth tens of thousands of dollars, and then promptly deserted. But there was a hard-bitten core on both sides, several hundred thousand strong, who "saw the elephant" and saw that it was nothing more than the face of death, but that death was secondary to the ideals they fought for, and returned to the battlefield again and again. Be it for states' rights, or the far more primal "you are on my land," or a loftier ideal of "for the Union," or finally "that all men are created equal" . . . they endured.

They endured. And when it was finished, one survivor would declare, "We tested steel against steel," and in so doing reforged that steel into a single nation.

They must forever remain "everlasting in the hearts of their countrymen."

A Rifleman in the Meuse-Argonne Campaign

First Division, AEF, October 1918

"Doughboys!"

BY ROLAND GREEN

The changing ways a soldier fought during the American Civil War became even more so by World War I. Artillery, machine guns, and rifles effective at ten times the range of half a century earlier dominated the battlefield. New elements such as poison gas shells and telephones were introduced, followed by armored vehicles, the tanks. The experience of being a soldier changed with the technology, and generally not for the better from the rifle carrier's point of view.

ROLAND GREEN is the author of dozens of novels and nonfiction historical articles. He is also the literary reviewer for a major newspaper. As a military historian he has always been fascinated by World War I and the men who fought in it.

[*]

SEPTEMBER 17, 1918, PONT L'ABBE, 1600

Sergeant Richard Beim stood at ease in front of the clerk's desk. He was getting tired of the clattering typewriter. His letter of discharge from the hospital seemed to be as long as a novel. Or maybe the clerk was just making him sweat. They liked to do that. They even got away with it, sometimes even with field-grade officers.

The clattering finally stopped. A chair squeaked and a door banged. Beim looked past the clerk to see Dr. Gates coming out of his office.

Beim not only stood to attention, he saluted. Gates was not just a good doctor and a captain, he was a fellow Chicagoan. And he'd never made Beim feel ashamed of being one of the First Division's handful of casualties in the St. Mihiel Salient.

"Still sure you don't want to stay here?" Gates asked.

"You'll need my bed, and I can't see myself as a three-stripe bedpan jockey—ah, orderly, sir," Beim said. (A bullet crease on the left arm didn't really slow you down, and Beim was five-eight and 170 pounds, and had been in good shape even before he signed up in 1916.)

"That wasn't quite what I had in mind," Gates said. "But in that case—here's hoping I don't see you again."

Both Beim and Gates signed the authorization for Beim to return to the First Division as fit for duty, and the clerk added his scribble as witness. The only problem with using clerks for writing secret messages, Beim reflected, was that the American Expeditionary Force wouldn't be able to read them any better than the Germans.

In a fit of generosity, the clerk handed Beim a receipt for his equipment and personally led him down to the supply room. Rather to his surprise, Beim didn't find too much missing—nothing that he probably wouldn't be issued when he got back to the division, and he hadn't let Rose's picture out of his sight.

Uniform—olive-drab. Long underwear. Pants. Puttees—thank God the leggings and all the mud they scooped up on the march were gone. Shirt—one button missing and the darned patch on the elbow, definitely his. Tunic with the Big Red One shoulder patch, the first in the AEF and still the one you saw most often.

Pack with spare clothing, including a few pairs of extra socks that Beim had scrounged in the hospital. It was getting on into autumn, and living in cold wet mud meant trench foot if you couldn't change your socks, or sometimes even if you could. No spare boots, but his original pair would at least get him back to Division. "Housewife" with sewing kit. Spare bootlaces. Nail scissors. Shaving kit with straight razor (a gift from his stepfather), brush, shaving soap.

Web belt with canvas ammunition pouch but no ammunition. Pistol holster badly in need of polish and also of a pistol, but Beim doubted he was going to have to shoot his way back to the division.

Then came the haversack, hanging off the bottom of the pack, banging his rump, though not as hard as usual. Nothing in it now but a box of hard bread (probably reasonably fresh) and his mess kit (eating utensils, salt and pepper, and coffee cup, wrapped in an old undershirt so that they wouldn't rattle loud enough to be heard in Berlin). A flat leather wallet, where he kept Rose's picture, her last letters to him, and the letter he hoped to finish and send off to her before the next push.

Top the whole thing off with the helmet and the almost-new short overcoat (patch up that bullet rip before the shooting started again) and look at the whole rig in the full-length mirror by the door.

Not too terrible, Dick, in Rose's voice, and if a soldier of twenty-two didn't have the right to imagine his fiancée's voice, then what the hell could he imagine?

He stepped back from the mirror, turned, and went out into the corridor that led to the outside rear door.

* * *

The hospital at Pont l'Abbe wasn't an old-fashioned château, it was some industrialist's mansion. This meant a big parking lot, now crowded with Model T and Renault ambulances bringing in the last casualties from the Salient, and big Liberty trucks unloading crated medical supplies and rations. It looked as if the hospital was getting ready for when the First Army went up against the Meuse-Argonne defenses.

It was no secret that was the AEF's next objective. It was no secret, either, that the Germans had been fortifying that area for three, maybe four years. Beim hoped that the German commander von Gallwitz was really a half-wit, but he wasn't too hopeful. The Germans might be on the ropes, but you couldn't count them out yet until they were flat on the canvas and you'd kicked them in the head a few times.

Meanwhile, it was raining, and none of the trucks seemed to be going back toward the front or even down to the railroad station. At least it wasn't too cold. Beim cast a watchful eye around for MPs and started walking.

As he walked, Beim wondered if there really was a place called "Sunny France." Maybe the French kept it hidden away and didn't give foreigners the keys. (At least not in wartime.)

His luck turned halfway to the station, as a Model T sedan stopped to give him a lift. It improved still more when he reached the station and only had to wait half an hour before a train stopped within spitting distance, with an American Pacific pulling it and an American engineer in the cab.

Beim was still careful about slipping on board. The boxcar he picked held neither the forty men nor the eight horses painted on the outside as its capacity. Instead it was half-filled with bales of hay and bags of oats (draft and artillery horses needed their rations, too) and three sleeping French laborers.

Or at least they wore French laborers' clothes, even though they looked more like Chinese. Probably what the French called Tonkinese, from Asia, and definitely not French West African soldiers, who were darker than any American Negro. They also had a reputation for carrying big knives and using them anytime they didn't like your looks. The Tonkinese were better traveling companions, for a man who wanted to report to his division with his head still on his shoulders.

The train chuffed out through the twilight and on into the night. Once they swung onto a siding for something with two engines in a big hurry. Maybe ammunition, maybe just some French general hot to see his mistress.

Nice to have a train that fast to take me back from Hoboken to Chicago when the war's over.

On that thought, Beim fell asleep.

September 18, 1918,
Somewhere in the Meuse Valley, 0700

Beim woke up the second time the train stopped, because somebody was shouting the name of the station. He vaguely remembered that it was one up toward the Meuse-Argonne, about sixty-odd miles from the St. Mihiel battlefield.

His thoughts stopped being vague about a minute later, when an MP climbed into the car. The Tonkinese looked petrified, because the MP was a huge blond guy with a .45. Beim wasn't scared, but he was slow and careful about pulling out his dog tags and the hospital letter. The MP grunted and motioned for him to climb down from the boxcar.

It looked as if someone had volunteered the MP detachment from one of those National Guard regiments from Wisconsin or Minnesota, all Scandinavian farm boys. Fortunately their lieutenant was only a little larger than Beim, who hated being towered over.

The lieutenant didn't stop giving Beim dirty looks until he also had checked the tags and letter. Then he gave the sergeant a tight little smile.

"I figured that nobody was trying to desert toward the front— although come to think of it, Beim's a German name, isn't it?"

Weary sighs didn't go over too well with officers, even as answers to dumb questions. "My folks were German. My dad and my older sister died in the Iroquois Theater fire. My mother remarried a Scotsman. The F in my name stands for Fitzroy."

"Ach. Sprechen sie Deutsch?"

"Aber naturlich."

They talked for a minute in German, with the lieutenant asking if Beim wanted to join the MPs and guard prisoners. It was the old army game—"I need three volunteers to take out that machine gun. You, you, and you." But the lieutenant didn't dare play it quite as hard with an infantry sergeant from the Big Red One with two wound stripes as he would have with, say, a National Army private without even one service stripe for six months overseas.

"Well," the lieutenant said, switching back to English, "I suspect you'll have enough chances to talk Fritz when we advance. Meanwhile. Report to the mess tent." A jerked thumb told Beim where. "We've got eleven more First Division orphans just finishing breakfast.

"Your new assignment is to take them up with you. Maybe you can fill them with some of your enthusiasm. I'm sure you've led squads before?"

It occurred to Beim that the lieutenant was pretty good at getting revenge, but it wouldn't have been smart to say that, in any language.

* * *

The mess tent lived down to the standard nonmilitary meaning of the word. The second thing Beim saw was eleven men sitting in a circle on the garbage-strewn floor. His next thought was to send them to the cook as KPs, to clean everything that didn't run away, and maybe chase the cook and clean him, too, if necessary.

But this wasn't his duty post, and the men were slowly standing up and pulling themselves together. Standing, they didn't look too bad. New packs, reasonably clean and complete uniforms, and Springfield rifles.

Thank God. If they're down to giving the First Division Enfields, we could still lose the war.

Beim had shot "Expert" with the '03 Springfield when he was a recruit. Over here, he'd tried out the heavier and less accurate American-made version of the British Enfield. He knew there'd never be enough Springfields to arm a three-million-man AEF, but he'd still rather jump off in his underwear than with an Enfield.

"I'm Sergeant Richard Beim. If you're going to the First Division, you're going with me. What did you have for breakfast?"

"Ah," said the largest of the men, with tattoos all over the backs of both hands. "The cook on my last ship called it skillygallee. That's when he didn't want us to know what was in it. Private Winowski, sir," he added.

"I'm a sergeant, not an officer," Beim snapped. "Now let's see one of those Springfields." He pointed at the thinnest and smallest (and probably Jewish) private. "Yours."

If the rifle had been a pair of boots, you could have seen your face in them. "What's your name?"

"Feldman, Sergeant."

"I see you take your rifle seriously. That's important, even if General Pershing says so." Like the rest of the AEF, Beim knew of Pershing's emphasis on the rifle as the weapon for warfare in open country. The problem was reaching the open country.

Beim did a quick and random inspection of other rifles and packs. He found only one dirty rifle, but the soldier—a Cajun named Moussin—had a trench knife you could shave with. Beim damned the rifle and praised the knife, and stepped back. A private named Goose had only nine ammunition clips in his pouches; the tenth held a pocket Bible.

"All right. Clean your mess gear. I'll try to scare up some rations. Feldman is acting corporal."

"Why a Jewboy as—?" began Moussin.

Beim glared. "Because I say so. And because there are enough MPs within earshot to jam that pig sticker up your ass sideways. If I don't do it first."

Moussin shrugged. "*Bien.*"

* * *

Beim suggested to the cook that if he didn't want his mess hall described in detail to the nearest officer, he would part with some marching rations. Beim had once made a two-day route march on an empty stomach and wasn't going to do it again, or inflict it on eleven new soldiers.

The payoff for blackmail was a can of French "monkey meat," a box of hard bread for every two men, and a can of "goldfish" (Beim couldn't tell if it wasn't salmon or sardines) for each man. Also full canteens, even if the water tasted like it had come out of a Park District swimming pool back home.

Then Beim took the lead, Feldman took the rear, and the little detachment moved off in search of a ride.

* * *

It was a noisy night for a road march, with motors grumbling, horses neighing, mules braying, curses in English, French, and maybe Tonkinese, rain pattering, mud squelching, harness creaking, and sometimes in a lull another sound that made Beim feel just a little chillier than the rain.

Artillery. Somewhere not too far away, the big guns were firing. This far in the rear, they had to be the super-heavy, the railroad guns and the like, feeling for German railroad junctions and supply dumps.

Traffic seemed to be moving in every direction except possibly straight up, and once Beim heard the buzz of an airplane whose pilot might be crazy enough to do that, since he was crazy enough to fly on a night like this. As for going down into the ground, a lot of animals and carts were doing that, whole or in pieces (it looked like a German bomb had taken out a team earlier in the day).

The march turned into a stagger. Beim now wished a curse on his puttees and thought longingly of the new trousers that were supposed to be ready for the spring campaign.

Round a bend, Beim smelled coffee. The Red Cross? No, it looked like just men brewing up while waiting out a hellacious roadblock. The wheel had come off a 155mm howitzer and ten tons of inert metal had slewed across the road. Somebody was trying to jack up the gun, somebody else to hitch up a double team to move it once it was jacked.

"Nobody's going anywhere until that gun's out of the road," Beim said, loud enough to make heads turn. He hoped that would scare up an officer to take charge.

"Any ideas?" Moussin asked acidly.

Beim looked again. The howitzer's carriage only blocked one lane. The barrel jutted across the other.

A great big blowtorch would come in handy right now.

"Okay," he shouted. "We've got to swing this piece around until the barrel's parallel to traffic. Then we have to—"

A burst of what had to be very rude French interrupted him. To his surprise, Feldman replied in the same language. Moussin shouted something into the darkness where the French had to be, and then something at Feldman.

Beim heard the word "Jewboy" and cringed.

Of all possible times for a brawl.

Except that it wasn't a brawl. Winowski stepped up to Moussin.

"Feldman's busy. So—"

It was dark, so Beim wasn't quite sure that he saw Moussin drop his rifle, draw his knife, and take a large tattooed fist on the point of his jaw, all in the same moment. But that's what it looked like.

By the time he'd looked over the French—whatever—that had come up behind them, Moussin was propped up against a tree, taking no interest in anything around him.

"Guess the swamp hunter took it personal, that they don't understand his Frog," Winowski said.

The French were bringing up a huge artillery piece, on two tracked vehicles. One (or so Feldman said) carried a gasoline engine that drove it and also powered the electric motor in the gun carriage. How big the gun was vanished in a roll of thunder, but Beim didn't need his ears to see what the French were doing.

Uncouple power cable and tow chains that linked the two machines. Swing the tractor around until its blunt nose was against the howitzer.

Then gun the engine until the howitzer shivered, started to tilt, then rose up and slid into the ditch with a horrible screech of bending metal and cracking wood. Also cheers from everybody on both sides of the roadblock, while Beim kept a lookout for officious officers.

It wasn't my gun probably wouldn't be enough of an explanation.

Then Feldman was shouting in his ear, "Come on, Sarge, the French are giving a ride," and Winowski helped Feldman and loaded Moussin onto a French truck that seemed to have sprung from the earth.

A sergeant had to preserve a little dignity, so Beim climbed on by himself. He lost that dignity a moment later, as he tried to shoehorn himself in and around several large heavy wooden crates.

"Ask the driver if we can smoke," Beim called out, hoping that Feldman was the only French-speaker with a working jaw. He also hoped the answer would be "Yes." Right now he'd walk barefoot over barbed wire for a fag.

The answer was more of a scream than a word, but Beim thought it sounded like "No."

Then came a torrent of French that outran Feldman's ability to translate. Feldman's voice struggled along behind and finally got the message across to his comrades.

They were riding in the back of an ammunition truck, loaded with 194mm shells (about eight inches) and powder charges for that big tracked gun.

I suppose it wouldn't be nice to thank the French for their help by blowing them up.

"*Peste.*" Moussin's voice sounded slurred but calm.

"You heard the man," came a voice followed by a lot of coughing and sneezing.

Hope this doesn't give anybody the influenza.

With a squeal like a whole pen full of slaughtered pigs, the truck lurched into motion.

September 25, 1918, Rear Area of the First Division, Near the Argonne Forest, 1800

Beim dipped his pen in the ink bottle. It was a small bottle, shared among the company's sergeants, but it was going to be a short letter and the new pen nib didn't turn half the ink into spatters and blots instead of words.

Dear Rose,

Your last letter was return-addressed SOMEWHERE IN FRANCE, like mine. So I guess you and your Red Cross people made it safely across the Atlantic. Not hard to do, these days, since the U-boats are supposed to be on the run. I also hope you beat the fall storms. I crossed in the early summer, and was still seasick half the time.

Of course, France is about the size of Texas, so that won't tell a German agent where my outfit or your Red Cross unit is. I hope things ease up before we both get leave at the same time. I want to spend the whole leave with you, not looking for you.

Find a good estaminet (that means a family restaurant) in walking distance from your quarters. You won't know much about France until you see what they can do with rationed or scarce supplies. Don't waste your time looking for good wine unless your name's Rockefeller or Mellon.

Beim thought of the restaurant near the hospital, run by a widowed mother, a widowed daughter, and two younger daughters who God willing might find somebody left to marry after the war was over. He thought of his platoon commander Lieutenant Allison's remark that France made him think of the South after the Civil War. Unlike the South, though, France had some foreign allies, so they just might win.

That train of thought brought his mind around to the letter he really wanted to write, about how this might be his last before the First Division was jumping off into the Meuse-Argonne battle. They wouldn't be in the first attack, because they were still assembling their four infantry regiments, two artillery regiments, engineers, medics, signal corps wiremen, old Uncle Tom Cobbley and all—supposedly 28,000 men but probably a little less.

Still the strength of an English, French, or German corps.

His mind turned phrases that would never pass the censor—

Most of the First Division's supplies have been delivered and most of them unloaded, even if they do kidnap infantrymen for fatigues every so often. The colored labor troops are working hard, even if they get rags to wear and garbage to eat.

I think they might be fit to fight if they were treated and trained better. I saw some of the coloreds under French command, who spout them into the trenches, and they looked like fighters.

Traffic on the roads is still pretty horrible. We're still trying to bring up our men and the French are trying to get theirs out. We're not getting bombed much, but that may be the weather more than anything General Mitchell promised.

If you look at a map, though, you can see how important the Meuse-Argonne could be if we win. The Germans drove this huge salient into the Allied lines in their spring offensive, almost all the way to Paris. We and the French held them just in time.

Now the British are pushing into Belgium, on the north side of the salient. We and the French are pushing into the south side, toward big coal fields and iron mines. If we meet, it'll wreck the German armaments industry. Also, they won't be able to get all their men out of the salient, and they can't afford to lose that many. They have to be able to hold their old frontier for a while in order to get a negotiated peace.

I am now one of the three senior NCOs in the platoon. We're supposed to have sixty-five men but we've only got fifty-eight. They say that rifle-company strength is going to be cut by about a quarter. So they may just leave us this way.

I'm happy with our platoon commander, David Allison. Like me, he joined up before the war. From Texas. After Cantigny they sent him to OTC at Langres. He's so thin there's barely room on his chest to hang his Croix de Guerre. Of course, that means it'll be awfully hard for the Germans to hit him—

"Hey, Chicago! The looie wants you!"

The platoon top, Hurlburt, had his head stuck through the tent flap.

Beim jerked his mind back from forbidden territory, scribbled at the bottom of what he'd written before,

All my love until we meet again and forever after that.

Your Dick

and stood up. "Lead the way."

Allison had a mustache so large that it almost swallowed his nose. It made him look as much like a French *poilou* ("hairy fellow") as a Texan.

He also gave Hurlburt a look that said the top's presence was not desired and his absence would be welcomed. Hurlburt started to open his mouth. Allison repeated the look. Hurlburt took the hint, and his leave.

"Okay," the lieutenant said. "How do you see the war going?"

Beim didn't quite gape. "You don't look much like General Pershing, sir."

"What does that matter? Or not?"

Beim considered his best course of action for about two seconds. He held his peace for enough longer to let a trio of trucks clatter by—one loaded with stovepipe-like Stokes mortars, the other two towing 37mm "trench guns."

Then he gave an edited version of the imaginary portions of the letter to Rose. The AEF had just reached the coal fields when Allison held up a hand.

"About what the Old Man reckoned. Question is, you want to go to Langres now or after we join the push?"

That consideration didn't even take two seconds.

"After."

"Good. Hurlburt's showing signs of boozing too much. The battalion MGs are about to kidnap Katzenmeyer. If Hurlburt folds, you're platoon top. If I go west, you've got the platoon." Allison grinned. "Still want to wait?"

"I'd be a damned fool not to."

"That you would. Oh, and Moussin's going to be a sniper, and two of your orphans are in the hospital with influenza."

"Damn."

"I know. I signed up to fight the Germans, not diseases. But what can you do?"

A mile away, some ack-ack was firing at German planes. Beim listened for the heavier report of bombs.

Silence slowly crept back over the First Division. Beim saluted. "By your leave, sir?"

Allison returned the salute. "Dismissed—and good luck."

October 1, 1918, First Division Area, 0800

That morning, runners had summoned the platoon and squad leaders to the company commander's tent. After that, Beim knew what was coming at them.

It was certainly a lot of Germans with guns, and Captain Stitt, the company commander, seemed to want Company D to wipe them out all by itself. Beim thought that the rest of the Division could be some help, but experience told him that the captain had a point.

In combat, what you had to do, and who you had to do it to, and who and what you had to do it with, could all change from one minute to the next. That meant you had to change with them.

"No battle plan survives contact with the enemy" was one of Allison's favorite quotations. "It was a Fritz who said that, so maybe that's why they're so good at fucking over other people.

"We, however, are gonna fuck them right back."

The first assault, beginning on September 26, had actually done fairly well, penetrating the German forward defense. Then they came up against defenses strongly held by German reserves, and they couldn't bring their artillery up to support another attack because the roads were too crowded and too muddy.

It didn't help that for the next three days of preparing to jump off, Beim felt like a pack mule in a Zane Grey novel.

Or maybe the lead mule, with Allison as the mule skinner.

Check everybody's gear, from the skin out. Issue ammo—twenty-five-round clips for the riflemen, twenty magazines for each of the teams with Chitchat automatic rifles (which would probably fall apart before they'd fired half that load, but never mind), eight grenades for each of the rifles with a French VB launcher, two hand grenades apiece for everybody except the Chauchaut gunners and their ammunition carriers, extra magazines for everybody with a .45—

"Where'd you get these?" Beim asked Hurlburt as he added a pouch of seven-round pistol magazines to his load.

"Traded a little ving blonk to one of the ordnance guys," Hurlburt said with a grin. "Hey, I may be a lush but I can't drink it all."

Beim sighed. Both he and Allison were also carrying Springfields with bayonets. Allison said that the .45 by itself was a dead giveaway to German snipers that you were a man in charge. And the big automatic was pretty good at the kind of range you had in trench fighting.

Although a shotgun is even better, but don't think that too loudly or Hurlburt will sure as the deuce come up with one.

They were forming up for the march when Feldman spoke for them all:

"I think I know what happened to Goliath now. The Philistine ordnance people loaded him up so that David got on his blind side and whacked him with the sling stone from a distance."

"That's why everyone keeps an eye peeled for his buddy as well as himself," Beim said, loud enough to reach the whole platoon.

October 4, 1918, The Argonne Forest, 0300

The battalion was the second wave. If the first-wave battalion hadn't broken through, the job was up to them. If it had, their battalion was to penetrate another half mile into the Kremhilde Stellung. Beim's company was supposed to clean out something called the Bois des Pinons, which Feldman said meant the "Feather Woods."

"Probably some Frog countess liked to keep a birdfeeder there" was Hurlburt's guess.

The bombardment from the first wave was reaching its climax. Half-deafened as he was, Beim could still tell the flat-trajectory seventy-fives skimming over the heads of the waiting infantry. He really hoped they weren't also skimming over the heads of the waiting German machine gunners.

Not to mention that even if they hit a bunker, they won't do much more than give the Fritzes inside a headache. Give me a one-five-five every time.

Somewhere off beyond the fireworks on the German position, the one-five-fives probably were hitting. Hitting the German artillery and reserves, if they were lucky. Hitting trees and rocks, otherwise, turning them into a tangle of churned-up ground and splinters that was almost as hard to get through as barbed wire.

The pulsing fire and ear-bruising thunder died as if a hangman's noose had choked it off. Then flares and the rattle of machine-gun fire took its place.

Allison's voice came in Beim's ringing ear. "Those are German fireworks." He looked to the left, where an engineer squad sat amid a pile of wire cutters and lengths of pipe, bangalore torpedoes for blowing quick and dirty paths through uncut wire. Beim thought that somebody higher up had a cool head, not betting on the first wave to do all the wire-cutting.

If we were British, we'd have heavy tanks to rip up the wire. But those little French Renaults can barely get through a picket fence or survive a machine-gun burst, and we lost most of what we had on the 26th.

The first Meuse-Argonne tank attack was rumored to have been a fiasco, even though the tank battalion commander got out and led the tanks forward on foot so he could direct their gunners on to targets. A job that an infantry sergeant named Richard Beim might just be doing for his own outfit's automatic weapons before too long . . .

"Time to go," came Allison's voice again.

The words didn't have to fight their way through the din quite as much. Beim lurched to his feet.

One day, they might have wireless sets small enough for a man to carry. Or at least small enough to fit in a tank.

He cupped his hands around his mouth, as a poor substitute for a speaking trumpet, to make his voice carry.

"Third platoon, let's go get some Fritz scalps!"

* * *

The battalion was supposed to advance four companies abreast, with a machine gun team in the rear of each company. Each company in turn was to be in a column of sections, like fat beads on a string. The rear section of each platoon was to act as a guide for the lead of the platoon following. That way they could either carry out an assault on unbroken German defenses or quickly reinforce a breakthrough.

As a plan, fine. In practice, when Third Platoon ran into a patch of shell-chewed ground where a herd of elephants might have gotten lost and didn't find a guide or any other Americans— not so fine.

Allison sent a runner back to bring up the platoon's Chauchaut teams. Beim took half a section to probe the crater field. It was nice to see that the one-five-fives probably had been on the job— chunks of barbed wire, chunks of German weapons, and chunks of German lay scattered. Some of the greener doughboys knelt, vomiting.

"Keep a sharp lookout," Beim called. He was scanning the tattered remains of the forest for any sign of movement. Surviving Germans could have ambushed the guides from the platoon ahead and be waiting until his platoon was gathered in the open, standing around with their thumbs in their mouths.

"And don't touch anything," he added. The Germans would

have had to work fast to booby-trap any of the bodies or weapons here, but "work fast" might be the German Army's motto.

Spreading out would be a good way to make the platoon a harder target, but also get it thoroughly lost. It was almost two hours to dawn, the bombardment had moved on, and the platoon didn't have enough flares to keep its position lit up until then.

At least the platoon behind them had made contact, sending up a runner asking for orders. Allison ordered them forward, and looked relieved when the company machine gun section came up with them.

The machine gunners were just setting up their weapon when Beim heard a thin cry of "*Kamerad!*"

"Anybody got a handkerchief?" asked Beim. "I think I'm the one to go in and—"

"*With* the typewriters ready to cover you," Allison interrupted.

Beim clicked his heels as best he could with mud-caked boots. "*Jawohl, Herr Ooberleutnant.*"

The whitest thing around turned out to be a pair of faded socks, so Beim tied them to the end of a salvaged picket stake and started walking toward the woods. The cries of "*Kamerad!*" were growing weaker—whoever was in there was either really hurt or a very good actor.

Then suddenly nobody was acting at all. A young German soldier in a positively mangled uniform jumped out from behind a tree, waving a Red Cross armband. A slightly older German followed him, trying to pull him back out of sight.

Then something like a large automatic pistol hammered out six rounds. The second German toppled to the ground, the first ducked behind a tree, and Beim had a grenade in the air before the toppling German hit the ground. Beim followed up the grenade with a running dive into the trees, bayoneted rifle extended.

More pistol-like sounds and the *whuff!* of bullets passing close, the carpenter-shop noises they made hitting a tree, and the scream as Beim lunged at a moving shape not quite as concealed as he must have thought he was.

A German officer rolled into the open, trying to claw the bayonet out of his belly with one hand and lift a strange-looking short rifle with the other. Beim jerked his bayonet out and thrust again, this time into the German's throat. He coughed a spray of blood and died.

Looking up, Beim saw the ragged German standing with both hands in the air and the Red Cross armband dangling from one.

"*Du—sanitater?*" Beim asked.

"*Jawohl,*" the other replied, confirming that he was a first-aid man.

"*Und er?*" Beim asked, not quite daring to call the dead officer names or kick him in the head.

That brought an explanation long enough for about six of the platoon to join Beim and start counting the wounded Germans.

Apparently the dead man was a former officer of the elite assault infantry, the storm troops, who had been sent to a regular infantry battalion for some offense. He had already killed or gotten killed several of his own men trying to find an honorable death for himself. Fortunately the other dead man, one of the aid man's friends, would be the last. And Beim's grenade had put most of its fragments into the trees or the already dead, not adding too much to the Germans' suffering.

Which I would have willingly done to Germans still fighting. Not these sorry bastards.

The officer's weapon was a Bergman machine pistol, something like a Chauchaut except that it fired a 9mm pistol round—and was, Beim suspected, incredibly more reliable.

All this he translated for Lieutenant Allison, then translated Allison's orders that the aid man go on aiding his wounded until they could be evacuated. He carefully didn't go into detail about how long that might be, and Beim ignored the mournful looks from the German wounded.

Fortunately Beim's conscience had only just started to nag him when the company commander, Captain Stitt, showed up and informed them that the platoon had not only captured about fifty Germans, they had also capped the Bois des Pinons.

"It looks a little plucked right now," Stitt added. "But congratulations."

"Thank you, sir," Allison said. "We'll plan on being dug in by daylight."

Beim crossed his fingers. The platoon could do it, but he wondered how much of the rest of the battalion was still in fighting shape.

* * *

Captain Stitt sent runners both forward and back in search of their own (or at least some) battalion headquarters, hoping that somebody would be able to make sense of the situation of D Company and tell them what to do next.

Lieutenant Allison thought this was no time to stay put and wait for orders. "I think we caught the Fritzes in this position before they could bring up their reserves. I think we should reinforce the first wave at its deepest penetration, and catch their reserves as they come up."

"What about leaving the job to the artillery?" Beim asked.

"The seventy-fives'll have to pick up and move forward, and the one-five-fives will be at extreme range."

That was about thirteen thousand yards, against nine thousand for the seventy-fives. Getting hit by a "short" from your own artillery could ruin your whole day.

Third Platoon needed no orders from anybody to turn itself into a combined outpost and field dressing station. Under the direction of the German *sanitater* (who turned out to be a Sergeant Walther

Rudely), they used the Germans' own first-aid kits to patch them up as best they could. The Americans, with few casualties of their own, worked willingly, while swearing under their breath at the German paper bandages, which easily got wet and then sometimes even more easily came apart.

Some of the Germans were beyond help, except, surprisingly, from Private Goose and his pocket Bible. He didn't speak a word of German, but some of the Germans spoke enough English to translate what he was reading for their dying comrades.

Beim personally thought that they were more in the swamp of the shadow of death than the valley, and they weren't doing much walking. But Goose helped remind them that they just might possibly not be alone.

Daylight oozed across the battlefield, to a distant accompaniment of artillery. At what they estimated was around noon Captain Stitt ordered a break for lunch. Beim had just opened a can of goldfish (recognizably sardine variety, this time) when a runner came in to report a convoy of mule carts in sight.

Some of the mules turned out to be horses, which got the runner a dirty look from Allison, plus a few under-the-breath remarks about "damnyankees" (clearly one word) who couldn't tell horses from mules from jackrabbits. Although he'd like to see the runner break his neck trying to ride a jackrabbit—

"You ride, Lieutenant?" Beim asked.

"In Texas?" Allison asked, with the sharklike grin he reserved for damn fool questions.

"Sorry, Lieutenant."

"No need to be. I'm engaged to a gal whose grandpa rode with Jeb Stuart. He's got a horse ranch outside of Waco big enough to fight this battle on. If I come back and marry her, he's promised to send me to veterinary school at Texas A & M."

"Sounds like the arrangement I have with Rose's father," Beim said. "Except he's going to send me to teacher's college. My stepdad's machine shop is doing pretty well, but he's sick a lot, and Mom has to stay close to home to take care of him."

Allison thrust out a hand. "Let's shake on lovely ladies with generous families."

"Yes, *sir*."

* * *

Mules or horses or jackrabbits or dragons, the creatures drawing the carts hauled all the Germans who couldn't walk to the rear, followed by the walking wounded guarded by a detail including Private Goose. Beim was glad to see him out of danger for even a couple of days.

Goose had confessed that he wanted to be a minister after the war, and Beim and Allison had agreed on another thing. If they found Goose's church later on, they would attend a service there, even though neither of them was as much a regular churchgoer as their families would have liked.

Sergeant Rudel brought up the rear, in one of two Model T ambulances that were carrying the dead Germans, including the storm trooper lieutenant. Beim personally would rather have buried the SOB in a slit-trench latrine, just before they filled it in. But in war or peace, you couldn't give everybody what they deserved.

The Model Ts were a good sign in another way. Somewhere leading back to the rear was a sort of road (the Model Ts weren't fussy), probably built by the Germans, wrecked by the AEF's artillery, and now being restored by the engineers.

Regular supplies at the front? Next thing you know, Red Cross girls. No, better not. Rose will insist on coming.

They moved up to join the rest of the battalion that afternoon, just ahead of a short, sharp bombardment of mustard gas shells. Beim thanked his stars that the Germans were gone, and that all he had to do was help the men who'd let their gas masks get out of order.

The American version of the British Small Box Respirator was pretty foolproof. Pull on the mask and seal it. Bring the filter box around in front of you. Hook the hose from the filter box to the mask, and breathe through the hose until either all the charcoal and other stuff in the filters got saturated or until you were out of the gas area.

It wasn't damn foolproof, and there were damn fools everywhere. Also, the hose could snag on bushes or be cut by shell fragments, the filter box could spring a leak and get wet, and the eyepieces of the mask often steamed up so that if you had to see clearly you were in trouble.

Certainly Captain Stitt seemed to be having trouble with his mask—or maybe he just didn't like mustard gas? (Not that Beim blamed him. If he ever found somebody who *liked* that damnable stuff, he'd try to find him a good insane asylum where he could share a cell with somebody who thought he was Napoleon . . .)

Captain Stitt was white-faced behind his mask when they marched out, but at least his mask was in place.

* * *

Captain Stitt's face wasn't the only white one in the company, a few hours later. Beim was in the newly cleaned out German bunker that served as the battalion command post, standing in front of Major Dubin, the battalion commander, trying to give as little information about Stitt as he could get away with.

Officers had ways of making trouble for sergeants who badmouthed them—or whom they thought had bad-mouthed them. This close to the enemy, that trouble could kill you.

"No, sir," Beim said, finally, "I wouldn't say that Captain Stitt had trouble with anything except his gas mask. If I've helped one man with those damned Tommy rig-outs, I've helped a hundred. I wish we'd adopted the Tissot mask from the French. It's all in one piece."

"I'm sure the War Department looked it over very carefully,"

Dubin said. "Probably found that the French couldn't spare enough for a division, let alone an army. And you don't seem to have much trouble with your equipment."

"I worked in my father's machine shop before I joined up, sir."

"So I recall. And you joined up in 1916. Why?"

"I knew we were going to get in the war sooner or later," Beim said. "So I wanted to be trained by the old Regulars before the shooting started."

"I think you're trying to flatter your officers," Dubin said, with a tight smile. "That's a breach of military etiquette. But I take your point. And *you* are taking out a patrol tonight. Brigade orders, to Moulin d'Islay."

"Yes, sir."

* * *

The first person Beim met after leaving the battalion CP was Hurlburt. He wasn't quite sober, but as always, he was a good-natured drunk.

At least until he started singing the song about the faithless girl who'd developed a taste for officers, who wore Sam Browne belts across their chests:

They say that love is a blessing.
A blessing I could never see,
For the only girl I ever loved
Has gone and made a sucker out of me.
She can Sam Browne out of Bordeaux,
She can Sam Browne all over Paree,
She can fuck herself to death with the AEF,
But she'll never find a sucker like me.

Beim grinned. "Hey, why don't you take that song up to the trenches? Sing the Germans to death?"

"Nah. Ain't enough beer to let me do that."

The second man Beim met was Lieutenant Allison, who explained the remark about beer. "The Fritzes had a whole truckload of the stuff in a bunker. And you know Hurlburt—he can smell the stuff a mile upwind. He also knows that your girl's over here with the Red Cross."

Beim's fists and teeth clenched. "Hey, don't do anything that'll get you into the stockade," Allison said. "You don't want to fuck up the platoon, do you?" He lowered his voice. "Who are you taking on the patrol?"

"Feldman, Winowski, and one of the Sure-Shit teams."

"Try Blaskowic's. He takes better care of his gun than Fesser."

Another reason for not taking over the platoon unless he had to—Allison had a knack for plucking information apparently out of thin air. One of the things they taught at Langres, or just natural talent? And could you be a good officer without it?

For tonight, concentrate on being a good patrol leader. And on coming back.

* * *

With a mud-covered hand, Beim made the "Halt" signal. The men behind him sighed so loudly with relief that Beim was sure that the Germans in the trenches two hundred yards away must have heard them.

He didn't blame the men—much. They were carrying their Hotchkiss machine gun fully assembled and ready to fire, weighing a good seventy pounds. Otherwise they had pistols and boxes of the twenty-five-round strips that the Hotchkiss used. Not an easy load to tote silently into range of the German wire.

A flare sailed up from the German lines, and somebody who just *had* to do everything the Germans did fired one in reply. The patrol froze in place, waiting for the light to die and for their night vision to come back.

Beim wondered if when the American flare-popper got home, he would run for Kaiser instead of President. A lot of people would run *from* him if he did, Beim included.

The loader must have had a strip in the Hotchkiss and the gunner his finger on the trigger, because muzzle flare and muzzle blast ripped through the night just as Beim was recovering from the flares. The rounds from the first strip sailed off into the night and out of human knowledge, but the second clicked into place almost before the echoes died.

This one did its job—and the next, and the three after that, as the gunner slowly traversed the gun to sweep the bullet stream along the German wire. As the bullets hit the hardened steel, they struck sparks in what seemed all the colors of the rainbow, tracing the position of the wire as clearly as if it had been coated with luminous paint.

Just to make sure, the second loader had a notebook in one hand and a pencil in the other, and every time his partner loaded in the next strip, he jotted down information about the height and depth of the wire.

A flicker of light, a dull thud amid the rattling of machine guns (the Germans were replying now, and it was all right with Beim if they wanted to give away their guns' positions), and a resounding crash ten yards away at most.

"*Minenwerfer,*" Winowski said. He knelt, slammed a rifle grenade onto the VB launcher on the muzzle of his Springfield, and pulled the trigger the moment the butt touched the ground. Even somebody as big as Winowski couldn't fire a rifle grenade from the shoulder without breaking something.

"That'll keep their heads down," Winowski growled.

Beim hoped he was right. The German trench mortar had to be one of their smaller models, but mortar rounds carried more explosive and threw more fragments in proportion to their size than artillery shells. The ideal place for a German trench mortar tonight was in Luxembourg. The fourth grenade and the second mortar round exploded almost together. Yellow light seared eyes as the grenade found the mortar's ammunition supply. Then Winowski swore, dropped his rifle, and clapped a hand to his thigh.

From somewhere to their left rear, a rifle cracked off five rounds rapid-fire, and to the left rear the Chauchaut team sprayed half a magazine into the night before their gun jammed.

Then Beim's blood went cold as three shots sounded from directly behind his position—and colder still as part of the darkness that seemed no more than arm's length away moved.

"'Halt!" Feldman and Beim shouted together, as another mortar shell showered them with clods of earth. One of the loaders cursed and started cleaning the dirt off his ammunition strips. The Hotchkiss had a reputation for jamming at a dirty thought, let alone dirty ammunition.

"Pardon," came a familiar voice. "I wanted another shot at him, but he run too fast and you fellas got good eyes."

It was Moussin the sniper, crouching in plain sight with his rifle across his knees. His face and hands were blackened, and Beim noted that the once-white telescopic sight bolted to the top of the rifle was also black.

Question: who had he been hunting?

"He's all right," Feldman's voice came out of the night. "That first shot came from nowhere near Swampman's position."

"And I adore you, too, college boy," Moussin said. "Did you see who it was?"

"Normal size, American helmet. That's all," Feldman said.

Beim felt a small wave of relief. They wouldn't have to go beating the bushes or the barbed wire tonight for the mystery traitor of a sniper—better not even think the name "Captain Stitt."

"Okay," the sniper said, "if somebody can take over the rifle grenades before Brother Fritz brings up more ammo for the mortar—"

"First we get Winowski back to an aid post," Beim said. He saw a rebellious look on the gunner's face and added, "Or I will shove that Frog gun up your ass and pull the trigger."

Beim's threat would have settled matters even if Feldman and Moussin hadn't backed him. The only thing the gunner asked after that was some help in carrying their gun, in return for help in carrying Winowski.

As the patrol struggled back toward their own lines, the German trench mortar reopened rapid fire, slamming five rounds into the patrol's empty position and then feeling for them with five more, which made all their loads feel lighter and their feet a lot faster. And far off to their left, they saw the flare and sparking of another machine gun, feeling for the German wire.

Going to be nice to get back home, where you aren't getting shot at from both sides.

* * *

Beim woke up the next morning dreading having to ask anybody about the mysterious goings-on in the rear of his patrol last night. He most dreaded somebody telling him that nothing had happened, and he wasn't to argue the point.

He had too many witnesses, besides the bullet wound in Winowski's thigh, which was probably going to put him in a rear-area hospital for the rest of the war, and maybe keep him from ever going to sea again. However, nobody would listen to them from the stockade, which was where they'd be if somebody decided to circle the wagons around Captain Stitt.

It was a good thing that he'd already decided not to write a book about *What I Did in the Great War for Democracy,* because there'd already been too much stuff happening that nobody would believe. (Well, maybe Rose, but she was special.)

A cup of coffee helped. So did a second cup, and a hot breakfast, even if it was just fried hard bread with canned butter and chemical-flavored jam on it. Then something to do with his hands, because nobody who didn't rank him dared disturb Sergeant Beim when he was cleaning his rifle.

Somebody with more rank did interrupt him, but it was Lieutenant Allison. They walked quietly together across the regiment's position, keeping an eye out for soldiers who were obviously slacking off—and for handy shell craters to dive into if German artillery started coming in. The position had a bunch of German bunkers, some of them going down three stories underground, plus the cellars of what had been a small town. But half of these handy shelters were contaminated with mustard gas or booby-trapped, and the useable ones had already been grabbed by either headquarters units or, more respectably, the dressing stations.

"They couldn't account for Stitt's movements last night," Allison said. "So Colonel Dubin—"

"Colonel?"

"Light colonel since last night. I think they're grooming him to take a regiment. A lot of the West Point field-grades who started the war are either too worn out or too badly needed on the staff. This army's going to cross the Rhine with a lot of officers who were company-grade or even enlisted or civilian two years ago."

Beim started to whistle the popular song "Just Like Washington Crossed the Delaware, General Pershing Will Cross the Rhine."

Allison gave him a sour look. "Just wait until we do that. If you haven't put up bars yourself by then, you're going to help row my boat."

"I suppose we can't escape fate," Beim said, with a grin. "But I'll try to run from it as fast as I can."

"Well, you won't have too many worries for now," Allison said. "Stitt has been bloodied."

That meant sent to Blois, where AEF officers who didn't measure up were sent, to be examined for what they *were* good for.

"If Stitt spends the rest of the war in the Service of Supply, that's enough," Beim said. "He's pretty good at moving boxes and crates around and even moving them to the right places."

"Could be," Allison said. "I won't get the company—I'm too junior. They're sending somebody down from Brigade. Wounded at Cantigny and rarin' to get back into the fight.

"On the other hand, Fourth Platoon's understrength—gas and the influenza. So they're combining what's left of it with us. You and Hurlburt each take half of the new platoon, at least as long as he stays sober."

"Can't we get Kastenmeyer back from the machine gunners?"

"He was killed last night, making the same kind of patrol you did."

Beim thought a dirty word, then several more. Then he walked away, without waiting to be dismissed. He and Kastenmeyer hadn't been close, but he remembered seeing a picture of the man's three children. Who was going to tell them where their father had gone?

His dark mood nearly made him run straight into an unlikely pair, Moussin and Feldman, waving their arms and arguing, apparently, about whether catfish were kosher or not.

"Sergeant," Moussin said, "this college boy says he can't eat catfish because they don't have scales. Is that right?"

Beim frowned. He couldn't remember ever eating catfish at a Jewish restaurant. "What about chicken?"

"But it's my *maman's* catfish that people kill for." He turned to Feldman. "Tell you this—you try the catfish, I don't call you Jewboy ever again until you make General."

Feldman chuckled. "General Jewboy. Not in this war, I think."

"What about the next one?"

"Hey, Louis, this is the war to end wars, remember?"

"Yeah. And tomorrow the Mississippi run backward."

Beim walked on. At least one human problem in Third Platoon was solved—or at least it wasn't going to kill anybody before the Germans got to them.

* * *

Beim had about two hours to taste the pleasures of being a platoon sergeant, or even sometimes an officer.

He asked about Kastenmeyer's machine gun, and it turned out that the battalion hadn't bothered to ask for its return to the MG company. Which, as far as Beim was concerned, made it the legitimate property of D Company. A chat with Lieutenant Allison found a good hiding place for the gun; a hint to Hurlburt sent out a raiding party (that's what it was, even if it was against their own supply people) to find more ammunition.

Beim even had two whole minutes to admire the gun. It was one of the new water-cooled Brownings, with a water jacket around the barrel instead of the measly Hotchkiss cooling fins, and a 250-round belt instead of an endless series of 25-round strips.

"Like my grandpa said about the Yankee repeaters in the War," one private said. "Load on Sunday and fire all week."

"Want to be a Yankee for once?" Beim asked. "Then you have just volunteered to be on this gun."

The private looked at Beim, decided this wasn't a joke, and nodded.

A road was definitely open to the left rear of the battalion's position—a four-horse team plodded up with a seventy-five, another with a load of three-inch Stoke mortars, and a third with a "slum gun"—a mobile kitchen.

Goose jumped off the slum gun and walked up to Beim. "Rudel speaks some English, Sergeant. He said that when his unit was coming upon the train, men were shouting to them not to go up and prolong the war."

"But they came up anyway, didn't they?"

"Yes, but if there are enough Germans like Rudel—the Lord would have saved Sodom, if He had found ten righteous men in it."

"So he would. But right now we're facing a lot of the unrighteous, and the fighting isn't over. Remember that God helps those who help themselves, and keep your rifle oiled."

"Oh, I will, Sergeant."

The slum gun fired off a lunchtime salvo of canned tomatoes mixed with monkey meat, rehydrated potatoes the consistency of glue, and canned apples. It stuck to the ribs, and Beim wondered if it would come unstuck before the Germans gave them a chance for some vigorous exercise.

The attack in which the First Division had participated was working around the flank of the Germans defending against the first attack. The Germans had thrown reserves from as far away as Flanders into stopping that one. If the Americans could get into their rear, it would be a miniature version of the big encirclement that somebody (probably Marshal Foch) was dreaming of.

The Germans couldn't afford to lose even that many men.

And Richard Beim couldn't afford to lose Richard Beim, which probably didn't make much difference to Marshal Foch.

The new company commander, Lieutenant Engel, came running up. He was almost ridiculously short and thick, but from the way he covered ground it had to be all muscle.

"The Air Service reports a German counterattack moving toward the low ground between us and Moulin d'Islay. They might cut off our observers on the top before we can string a telephone to the artillery. They have brought up the one-five-fives, so if we can hold the infantry—"

"Don't those Fritzes know they're prolonging the war?" Beim asked rhetorically.

"Hunh?" Engel replied, inspiringly.

"Never mind, sir. I'll get the platoon moving."

* * *

The platoon wasn't the only thing moving, and for a few minutes Beim was thinking they had more of a traffic jam than a tactical maneuver. Somebody was setting up one of the 37mm close-support guns overlooking the low ground, and Beim told each section to steer wide of him.

"Those little bastards are great for killing machine guns, but they attract artillery like garbage draws flies. And they always figure that the infantry has to protect them, even if it means we're staying in the target area."

"I hear you," someone said, and another someone asked, "What about gas?"

"The Germans aren't going to mustard-gas in an area if they're planning on moving through it," Beim said. "If they go around another way, watch out and keep your masks ready."

He had a lot of exchanges like that on the way to the low ground, and saw Lieutenant Allison having some of his own. No time to put up their own wire, but the Germans had strung plenty in places where they would now be wanting to get through. And some prudent person had stolen a few rolls of chicken wire from the engineers. Laid down across the barbed wire, it would let the Americans move forward and back with safety, and when it was pulled up, the Germans would be stuck on the wrong side of their own wire.

With luck.

* * *

The Germans were holding off with their artillery. Maybe they were finally short of ammunition? Or maybe they were just going to deliver one of those short and nasty bombardments they'd used in Flanders and Champagne. Everybody had given up the three-day bombardments from earlier in the war, that ran you out of ammunition, wore out your guns, and told the enemy exactly where you were going to hit him.

Right now, the Germans seemed to want to annoy all the Americans equally. Random shells, mostly the heavier "Jack Johnsons" instead of the lighter "whizz-bangs" ripped up ground, trees, wire, and what was left of buildings. Planes zoomed low, some of them pursuits chasing other planes, others strafers (mostly German), trying to make trouble on the ground. From the German positions, machine guns fired at the occasional American plane.

The 37mm gun off to one side fired a few wild shots at the German machine guns. Some of the riflemen and Chauchaut gunners among the Americans raised their weapons to fire at the German planes.

Allison shouted to them to hold their fire. "Let them give away their positions, not us!"

To Beim, he added, "Have they got that telephone line connected yet?"

The nearest person to send looked to be Moussin. "Run up to the mill and ask them if the artillery's on the horn yet. And if it is, do they want us to move back?"

It wouldn't be easy shifting position under fire, but better than being smashed by their own artillery.

Moussin vanished. Allison studied the ground ahead, carefully holding the binoculars so that any stray rays of sunlight wouldn't make a revealing reflection off the lenses.

"You know," he said, as quietly as he could and still make himself heard, "I wish we had one German weapon. Machine gun seeds."

"Sir?"

"Ever wondered how the Germans always have so many machine guns? They go out and plant seeds at night, and the next morning the guns are ready to go. All they need is ammunition and some gunners ready to die by their guns."

"Well, we might just have—"

The German bombardment erupted, if not a hurricane, then at least a squall, stretching all the way from the battalion on the left up to the Moulin on the top of the hill.

Beim heard screams. Some of them might be his. He saw bodies flying, who couldn't be his, because he was still flat on the ground, gripping it for all he was worth. Then he didn't see anything except a vast wall of smoke rolling toward him, and he couldn't hear anything at all.

He had the odd thought that he would have liked to hear some music in his last moments. But he didn't need to hear any orders.

Hold the Germans.

The bombardment must have halted now, because he saw human figures advancing toward him out of the smoke, firing rifles and machine pistols. They wore their pig-snouted gas masks, and were they using gas or just keeping out their own smoke? Beim contemplated the questions for all of two heartbeats, then squeezed off his first shot, a second, a third—

And he could hear them. He wasn't deaf. He could also hear the whine and *wheet* of bullets passing close, and the thump of grenades. A German loomed out of the smoke, holding one ready to throw, and Beim fired, then rolled to one side in case the German dropped the grenade—Beim snatched it up and threw it wildly forward, hoping it would land among the Germans.

He never heard it land. The world turned to solid sound, as the first salvos of one-five-fives stormed out of the sky onto the advancing Germans.

This time he knew that his own body was flying. He didn't know if it was flying in pieces or whole. He knew—or thought he knew—when he landed.

Then he stopped knowing.

* * *

He had knowledge again, but it was only darkness, and the creak of metal, and a human voice not too far from his ear reciting the Twenty-third Psalm—

"He restoreth my soul—" and a fit of coughing.

" 'Goose?" If that was Goose, he sounded as if he was strangling. Gas? No, it sounded more like excitement.

And if he could make that kind of distinction, he himself wasn't dead.

"Hey, the Sarge is alive!"

Beim's head was aching. Goose's shout made it worse. "Of course I am, you little Bible-thumper."

October 28, 1918, A Hospital Near Verdun, 1730

"Sergeant, you have some visitors."

Just in time, Beim remembered his crutches. He had actually stood up a couple of times when nobody was around, holding on to the arms of the wheelchair.

It had helped him feel less guilty about being in the hospital with such—he thought—minor wounds. A bit of gas. Temporary partial deafness. Lots of bruises. A greenstick fracture of his right ankle and a sprained left wrist.

But Moussin was missing in action. Goose had taken so much gas that when he caught the influenza it turned into fatal pneumonia. And Beim had seen Feldman, looking like a wreck of himself, while a Dakin-Carrel apparatus dripped antiseptic into several wounds in his legs. (The fluid, Beim had learned, was basically diluted chlorine, the same stuff they used to scrub locker room floors and make into poison gas.)

But Nurse Ryan wouldn't listen to any excuses for his walking around, and her word was law even though with him she thought she didn't need to throw a fit.

Then Beim desperately wanted to stand, but couldn't have done it to save his life.

Rose was in front of him, her pretty face as wet as if she'd been out in the rain.

Beim lifted one hand. "Hey. Don't cry. They only blew me up. They didn't blow anything off."

"Really?"

He'd heard the same sort of skepticism—only weeks ago—about the Air Service.

"Cross my heart"—he made the gesture as well as a healing sprain allowed—"and hope to be out of this wheelchair soon." He decided that nothing else was going to happen until he had kissed Rose.

He held out both arms—and that was the last thing he was aware of until he suddenly saw Rose standing again, blushing almost the color of the Red Cross on her uniform.

And heard the cheers, the whistles, the calls of "Come on over and give me some of that."

"Damned rats don't know how to treat a lady," said Lieutenant Allison.

"I quite agree," Nurse Ryan said. "Can I get you—?"

"Coffees, please," Rose said. "And can you use one hand, Lieutenant?"

"I'll try. I'd hate to put you to work when you've just got back together with your fellow."

Rose blinked, and Beim had a horrible, irrational moment of fear that she was about to tell him that their engagement was off.

Then he remembered that climbing-into-his-lap kiss, and realized that she was trying not to cry again.

"Oh, Dick has told me enough about you to make me know that you're one of the good guys. If you can't hold a coffee cup—"

Beim realized for the first time that both of Allison's arms and part of his scalp were covered in bandages. "Do I dare ask what happened to you, sir?"

"Almost as silly as your going ass-over-elbow—sorry, ma'am. The battalion was just going back into reserve when the Germans started one of their hates. Gas, high explosive, air raids, everything but the kitchen stove. I got a knock on the head, and it threw me forward so that I landed with both arms in a pool of mustard gas.

"Lucky for me I didn't breathe any of it."

They talked about those who were gone. "Rose is going to send that little Bible of Goose's back to his family," Allison said.

"That's part of our job in the Red Cross," Rose said, in a voice that was almost steady.

It didn't take Allison long to decide that three was a crowd. He finished his coffee, gallantly tried to lift Rose's hand to his lips, and left.

"So?"

"Well, I can't go to Langres until I get out of here. Three wounds may get me sent home anyway. And the war may be over soon. We're hitting the Germans from both sides, the AEF is getting stronger and better every month, and the new German chancellor is supposed to be a reasonable man. Or at least he's not one of the old-line Prussians."

"Sometimes I wonder where the reasonable Germans have gone," Rose said dully. "Or the reasonable anybodies, for that matter."

"Oh, Goose met one. And I certainly believe in reasonable people, or why am I going to marry you?"

This time she kissed him gently on the forehead.

Epilogue

Chicago Tribune, November 28, 1958:

RICHARD FITZROY BEIM. On November 23, at Swedish Covenant Hospital, of pneumonia and other complications of the Asiatic flu. Mr. Beim, a distinguished educator, graduated from Chicago Teacher's College in 1923, after serving in the AEF in World War I. He taught in the Chicago public schools for the rest of his life, except for service in the Quartermaster Corps during World War II. At the time of his death he was Principal of Von Steuben High School.

He is survived by his wife Rose, three daughters, and five grandchildren. At the funeral at St. Luke's Lutheran Church, eulogies were delivered by Major-General David Allison (USA, Ret.) and Nathan Feldman, Professor of Romance Languages at Hofstra College.

Donations may be sent to the Richard Beim Memorial Scholarship c/o Von Steuben High School.

Historical Note

All persons named in this story are fictional, except for Generals Pershing, Mitchell, von Gallwitz, and Marshal Foch. They probably each wished that the other three were fictional, but authors have only so much power over Clio, the Muse of History. The topography and tactics of the Meuse-Argonne campaign has been edited to make it more understandable. No changes have been necessary to present the First Division (now the First Infantry Division) in a good light. Its record speaks for itself.

Americans Landing at Normandy Beach

France, 1944

BY WILLIAM H. KEITH

The period from World War I to World War II is often referred to as being more a period of truce, during which all sides re-armed and developed even deadlier weapons. The tank and airplane became an integral part of the battle. Weapons shot farther and more accurately. Bombs fell and artillery could fire from miles away. As seems to be the theme, soldiers learned how to kill even more efficiently. Though with so much changed, a Primus Pilus from Caesar's Tenth Legion who found himself commanding a squad of the American First Infantry Division on Omaha Beach would in many ways have felt at home. Looking at soldiers who fought very differently and for a variety of reasons in this book, you have probably by now noted how much remained the same. The loyalty and concern a soldier feels for his comrades; the everyday concerns of staying warm, dry, and well fed; and the realization that uncommon valor often isn't that uncommon, just rarely recognized— all were shared by a legionnaire and a paratrooper two thousand years later.

WILLIAM H. KEITH is the author of more than eighty-five novels and is known for his well-researched and well-written historical military books, many written as H. Jay Riker.

[★]

0630 HOURS

The first artillery round whistled and struck the water just twenty yards to the left of the LCVP, sending a towering geyser of white spray high into the overcast sky. Thirty men, packed shoulder to shoulder within the claustrophobic confines of the tiny craft, felt the hard slap of the concussion and pulled themselves in and down a little tighter. A second round detonated to the right, this one even closer, and sheets of falling water cascaded into the landing craft, further drenching men already soaked to the skin after hours of circling in the rough, predawn seas off Normandy.

Several of the men were vomiting noisily into their issued puke bags, their plastic helmet liners, the oily surge of bilge roiling across the LCVP's deck, or over themselves and their neighbors. One recited the Hail Mary over and over in a rapid-fire mutter, his fingers working their way along the beaded length of a rosary. Some used their helmets to bail with a grim and desperate stoicism. Others clutched weapons and equipment and braced themselves against the stomach-wrenching lurch-and-roll of the landing craft, wondering if they were going to survive the next few minutes.

One, Private First Class Joe Smith, raised his head above the boat's port-side gunwale just enough to get a glimpse of the beach half a mile ahead, and found himself staring into Hell. Beneath billowing clouds of smoke, the bluffs rising behind the beach seemed unnaturally green, and he could see the church tower rising from the tiny French town of Vierville.

And that fact terrified him more than the smoke, the ungodly noise, the rising splashes of shells hitting the water, the occasional flash and gout of flame as a landing craft ahead took a direct hit. The men of A Company, 116th Infantry of the Twenty-ninth Division, had been told that the beach defenses would be obliterated by the time they got there—first by waves of B-24 bombers spilling thirteen thousand bombs across beach and bluff, then by the devastating bombardment of dozens of Allied warships offshore, and finally by swarms of explosive rockets fired by specially modified landing craft, the LCI(R)s. So far as Joe could see, however, the German defenses appeared to be intact, even pristine. The green bluffs looked untouched; the church steeple was still standing.

And artillery, mortar, smalls arms, and machine-gun fire from hundreds of prepared positions were hammering at the men and boats of the invasion's first wave. From half a mile away, he could see handfuls of tiny black shapes huddled at the water's edge—the survivors of the first boats ashore.

Something struck the LCVP's ramp close by Joe's ear, a shriek of metal deflecting metal. "Get your damned head down, Smith!" his platoon sergeant bellowed from the rear of the well deck. "You wanna get yourself killed?"

"I'm already dying of seasickness, Sarge," Joe replied, dropping into a sheltering half crouch once more. "It don't make much difference."

It was Tuesday, the 6th of June, 1944, and A Company rode the surging swells a half mile off a flat shelf of a beach code-named Omaha, at a sector designated as Dog Green. It was H-Hour of

D-Day, the start of the largest, most complex, most monumental sea-air-land invasion in history.

And the grand crusade to liberate German-occupied Europe would soon depend upon Joe and a few thousand others like him—scared, wet, seasick men flung against the steel and concrete bastions of Hitler's *Festung Europa*.

The outcome of World War II would in large part be decided in blood, desperation, and raw courage on the sands of Normandy.

The Men

The invasion force that gray June morning numbered some 130,000 men—Americans, British, and Canadians most of them—backed by 195,700 naval and merchant marine personnel in a cross-Channel armada of 6,939 vessels, including 1,213 warships, 736 ancillary craft, 864 merchant vessels, and 4,126 transports of all sizes, ranging from troop ships through LSTs and LCI(L)s down to thirty-six-foot LCVPs like the one ferrying PFC Smith toward the beach. Overhead, an air armada of 13,000 aircraft filled the skies, each with its distinctive array of identifying alternating stripes—two black and three white—painted on wings and fuselage. Fifty thousand vehicles, from motorcycles to tanks and heavy bulldozers, made the passage with the troops, a colossal traffic jam waiting to happen.

The United States Army's contribution to the Allied assault that gray June morning included some 73,000 men. Of these, 15,500 of the 82nd and 101st Airborne Divisions landed by parachute and glider behind the beaches shortly after midnight. The rest, some 57,500 men of V and VII Corps, were crammed into landing craft corkscrewing through four- to six-foot waves off the beaches of northern France. Of these, 23,250 men of VII Corps were headed for Utah Beach, which ran northwest to southeast along the base of the Cotentin Peninsula. The rest, 34,250 men of V Corps, were being deployed to Omaha Beach, running east-west along a six-thousand-yard stretch of the Normandy coast twelve miles to the southeast.

Private First Class Joe Smith is in fact a composite character, a deliberate fictional representative of tens of thousands of others like him. His personal statistics match the average for the American soldiers coming ashore on D-Day: he was twenty-six years old, stood five feet, eight inches tall, and weighed 144 pounds. Like 60 percent of the men of Company A, 116th Regiment of the Twenty-ninth Infantry Division, Joe was from Bedford, Virginia, though, of course, the men wading ashore at the Omaha and Utah beachheads hailed from cities, towns, villages, and farms all over the eastern two-thirds of the United States. Like roughly half of his buddies in the LCVP, Joe had been drafted. Like roughly half, he was a high school graduate. About 10 percent of America's enlisted men even had a year or two of college behind them, making the U.S. Army, on average, the best educated in the world at the time.

The American Army was also the *greenest* army in a world that had, for the most part, been at war for more than four years. The troops coming ashore at Utah and Omaha included the Fourth, the First, and the Twenty-ninth Infantry Divisions and, in the parachute assault inland, the Eighty-second and 101st Airborne Divisions. Of all of these, only the few old hands of the First and the Eighty-second had seen combat previously, in North Africa and in Sicily.

For the vast majority, the Normandy beaches would be their baptism of fire.

0640 HOURS

The coxswain of Joe's LCVP gunned the 225-horsepower diesel engine, starting the final leg of the run in toward the beach. The sea was running high here, with waves averaging four feet; the flat-bottomed landing craft hit each in succession like a solid wall, lurching and pounding, rising and falling, adding to the *mal-de-mer* misery of men who'd already spent much of the past forty-eight hours fighting rebellious stomachs. Shell splashes continued to rise and fall, accompanied by a cacophony of thunder that even the landing craft's pounding engine could not mask.

Joe, among the first in the mass of troops immediately behind the LCVP's ramp, risked another peek up over the gunwale and past the ramp's edge. The ramp itself was too high for him to peer over, and provided at least the illusion of shelter. Joe was very much aware of the fact that while the sturdy little boat's ramp was made of steel, most of the rest of the craft was plywood, providing exactly zero protection from the small arms and machine-gun fire hammering at the advancing troops.

From his vantage point just behind the section leader on the left side of the ramp, Joe could see the entire stretch of Omaha Beach, from the concrete-block Vierville draw almost dead ahead, sweeping east past Les Moulins, and reaching all the way toward Colleville, though the farthest landing areas were now shrouded in heavy smoke.

In point of fact, the only town name Joe remembered was Vierville-du-Mer, because it had given its name to the westernmost of five small ravines leading from the beach up onto the table-land behind the bluff. Those ravines, or draws, provided the only routes by which vehicles could get off of the beach; the Vierville draw, labeled Exit D-1, was part of A Company's initial objective in the massive and meticulous strategic battle plan called Operation Overlord. A Company's orders were to secure the draw, move up the draw into what was confidently expected to be the flattened rubble of Vierville itself, and engage the dazed survivors of the German defenses—those who didn't surrender outright—somewhere in the flat *bocage* country beyond.

At the moment, however, it didn't appear that the defenders were either dazed or inclined to surrender. According to the operational orders, the very first to hit the beach would be engineers and NCDUs—naval combat demolition units—men trained to use high explosives to clear lanes through the forest of beach obstacles and mines, and to demolish the concrete barriers across the beach exits. With them would be sixty-four DD tanks—Sherman tanks equipped with rubber flotation collars that would allow them to be dropped into the Channel well off the beach and swim ashore with their duplex drives—the "DD" of their name. Emerging from the water onto the beach, their 75mm cannon would engage the German defenders and provide cover for the engineers blowing paths through the obstacles.

Close behind would be the first wave of the main assault forces, including A Company, which would rush up the beach, seize the entrances to the five draws leading through the bluffs, and neutralize any surviving German defenders.

From where Joe stood, however, he couldn't see *any* movement up the beach. The initial ranks of landing craft had come to a halt perhaps fifty yards off the beach, and the surf was filled with men struggling to get ashore. Small, black masses of men huddled at the water's edge and around the bases of exposed obstacles, as German emplacements on the bluff towering above the beach poured fire into men and landing craft alike.

What he saw was a landing stopped cold at the water's edge, the men floundering and in total disorder as the meticulously crafted invasion plan fell apart.

And his LCVP was headed straight into that hell of fire, death, and chaos.

The Allied Plan

In the spring of 1944, continental Europe belonged to Nazi Germany. Since 1942, Allied troops had been gathering in England, preparing for the inevitable invasion of the continent. Everyone—Allies and Germans both—knew the invasion *would* come.

The only questions were when . . . and exactly where.

In March of 1943, British Lieutenant General Frederick Morgan had been appointed as chief of staff to the supreme Allied commander—although at that time the post of supreme Allied commander had not yet been filled—and ordered to begin planning for a possible cross-Channel invasion of France sometime in 1943 or 1944. Morgan created a working group called COSSAC, an acronym drawn from Morgan's title, which began choosing just where and when the invasion would take place.

COSSAC soon settled on the Normandy coast, sixty miles of beaches alternating with rocky cliffs between the Cotentin Peninsula and the mouth of the River Seine, as the best in an unfortunate series of possible choices. The obvious choice for a strike across the Channel—at the Pas-de-Calais just twenty miles across the Straits of Dover from England—was perfect in every way but one, the fact that it *was* the obvious choice. A landing at the Pas-de-Calais offered a direct-line path toward Germany and the strategically vital Rhine-Ruhr region and was located at the narrowest point of the English Channel, and so those ports and beaches were especially heavily fortified.

Other possible choices were equally fraught with disadvantages. Belgium and the Netherlands offered excellent ports—a key advantage for maintaining and building up any beachhead—but were too close to German reserves and Luftwaffe bases. Le Havre, in upper Normandy, was also a superb port, but to take it would require landings on both sides of the Seine, offering the Germans the chance to defeat both landings in detail.

Farther west, the coast of Brittany offered good ports, including the city of Brest, but a long voyage for the invasion armada, and the approaches were guarded by the German-occupied islands of Guernsey and Jersey. The Cotentin Peninsula itself had the port at Cherbourg to recommend it, but much of the area could be flooded by the Germans, and the narrowness of the peninsula itself might allow the enemy to bottle up the invasion force with no room to maneuver, just as they had in Italy.

And so, almost by default, COSSAC early on had settled on Normandy as the invasion site.

The overall invasion plan, from the marshaling of ships and men in England to the breakout into France, was code-named Overlord, while the plan for D-Day itself, the assault on the beaches, was called Neptune.

For the Allies, the basic strategy of Neptune was relatively simple: get as many men and vehicles ashore as quickly as possible, get off the beaches as quickly as possible, and push as far inland as quickly as possible. The *specifics* of how they were to do that, however, seemed overwhelming in their number and meticulous attention to detail. Precise times and movement schedules were created for everything—when each ship would be loaded and depart, when the air strikes and shore bombardments would begin and end, when each unit would go ashore and in what order, when each objective would be taken.

At one point, the supreme commander of the Allied effort, General Dwight D. Eisenhower, pointed out that while battle plans are everything, as soon as the battle was joined, plans became worthless.

The sentiment was echoed by many of his subordinates. After one briefing, Colonel Paul Good, commanding officer of the 175th Regiment, Twenty-ninth Division, held up the operational plans written just for his regiment—a sheaf of typewritten paper thicker than the thickest telephone book. After attempting unsuccessfully to tear the "phone book" in half, he tossed it over his shoulder and told his men, "Forget this goddamned thing. You get your ass on the beach. I'll be there waiting for you and I'll tell you what to do. There ain't nothing in this plan that is going to go right."

Good's words would prove to be prophetic.

By choosing Normandy as the invasion beachhead, COSSAC was able to turn several potential disadvantages into positive assets. If the Germans could be convinced that the invasion, when it came, would strike at the Pas-de-Calais, they would be tempted to believe that the Normandy landings were a decoy, part of an elaborate deception. Almost from the start, an elaborate deception program to that end, code-named Fortitude, was mounted by the Allies.

With that, a Normandy invasion would hold the vital element of surprise. The region east of the Cotentin Peninsula was relatively sheltered from Atlantic storms and wind, and the chosen beaches offered access to good roads and beach approaches leading inland. Once the enemy realized that Normandy was the real beachhead and not a feint, the Seine River would delay the movement of German reinforcements—especially their dreaded panzer divisions—southwest from the Pas-de-Calais.

In fact, there was only a single serious weak point to the Allied strategy, but it was a weakness that would come close to jeopardizing the entire invasion.

And the name of that weak point was Omaha Beach.

0645 HOURS

"Where the hell's the air corps?" one of Joe's buddies, PFC Tom Kowalski, demanded. He was looking up at the overcast with something approaching desperation. "Where the hell's all our damned air cover? Where the hell's the *plan*?"

"Stop whining, Ski," Corporal Vince Collins said, slapping the back of Ski's helmet. "With the big guns on the battleships pounding 'em, the Krauts won't know what hit 'em!"

And that ship bombardment *had* been impressive. Off Omaha Beach that morning, the battleships *Texas* and *Arkansas* and several cruisers and destroyers had opened up at 0550 hours—forty minutes before H-Hour and just as it was getting light—with a savage bombardment of the shore that had lasted for half an hour. When the shore bombardment began, Joe and the thousands of other soldiers in the first wave were already circling in their landing craft, awaiting the moment to turn toward shore.

Joe had been awed by the ferocity of that bombardment, had felt the concussion of each volley as it hammered across the water, had actually been able to *see* the flights of fourteen-inch shells from the *Arkansas* and *Texas* as they hurtled overhead on their way to the coast of France. Surely *nothing* could have lived through that hell-storm of fire . . .

And yet as Joe's LCVP motored yet closer to the beach, he could see that the defenses behind Omaha Beach were very much alive. From his roughly jouncing vantage point now five hundred yards offshore, it was clear that all of the men and equipment landed so far were still piled up along the water's edge; none had advanced as far as the flat shingle behind the beach and at the foot of the bluff.

He was aware now of another ominous sign that not everything had gone as planned. In the surf between sand and deep water and extending well up to the exposed tidal flat beyond, he could see a veritable forest of beach obstacles running along the water's edge. Many of those structures, Joe's unit had been informed, had mines attached to their business ends—either Teller antitank mines, each containing twelve pounds of TNT, or old French artillery shells looted from the defunct Maginot Line.

The beach obstacles represented a kind of Maginot Line on

their own—the fruit of German field marshal Erwin Rommel's conviction that any Allied invasion of France *must* be stopped on the beaches, and not be allowed to move inland. But what they told Joe was that the army engineer teams, naval combat demolition units, and navy Seabees who'd been tasked with blasting paths through those obstacles for the approaching troops had failed to carry out their assignments.

The engineers and NCDUs, if they'd made it ashore at all, must be trapped in that pileup at the water's edge, unable to move forward, unable to blow paths, as planned, through the obstacles, or to open up the concrete barriers blocking the exits off the beach.

What in the hell had gone wrong?

The German Plan

Field Marshal Erwin Rommel, the brilliant Desert Fox of the North African Campaign, was assigned in November of 1943 to take charge of the coastal defenses of France against the long-expected Allied invasion. In December, he went on an inspection tour from Norway to the border with Spain, and was appalled by what he saw. The much-ballyhooed Atlantic Wall was all but fiction, "a figment," as he put it, "of Hitler's *Wolkenkuckkucksheim*," his "cloud-cuckoo-land."

Fearing he had only months remaining before the invasion, Rommel instigated an almost frantic building program along the entire coast, erecting pillboxes, fortifications, artillery emplacements, entrenchments, beach obstacles, tank traps, and minefields. Most within the German High Command, including both Hitler and Rommel himself, felt the likeliest objective of an Allied invasion would be the beaches along the Pas-de-Calais, and most of the defensive efforts were concentrated there.

All agreed, however, that Normandy was also a possible target for invasion, and in January and February of 1944 Rommel personally supervised the strengthening of the Normandy beach defenses. Besides improving the gun positions and fortifications themselves, which included pillboxes, artillery batteries, coastal defense guns, and Tobruks—circular emplacements mounting machine guns, mortars, or a tank turret—he ordered the emplacement of tens of thousands of beach obstacles. These included Belgian gates, iron frames ten feet high and erected in belts 150 yards out from the high tide line; poles driven into the sand and angled toward the sea in a line 100 yards from the high tide mark; and, closer in still, fields of hedgehogs—easy-to-make obstacles consisting of three or four steel rails each about four yards long and welded together at the center to create angular structures like a titanic child's jacks, placed to rip the bottom out of an incoming landing craft at high tide.

Along the Normandy coast, the tidal flats extended for two hundred yards into the Channel, and the water could rise by ten feet or more in the six hours between low tide and high. At high tide, the beach obstacles, many with mines or artillery shells attached to them, were submerged and invisible to incoming landing craft. At low tide they formed a deadly and labyrinthine cordon that would delay the advance of troops across the beach and block the deployment of vehicles.

Rommel argued that the Allies didn't care where they landed—Normandy or the Pas-de-Calais—only that their landing be *successful*. Once ashore, they would begin a massive buildup of men and materiel that the thinly stretched German war machine could not possibly match.

0648 HOURS

Four aircraft howled low overhead—odd-looking, twin-boomed P-38 Lightnings with black-and-white invasion recognition stripes on wings and tail booms. "There's your flyboys, Ski!" PFC Coleman shouted as the aircraft vanished into the smoke clouds gathering above the bluff ahead. "Quit your damned yapping!"

Four planes seemed little enough a force to throw at the German defenses, but the sight cheered Joe and the others enormously. Kowalski didn't reply to Coleman's gibe. He was busy vomiting into his helmet again.

Many, if not most, of the men in the tiny landing craft had been sick for days. The invasion had originally been scheduled for yesterday, Monday, June 5, and they'd boarded troop transports days before. Some elements of the invasion fleet had departed England on June 3. When the landings were postponed because of bad weather—a storm was raging through the Channel—many troops had ridden it out at sea rather than return to port. Joe and the other members of his company had been on board the British troop transport *Empire Javelin*, which had left port late on the 4th.

They'd ridden out the storm throughout the 5th, wet, seasick, and miserable. Finally, that evening, the men had received the word that the invasion was a go. Off Omaha Beach at 0100 hours on the morning of June 6, Joe and the others in his section had clambered down the boarding nets and into the waiting LCVP. For the past five hours, then, they'd circled in the darkness, getting wetter, more seasick, and even more miserable.

The LCVP—landing craft, vehicles, and personnel—was a remarkable invention. Also called the Higgins Boat, after Andrew Jackson Higgins, its American designer, it offered a relatively cheap and easy means of ferrying thirty men at a time from transports to beach. Thirty-six feet long, with a twenty-six-inch draft forward and a thirty-six-inch draft aft, displacing nine tons, the craft could manage about twelve knots while hauling thirty men and their equipment, or a three-ton truck, or a jeep and a twelve-man squad, or 8,100 pounds of supplies.

Joe's LCVP, like most of the others around it, carried an assault section, half of a rifle platoon. The thirty men aboard included an officer and a senior NCO; five riflemen; a light machine gun team; BAR, bazooka, and mortar teams; a flamethrower team; and teams with wire cutters and bangalore torpedoes—lengths of pipe packed with explosives that could be attached end to end and used to blast open paths through barbed wire and minefields. The LCVP was part of the meticulous work that had gone into the invasion planning. Six landing craft carried a company's three rifle platoons, while a seventh carried the company command group and attached personnel—medics, gap teams, forward observers, guides, and liaisons for following units. In all, a company numbered about two hundred men.

They hit another series of heavy rollers. "Jesus!" Corporal Latham groaned in his thick, Brooklyn accent. He was standing just behind Joe, the assault section's assistant BAR man. "If I ever find the guy what invented this boat, I'm gonna have some words with him, know what I mean?"

"That guy Higgins ain't got nothin' to be proud about," said another.

It was an attitude common among the soldiers in those boats that morning. After circling for as long as five hours in the predawn darkness, many of the troops didn't care if they lived or died, so long as they could get to solid ground.

Off to port, two men floundered in the water, supported by their inflated Mae Wests. Either they were survivors from another boat, or, more likely, they were the crew of one of the DD tanks that were supposed to go in with the very first troops. Those tanks, supported by raised floatation skirts of rubberized canvas, had less than one foot of freeboard when they were deployed, and were at the nonexistent mercy of rough water.

"I think," Joe said to no one in particular, "that things are getting FUBAR."

It was soldier's slang for "fouled up beyond all recognition" . . . or words to that effect.

The Beaches

Operation Neptune called for the landings to be divided among five beaches. Toward the east, the British beaches, code-named Gold and Sword, straddled the Canadian beach, Juno. In the west were the American beaches: Utah, striking west at the base of the Cotentin Peninsula, and Omaha, holding the key sector adjoining the British landings.

The command of the operation represented a delicate balance of politics and personality. The supreme Allied commander, appointed in December of 1943, was five-star general Dwight D. Eisenhower, graduate of the West Point class of 1915, and a somewhat controversial choice since he had no actual combat experience and had never led men in combat. He was seen as a diplomatic choice, however, one who would work well with the British. Since two-thirds of the men committed to the invasion were Americans, an American supreme commander was a necessary choice.

Second in command was British General Bernard Law Montgomery—irascible, at times intemperate and hard to work with, but under Eisenhower's overall direction he would be in command of all Allied ground forces on D-Day, the Twenty-first Army Group, which was made up of the U.S. First Army and the British Second Army. His chief claim to fame was that he'd commanded the British Eighth Army in its decisive victory over Rommel's Afrika Korps in North Africa two years before. And now he would face Rommel once again in the hedgerows of northern France.

The American contingent of the Twenty-first Army Group was under the command of General Omar N. Bradley, a West Point classmate of Eisenhower's. The U.S. First Army consisted of two corps. The U.S. VII Corps, starting with the Fourth Infantry Division, would go ashore at Utah Beach. Omaha Beach would be assaulted by the U.S. V Corps, composed of the Twenty-ninth Infantry Division and the First Infantry Division—the latter the "Big Red One" that had already made a name for itself in North Africa and Sicily.

The American beaches were subdivided into sectors, each the assigned target of an individual regimental company. At Utah there were only two sectors, Green Beach to the north, Red Beach to the south. The beach itself had a broad, open shelf, and the land behind the beach rose and fell in sand dunes and gentle hummocks. Behind the beach, most of the land was low and in places quite swampy. As American paratroopers would discover in the darkness and confusion of their drop early in the morning of June 6, the Germans had flooded large tracts of land near the Merderet and Douve Rivers six to ten miles inland from the beaches. Roads leading off the beaches were built up slightly higher than the flooded areas and were called "causeways" by the American planners.

The German defenders at Utah were from the 709th and 716th Divisions, static troops, not exactly the best or the most finely tuned of the Third Reich's legions. Many were old men or teenagers, or were recovering from wounds suffered on the Eastern Front, or were Ost battalions of Poles or Russians of dubious loyalties. There were several tough positions, but overall the beach defenses were more porous here than elsewhere.

Omaha Beach, however, was quite a different story.

The landing areas were located in a shallow bight in the Normandy coast land, a seven-thousand-yard stretch of sandy beaches in a shallow crescent between sheer cliffs. Above the high tide line was a shingle of sand or loose stones leading up to—along much of the beach—a seawall of concrete and wood, four feet high in most places, as much as twelve feet high in others. Behind the seawall was an area called the shelf, flat, some of it swampy, all of it heavily mined by the Germans.

Beyond the shelf, the land rose in a steep bluff, a hill ninety to one hundred feet high, everywhere dominating the beach below. The bluff was split by five draws leading off the beach. Running from west to east, those ravine exits were labeled D-1, at the village of Vierville; D-3, at Les Moulins; E-1, E-3, and F-1. The first two had roads leading up onto the tableland beyond; the other three were nothing but footpaths. All five draws were blocked by concrete fortifications, minefields, and barbed wire, and covered by fire from machine-gun and mortar positions.

A further complication was a German emplacement of six 155mm cannons at Pointe-du-Hoc, four miles west of Omaha Beach, heavily fortified and positioned at the top of a vertical, 130-foot cliff. Those guns, it was believed, would have a clear line of fire onto the beaches at both Omaha and Utah, and were thought to be invulnerable to naval gunfire or bombing runs. They would have to be assaulted directly from the sea.

The invasion planners had divided Omaha Beach into two areas of responsibility. The western half, comprised of sectors Charlie, Dog Green, Dog White, Dog Red, and Easy Green, were to be assaulted by the 116th Regiment of the Twenty-ninth Infantry Division. The eastern half, comprised of sectors Easy Red, Fox Green, and Fox Red, were the responsibility of the Sixteenth Regiment of the First Infantry Division. Almost as an afterthought, the naval battery at Pointe-du-Hoc would be stormed by the U.S. Army Ranger Second Battalion.

The Allied planners had not wanted to land at Omaha at all. Because of the cliffs rising along most of this area of the coast, the *only* decent landing area between Utah to the west and the British beaches to the east was here, along this brief, sandy crescent . . . and it was here that the Germans could be expected to put the heaviest and strongest of their defenses.

But without a beachhead here, the Fourth Division's landing at Utah would be separated from the British right flank at Gold by over twenty-five miles. The Germans could be expected to exploit that gap almost immediately, allowing them to isolate and defeat the American and British landings separately. For that reason, Omaha Beach was critical to the invasion; without it, Overlord would almost certainly fail at the water's edge in blood and slaughter.

This, then, was the Allied plan—with little in the way of tactics, maneuvering, or finesse beyond the ongoing campaign of misdirection intended to fix the enemy's attention for as long as possible on the Pas-de-Calais. The British Sixth Airborne Division would seize critical bridges and strongpoints outside of the important town of Caen, on the Orne River south of Sword Beach, and secure the invasion's left flank. On the Cotentin Peninsula, the American 82nd and 101st Airborne Divisions would capture the town of Ste. Mère Église, disrupt the movement of German reinforcements and communications behind Utah Beach, and hold the right flank.

Between the two, more than 130,000 men would storm up out of the sea and rush the fortifications of steel, concrete, and wire, using tactics indistinguishable from those employed in the blood-drenched trenches of World War I.

The planners had one encouraging break, however. The defenders at Omaha, as at Utah, were believed to be the German 716th Division, static troops and Ost battalions—Polish or Russians given Hobson's choice between manning Hitler's Atlantic Wall and being herded into POW camps. After the naval bombardment, after the softening up by waves of B-24s, after clouds of rockets fired from LCI(R)s, Omaha's defenders would be dead, dazed, or surrendering.

0650 HOURS

His seasickness *almost* forgotten, Joe turned as the section leader, Lieutenant Dolan, standing directly between Joe and the ramp, yelled, "Listen up! Listen up, everybody!"

Another mortar round went off nearby, the concussion slapping the side of the LCVP like a hammer's blow. Dolan had to yell to make himself heard above the cacophony of shell fire, explosions, and the roar of the landing craft's diesels.

"All right, so it's not the walk in the park they told us it was gonna be! So what else is new?" That elicited a few grim chuckles from the listening men, and Dolan pushed on. "When the ramp goes down, I want you to haul ass, okay? Just get out of the water and get across that beach as fast as you can manage! Get to the seawall at the top of the beach. We have a mission to carry out, and by God we're gonna do it! Just remember your training, don't freeze up, and get your asses to that seawall! I'll see you at the top of the beach, and we'll go on from there. If for whatever reason I don't make it, you listen to Sergeant Morrison! You hear me?"

"Yes, sir!" a few men chorused.

Dolan cupped a hand behind his ear, leaning forward as if he couldn't hear. "What was that?"

"Yes, sir!"

"Twenty-nine, let's go!" Dolan yelled. It had been the division's battle cry throughout training.

The men packed into the LCVP answered Dolan with a roar.

Joe turned to look over the side of the LCVP again, and was just in time to see a German shell or a mine—he couldn't tell which—detonate at the bow of another LCVP just thirty yards away. The flash ripped the heavy bow ramp up and back and engulfed the forward third of the boat in flame and whirling splinters. A couple of bodies splashed into the sea between the boats as the other landing craft, shattered bow agape, nosed down into the water and flung its stern high. Dozens of soldiers struggled in the water, their Mae West life jackets blossoming over their shoulders and behind their heads. The landing craft turned turtle almost at once, and some of the men in the water tried to cling to it, as others struck out toward the distant beach.

For a moment, Joe wondered if the coxswain of his boat was going to slow to take some of the survivors ashore, but the LCVP kept gunning ahead, cresting each wave like a roller coaster. During the platoon's briefing, Dolan had told them that no boat would stop for any other. Rescuing survivors in the drink was a job for the navy or for the coast guard. The tight timing of the plan, the orderly ranks of incoming landing craft, could *not* be delayed by rescue efforts.

Remember your training, Dolan had said.

Somehow, thirteen weeks of boot camp, the combat training that had followed, and two years of practice exercises storming British beaches and crawling through obstacle courses just didn't seem to be enough for this thunderous excursion into Hell.

Training

The United States Army had entered combat in North Africa with the assumption that they were the best-trained soldiers in the world. They discovered their mistake at a place in Tunisia called Kasserine Pass. A counterattack by Rommel had hurled the confidently advancing Americans back—many had dropped their weapons, turned tail, and run—and though the overextended enemy had been stopped at last by Allied artillery fire, this first clash between U.S. troops and the battle-hardened Germans had been a sobering experience. Eisenhower had later written, "From now on I am going to make it a fixed rule that no unit from the time it reaches this theater until the war is won will ever stop training."

The Twenty-ninth Division had sailed from the United States to England on board the *Queen Mary* in September of 1942. They'd arrived with nothing to do, no clear mission, since the invasion wasn't even in the planning stages as yet, and the threat of the Germans crossing the Channel had receded since Hitler's invasion of Russia fifteen months before. This led to friction. American GIs were used to better food than was available in England, and better living conditions in the barracks. Their pay was more than twice that of their British Army counterparts, and their uniforms were newer and sharper. British Tommies began complaining that the Yanks were stealing their girls. As their popular saying succinctly summed it up, "The Americans are overpaid, oversexed, and over here." The Americans, of course, had a brash comeback. The British, they replied, were "underpaid, undersexed, and under Eisenhower."

The best antidote for boredom and too much free time was training, and lots of it. In America, boot camp had turned raw recruits into soldiers, breaking down their individuality and building them up into a unit that could work together. In England they began working at combat training, marching endlessly, running obstacle courses, crawling under barbed wire with live machine-gun rounds cracking overhead, spending nights out in the field, learning to dig foxholes, learning to *live* in foxholes, learning to read the land as well as learning to read maps.

The U.S. Assault Training Center was established at Woolacomb, and practice beaches were set up all over England. The most extensive was in Devonshire on the south coast, at Slapton Sands, where the topography was a close match to Utah Beach—a coarse gravel beach leading to swampy ground and shallow lagoons beyond. Almost three thousand local residents were evacuated from the area, and in August of 1943, the beach at Slapton Sands began to bristle with hedgehogs and other German beach defenses.

Here they practiced debarking from all types of landing craft, from little LCVPs up to LCIs, LSTs, and troopships. They worked out fire exercises, and practiced assaulting all types of targets, with and without fire support. They learned how two men could work forward, each in turn covering the other, to attack a pillbox with hand grenades or a satchel charge. They learned how to use bangalore torpedoes to blow holes through wire or a minefield, and how to use wire cutters to cut through the wire.

Since about one-quarter of the troops going ashore in the first wave would be combat engineers tasked with clearing beach obstacles, a special facility for engineers was set up here as well.

The focus, always, was on *offensive* tactics. Once they hit the beach, they were to move forward and assault their assigned objectives. All other considerations came second: they were *not* to try to help wounded, for instance. That was the job of the medics. The mission objective always came first.

Assault training was divided into four phases—individual training on the obstacle course, team training for wire cutters and demolition teams, company-level exercises involving two hundred men, and battalion-level exercises involving eight hundred or more. The training was unrelenting, realistic, and dangerous. In December of 1943, a live artillery round fell short and killed four men. A few days later, three landing craft capsized and fourteen men were drowned.

Besides honing the men, the training helped the commanders spot flaws and fix problems. On the night of April 27–28, Operation Tiger, a major rehearsal for VII Corps' landing at Utah, was held at Slapton Sands, and some serious shortcomings were revealed. Confusion with schedules and organization resulted in traffic jams off the beach. The British and Americans were using different radio frequencies, adding to the confusion. The real problems came when several E-boats—the larger German equivalent of American PT boats—snuck through the British destroyer screen, sank two LSTs, and damaged six more. Almost eight hundred men were killed, and about three hundred others were wounded in the attack. Lives were lost because the men had not been trained to use their inflatable life belts.

These deficiencies, and others, were corrected.

In the course of these exercises, the school leaders worked out the optimum makeup of each assault team—riflemen; BAR, bazooka, and 60mm mortar teams; and the rest—with an officer as section leader and a senior noncom as assistant section leader. Every man had his assigned place in the LCVP—rifle team in the lead, followed by the wire cutters, followed by BAR and bazooka teams, followed by mortar, machine-gun, and flamethrower teams, with the bangalore torpedoes and the assistant section leader bringing up the rear.

Every man had an assigned task once he hit the beach.

Of particular importance were the engineers and navy combat demolition units or NCDUs. Low tide at Omaha Beach would be at 0525 hours and H-Hour was set for 0630, just an hour and five minutes later. When the first waves went ashore, the forest of beach obstacles would be exposed. Paths *had* to be blown through those obstacles and the paths marked *as the water was rising*. If this vital task wasn't accomplished, later waves of landing craft—bringing in reinforcements and equipment and taking out the wounded—would find those obstacles, and the deadly mines attached to them, submerged.

Timing and training both would have to be perfect, or the landings could quickly deteriorate into utter chaos. Techniques were developed and practiced at Slapton Sands and elsewhere but, ultimately, their final proof would be the invasion itself.

Most of the troops shared the attitude of one airborne soldier, who wrote that after a particularly grueling training exercise, "you finally dragged your weary body those last few torturous miles, and throwing yourself across the bunk you said—'Combat can't be that rough!' "

They would soon learn otherwise.

0652 HOURS

Joe's mouth was dry—perhaps the only part of him that was. As the LCVP got closer and closer to the beach, he found himself hunching over, as if by pulling in his body he could make himself a smaller target. His gear seemed to drag at him—his M-1 rifle slung over his shoulder; his belt with canteen and extra magazines, mess kit, and bayonet; the one musette bag over one shoulder with his gas mask, the other with some blocks of TNT for the demo guys. His battle jacket, impregnated with a waterproofing chemical, felt greasy and heavy. His left hand gripped the handle of a heavy metal ammo case he was hauling for the LMG team.

There was no more chatter, no banter, no more words of encouragement from Lieutenant Dolan. For the past few minutes, the noise had steadily increased, an ongoing and unrelenting thunder of explosions mingled with the roar of the boat's engine, the rapid-fire hammer of machine guns, and the steady crack of small arms fire.

There were two .30-caliber machine guns in the LCVP, in well mounts all the way aft, and both were firing continuously. When Joe glanced toward the stern of the boat, however, past the hunched bodies and drawn faces of the other troops, he saw that the navy gunners had ducked down inside the armored wells, with only their hands reaching up to blindly point the weapons and depress the butterfly triggers. The coxswain, too, had ducked below the cockpit's splash shield on the port side, just behind the well deck, and was steering blind.

The realization that the navy was driving them ashore without looking was not exactly an encouraging one.

Then the belly of the landing craft scraped sand. They jolted forward for a few feet, then slewed to an uncertain stop. The bow ramp dropped with a rattle of steel cable through cable guards and hawse pipes, and the three columns of close-packed men in the well deck surged forward.

Instantly, everything went wrong.

Dolan was immediately ahead of Joe, who was second in line in the left-hand column. As the lieutenant stepped out onto the ramp, the right side of his head exploded, his helmet and a spray of blood, bone, and brain stung Joe's face and splattered across his field jacket. Joe felt the bullet, deflected by Dolan's skull, snap past his right ear. Dolan tumbled backward into Joe, knocking him back a step as Latham collided with him from behind. On Joe's right, Kowalski folded his arms over his belly and sagged forward, crumpling to the boat's deck.

By chance, the landing craft had dropped its ramp directly opposite a German machine gun somewhere up on top of the bluff just a couple of hundred yards ahead. Rounds slashed through the close-packed men at the LCVP's bow, screeched off armor plate, and splashed in the water around the ramp, turning the passing swells into a seething froth.

Joe didn't think—he couldn't think. All he knew was that he had to get off the boat, out of that boxed-in death trap. He pushed the lieutenant's deadweight body forward and to the side, and Dolan's body toppled sideways off the ramp, hitting the water with a dull splash; Joe took three steps across the ramp, jumped into the water . . . and nearly drowned.

In theory, the water shouldn't have been more than a couple of feet. The LCVP's draft at the bow was just twenty-six inches. In practice, though, the physics of wind, tide, and surf tended to create sandbars beneath the surface, with deeper water inshore. There were also submerged craters scooped out by naval shells falling short, by German mortar and artillery fire falling on-target, and by exploding mines, and some of those holes were *quite* deep.

All Joe knew was that the expected firm shock of his boots hitting sand beneath knee-deep water wasn't there. He plunged straight down, the cold, murky water closing over his face and head with terrifying suddenness. He struggled, floundering.

Since the chaos of Operation Tiger at Slapton Sands, regimental orders required that no man carry more than forty-four pounds of equipment. In practice, most men carried much more, as platoon leaders piled on extra gear and ammunition, especially for the machine guns and mortars, and the men themselves found space to tuck in important extras—spare magazines for their rifles, cartons of cigarettes, copies of the Bible or of travel guides to France. The soldiers with specialized equipment couldn't hope to stay under the forty-four-pound limit; a flamethrower alone weighed over seventy pounds. Private George Roach, an assistant flamethrower operator, hit Omaha beach carrying over one hundred pounds of gear—M-1 rifle, ammunition, hand grenades, a five-gallon container of fuel, a cylinder of compressed nitrogen, and assorted wrenches and tools.

Roach himself weighed just 125 pounds.

Joe wasn't *that* heavily burdened, but he was carrying an extra musette bag with blocks of TNT for the demolition teams, and a heavy metal box of belt ammunition for the assault team's .30-caliber machine gun. It hadn't seemed like much back on board the *Empress Javelin*.

But now it was dragging him to his death.

Weapons and Gear

The equipment carried by each man at D-Day depended, of course, on his unit, his team, and on his mission. Engineers and demolition men had to carry the tools of their pyrotechnic trade with them, along with rifles, packs, and other gear; paratroops coming down on the Cotentin Peninsula had different designs of helmets, boots, and combat uniforms. The U.S. Ranger battalion had special gear for climbing the cliff at Pointe-du-Hoc, including rocket guns for firing grapnels attached to climbing ropes and twenty-five-yard ladders appropriated from a British fire department.

Most of the men wading ashore on the beaches at Utah and Omaha, however, were dressed in the standard-issue uniform that had evolved somewhat in the years since the beginning of the war. The United States Army in 1944 had actually enjoyed something of a breakthrough in the science of outfitting its troops, with the first army in history to be issued uniforms specifically for combat, distinct from dress uniforms for parade. Their German opponents wore tailored dress tunics complete with badges and braid through most of the war, and in temperate climates, at least, the British tommies wore standard battle dress for all occasions.

The GI's field jacket was either the hip-length M1941 or the much superior M1943, thigh-length, waterproof, windproof, and tear-resistant. For D-Day, his uniform was impregnated with a chemical designed to protect against German gas attacks. The stuff made uniforms greasy and stiff, scratchy and unpleasant. The cloth could no longer breathe, and so the soldier sweated profusely, froze when it got cold, and always stank.

His helmet was the familiar M1 steel helmet. It came in three parts—the outer steel shell, painted olive drab and sometimes covered with scrim net for holding camouflage; an inner plastic shell with straps to secure it to the head; and a soft, almost shapeless knit cap called a "beanie." This last was designed to cushion the head under the helmet, but was also frequently worn by itself when the soldier was not in combat.

In the time-honored tradition of the ingenuity and improvisation of the American fighting man, the helmet frequently did double duty—as a pot for cooking or for heating coffee, as a makeshift basket for eggs or produce liberated from a local farmer, as an entrenching tool, as a washing or shaving bowl, as a temporary repository for vomit, and as a bucket for bailing out sinking landing craft or rain-filled foxholes. Officers were identified by a single, short, vertical white stripe on the back of the helmet. Senior noncoms were identified by a single horizontal stripe.

The most vital item of an infantryman's load-out, of course, was his rifle. Most common was the M1 Garand, so-called after its inventor, John C. Garand. The M-1 was the first self-loading rifle ever accepted into military service as a standard weapon. It was a semiautomatic, gas-operated, .30-caliber weapon. Expensive and complicated to produce, it nevertheless was a sturdy and effective weapon, and by the end of the war, some 5.5 million had been produced. It weighed nine-and-a-half pounds.

The Garand had one serious flaw. It was loaded by forcing an eight-round clip down into the receiver housing—itself sometimes a painful process resulting in skinned knuckles—and this was an all-or-nothing affair; there was no way for a soldier to top off a half-empty clip. Worse, when the final shot was fired, the empty clip was ejected with a loud and distinctive *ping*. German troops quickly learned that the distinctive sound meant the firer's weapon was empty, and would wait until they heard it before rushing him.

Many soldiers actually preferred the M1903 rifle, commonly called the Springfield. The standard U.S. rifle of World War I, it was bolt-action, firing from an internal five-round magazine. Army snipers used the M1903A4 version mounting a Weaver telescopic sight. While the M1 had replaced the Springfield as the army's standard-issue weapon by 1939, Garand production could not keep up with demand as millions of recruits were inducted into the armed forces after Pearl Harbor, and so the cheaper and simpler M1903 was placed back into large-scale production to fill the gap. Many troops coming ashore on D-Day had Springfields rather than Garands; by that time, many Springfields had also been passed along to the French resistance.

Troops not issued with rifles, such as platoon- and company-level officers, the members of mortar and machine-gun crews, jeep and truck drivers, or special-duty personnel such as MPs, often carried the .30-caliber M1 carbine. Much lighter than the Garand at 5.2 pounds, it was gas-operated, firing from either a fifteen- or thirty-round box magazine. It was by far the most popular weapon in use by American troops, with more than 6 million produced by war's end. Its single disadvantage was that its shorter muzzle length made it far less accurate than a rifle, but its high rate of fire and large magazine capacity made it a winner in firefights. Later in the war, the M2 version was introduced, with a full-auto capability.

Another popular American weapon was the .45-caliber M1A1 Thompson submachine gun. Though the original drum-fed version had been made infamous by Chicago gangsters in the 1920s, the 1942 version fired only from twenty- or thirty-round box magazines and lacked the pistol grip under the barrel. It was heavy—10.5 pounds—and costly to produce, and so was available only in limited numbers. Preference for issuing the Thompson went to elite units such as airborne troops and Rangers. It was quite popular, however, among those regular soldiers who could get one.

Another submachine gun, the .45-caliber M3, was designed for mass production, made mostly of stamped sheet metal, and easy and cheap to produce in large numbers. Based on the British Sten gun, though with a vertical magazine rather than one coming off the side, it was reliable enough, but there were some ongoing issues with cocking levers breaking off, the wire stock bending, and internal parts breaking because they were made of softer metal. Troops in Europe preferred the more glamorous Thompson, while referring to the unlikable M3 as a "grease gun," which it did resemble. The M3 weighed 8.5 pounds unloaded, was considerably shorter, and more easily handled than the Thompson, and had an effective range of about a hundred yards. It could only fire on full-automatic, though an experienced user could squeeze off individual shots. It fired .45-caliber rounds from a thirty-round box magazine, though it could be modified to fire 9mm Parabellum as well.

For troops carrying pistols—again, officers, gun crews, and MPs—the most popular was the M1911A1 .45-caliber automatic pistol. Legend had it that it had been designed as a man-stopper after Marines in the Philippines had trouble bringing down Moro tribesmen with .38-caliber revolvers. Like most pistols, it was tough to fire with anything approaching accuracy and was considered to be a weapon of last resort only. It weighed two and a half pounds and fired seven rounds from a magazine inserted up the grip; some soldiers cheated by chambering a round, then inserting a full magazine, with "one up the spout" giving them eight rounds total.

Whatever weapon he carried, the U.S. infantryman was well drilled in its use, was enjoined constantly to keep it clean and to field-strip it frequently, and was taught *never* to lose it.

0654 HOURS

The first thing Joe lost was the box of ammo; the second thing was his rifle. He didn't intend to throw it away; his training had endlessly emphasized the need to hang onto his weapon above all else, and men who'd accidentally dropped them in exercises might be punished by being ordered to carry them held overhead on a march, or to sleep with them in their bunks.

As the water closed over his head and Joe lashed out with his arms, though, the M-1 slipped off. He felt soft mud under his knees, but he couldn't stand up, couldn't move, couldn't *breathe*. Struggling wildly, he tried to inflate his life belt.

A-Company had been issued with B-4 life jackets—popularly called "Mae Wests" by the troops, after the popular, full-bosomed movie actress—which could be inflated by mouth or by squeezing an attached device holding a small cylinder of CO_2. Joe felt the gas cartridge fire and the air bladders inflate, but his gear still weighed him down. Somehow, he managed to pull off the bags containing his gas mask and the spare demolition charges as well, struggling to get back to the surface.

His head broke into the open air. His thrashing feet touched the bottom and he lurched forward another few steps, managing somehow to keep his head, and now his shoulders, above the water. Gulping down air in panicked breaths, he started moving forward, half walking and half swimming until he was sure of his footing.

The water around him was filled with thrashing men from his LCVP. Some, having seen Joe step off into a hole, or trying to avoid the machine gun slaughter on the ramp, were scrambling over the boat's side and picking their way forward through the water, their rifles held above their heads. Others had come off the ramp. Glancing back, Joe saw at least a dozen bodies on the ramp, in the well deck, or floating in the surf; machine-gun fire continued to stitch through the struggling men. A few feet away, PFC Sam Stevens, one of the wire cutters, suddenly pitched back in the water and was gone.

The water in front of the landing craft was stained red with men's blood.

Joe turned again and kept slogging toward the waterline ahead, trying to shut the death and blood and nightmare horror from his mind. But death and blood and horror were *everywhere*, ahead and to both sides as well as behind, and in seconds his mind became numb. He moved without thinking, without being *able* to think. Incoming mortar rounds splashed and *whoomped* ahead and to either side.

More men died. Ahead and to his right, Hodgkins, the flame-thrower operator, was suddenly wreathed in tongues of flame as he stepped out of the water. A round had hit his fuel tank, detonating it, and for several horrible seconds Hodgkins continued crawling forward, his body completely enveloped in fire. Foot-high geysers of water snapped and spat, running in long, straight lines as German machine gunners played their weapons back and forth along the water's edge.

By the time Joe reached water less than knee-deep, the number of men around him had thinned out somewhat. Though it was tough to make out details—and even harder to make sense of what he was seeing—it appeared that incoming landing craft had bunched up in some places, had missed their assigned beach areas in others. The result was that Joe could see empty swaths of beach to both left and right, and other places, including dead ahead, where the men had bunched up in a hopeless and chaotic tangle. As near as Joe could tell, A Company, or most of it, had come ashore right where it was supposed to be, in front of the Vierville draw. Many landing craft, however, had been swept off course—a strong current was running right to left off the beach—or had swung out of line to avoid wrecked landing craft ahead, with the result that many had beached much too far to the east. The Germans could ignore the empty spaces on the beach and concentrate their fire on the tightly packed masses of soldiers now huddling at the bases of the beach obstacles or crouching in the surf.

Joe splashed out of the water, utterly exhausted, totally spent. Ahead rose one of the logs slanted toward the sea with the ominous squat cylinder of an antitank mine attached to its end. It was all Joe could do to slog toward that dubious bit of shelter.

Another soldier lay at the obstacle's base. When the other man didn't move or say anything, Joe touched his shoulder. "Hey, buddy!" His own voice was raw, curiously distant. "You okay?"

Then he rolled the body to the side and saw that the man's face was missing, a blank expanse of raw hamburger and shattered bone lacking eyes, nose, or jaw. Joe's stomach twisted, but he was too exhausted, too drained to be sick again. He lay flat on the sand for a long moment as gunfire cracked and whined overhead. One bullet struck the obstacle with a solid *thunk*, and it crossed his mind that the Germans might be firing at the mine above him, hoping to set it off.

To his left, thirty yards away, he saw two DD tanks, their amphibious skirts collapsed. One was firing its 75mm gun at a pillbox nestled back up the draw, but greasy black smoke boiled from the other, and Joe could see one of its crewmen sprawled across the top of the turret, halfway out of the hatch. He wondered where the rest of the DD tanks were; there were supposed to be thirty-six of them at Omaha alone, half of them on the Twenty-ninth's half of the beach, but those were the only two he could see. A moment later, the live tank took a direct hit from a German 88, the blast peeling its turret up and back at a crazy angle. Its fuel tanks ignited— "brewing up" as the Brits called it.

Joe didn't see any of its crew escape.

Horror merged with horror. He saw Latham stumble out of the water, then vanish in a blast, hurling wet sand and smoke skyward and leaving nothing behind but scraps. A mine, a shell . . . Joe didn't know what had killed him. He saw Coleman on his back in the surf, his torso ripped wide open, his intestines strung out behind him like pink balloons. Corporal Collins staggered toward him along the water's edge, cradling a bundle awkwardly in his left arm. When Joe looked more closely, he saw that the bundle was Collins's right arm, blown off at the shoulder.

Joe wanted to go help him, but he couldn't move. The safety at the base of the obstacle was purely illusory, but at the moment he didn't think *anything* could make him venture back into the open again.

"C'mon, buddy! You gotta move!"

Joe became aware that someone had been shoving his shoulder for several moments. Turning, he saw a couple of engineers flat on the sand next to him, demolition specialists, recognizable by their satchel charges. One held a fuse igniter sealed inside a latex condom to keep it dry.

"You can't stay here, buddy!" the engineer shouted. "The tide's coming in!"

How long had he been here? Joe wondered. The tide was advancing, the surf already lapping around his boots.

"We're gonna blow these things," the other engineer shouted. "You can move, or you can die!"

Somehow, Joe started moving. Gunfire and artillery rounds continued to sweep across the beach, but the men of the first wave, he saw, were making their way up the shelf, past the obstacles, and taking cover beneath the seawall. The incoming tide was acting like a broom, sweeping clumps of men up from the water's edge. Eventually, he knew, the water would make it all the way to the seawall, but for now it offered sanctuary, a haven from the blood and slaughter at the water's edge.

It was the longest hundred yards he'd ever crossed. He couldn't run, but he found himself leaning forward, as if advancing against a harsh and blustering wind. With each step he expected death; with each step he was surprised, in a dull, emotionless, and unconnected way, that he was still moving. Around him, widely scattered across the beach, other men leaned into the wind with him.

Eventually he made it, dropping onto the top of the shingle beneath the wall. He pressed his head against cold concrete and shivered, as the cacophony of death and thunder continued to wash across him.

From the Sea

At Utah Beach, American forces came ashore under fire that was—by the standards set at Omaha just twelve miles away—light and scattered.

The initial landings, led personally by Brigadier General Theodore Roosevelt Jr.—son of the famous Rough Rider President and assistant division commander of the Fourth Infantry—came ashore about a mile south of their planned beachhead, thanks to the strong current that was helping to turn the Omaha landings into chaos. Here, the current worked in the soldiers' favor, for the enemy defenses at the planned landing zone were much stronger. With a very real danger that following waves bearing reinforcements, equipment, and vehicles would land at the right beach and leave the first wave stranded, Roosevelt made a strategic decision, saying, "We'll start the war from right here."

Resistance crumbled as U.S. troops knocked out beach defenses and began moving inland. In all, casualties for the Fourth Division that day totaled fewer than three hundred—fewer than died in the E-boat attack at Slapton Sands. Only at Utah did the attackers reach all assigned objectives, though combat inland remained fierce, where scattered groups of 82nd and 101st Airborne troops continued to fight disorganized German troops.

On the British beaches to the east, fierce fighting had ensued, especially at Juno, where the first waves of Canadian forces suffered horrific casualties. Here too, however, British, Canadian, and Free French forces were moving inland by afternoon, as troops and supplies continued to pour ashore behind them.

At Omaha, however, most shore-to-ship communications were knocked out. Few radios had made it ashore intact. From the ships watching off the beach, it appeared that the U.S. forces had been pinned down at the seawall and could not advance. Destroyers, notably the *McCook* and the *Harding*, but including numerous others, moved perilously close inshore, dueling with German batteries and emplacements.

Allied aircraft all but controlled the skies—the Luftwaffe managed to carry out only a few scattered and ineffective sorties. But the Allied planes were unable to deliver close support for fear of hitting friendly troops on the beach. The initial air bombardment failed because the heavy bombers were excessively cautious. The promised carpet of thirteen thousand bombs that was supposed to shatter German defenses and flatten obstacles had fallen far inland, killing a few cows and civilians, but leaving the defenses untouched. It had been the same with the hour-long bombardment by the fleet. Most of the rounds had been high, exploding inland. Those that were on-target—such as over the German bunkers at Pointe-du-Hoc—simply failed to make much, if any, impression on the superbly designed and reinforced structures.

* * *

One particularly nasty intelligence failure became clear only later in the day, as U.S. troops began capturing German soldiers. The troops defending those bluffs above Omaha Beach were not Ost battalions or the 716th Infantry. The American troops were up against the German 352nd Infantry, a solid, well-led, and well-equipped unit with combat experience in Russia. There was a regiment of the 352nd along the bluffs—close to two thousand men.

The men of the First and Twenty-ninth Divisions were up against first-rate troops. Worse, few tanks and few artillery pieces made it ashore, and many of the men in the first wave had lost their own weapons and equipment.

As the morning wore on, Allied commanders began giving thought to halting subsequent waves of troops, and even to the idea of attempting to pull the survivors off. At 0830, H-Hour plus two, the commander of the Seventh Naval Beach Battalion ordered a halt to the landing of all vehicles on the beach, and for all ships currently attempting to unload vehicles on the beach to withdraw and await further orders.

The Omaha landings appeared to be failing.

The appearance, however, was incredibly wrong.

0746 HOURS

Joe had a rifle again.

A soldier had dragged a wounded man to the seawall a few feet away, his left arm torn open from shoulder to elbow, and administered a styrette of morphine. Joe had taken the wounded man's M1 and begun looking for someone to shoot at.

His initial mind-numbing shock after nearly drowning and then making his way across the beach had worn off enough for him to begin to feel again . . . and what he was feeling now was *anger.* The air and naval bombardments had failed to put a dent in the enemy defenses. Some of the larger landing ships and landing craft appeared to be pulling back from the beach, many without unloading their vehicles, and some of the men at the seawall began saying they were being abandoned by the navy.

"We're getting slaughtered down here!" Joe told the GI sitting beside him. "We might as well go get slaughtered up there!"

Sliding over the top of the wall, Joe crawled under a tangle of concertina wire, then jogged across the shelf beyond and started climbing. The bluff at this end of the beach was about ninety feet high, but the slope was shallow enough that he could drag himself up hand over hand.

Joe was beyond tired, but all he wanted now was the chance to get a few shots off at the bastards who'd been shooting at his unit, keeping it pinned to the sand.

Eventually, the hill began leveling off. He could hear the yammer of a machine gun to his left and began crawling in that direction. Raising his head cautiously, he could see the coal-scuttle helmets of two Germans squatting in an open Tobruk behind an MG42, firing the weapon at the beach.

He wondered if that was the machine gun that had fired into the open bow of his LCVP. It didn't matter. It was firing at his buddies below. Raising his borrowed M1, he took aim and began squeezing the trigger, burning off eight rounds before the empty clip flew from the receiver with a sharp *ping*.

The machine gun was silent, the Germans behind it slumped over the rim of the emplacement.

Every Man a Hero

"I have returned many times to honor the valiant men who died on that beach," General Omar Bradley wrote three decades later. "They should never be forgotten. Nor should those who lived to carry the day by the slimmest of margins. Every man who set foot on Omaha Beach that day was a hero."

From the ships offshore, it seemed a foregone conclusion. The landing had failed. By noon, General Bradley, on board the cruiser *Augusta*, was wrestling with the decision of whether or not to begin trying to pick up the survivors.

And things *were* bad ashore. In A Company of the 116th Regiment, every single officer was dead, every senior noncom dead or wounded. The men in the shadow of the seawall at first were waiting for someone to tell them what to do.

A few officers had also made it to the seawall, however, and were doing their best to organize the men. Brigadier General Norman Cota, the assistant CO of the Twenty-ninth Division, walked up and down the beach, directing the placement of a BAR to provide cover for the obstacle-clearing units, then organized men to find bangalore torpedoes and explosives and set them to blowing holes in the wire beyond the seawall. The commander of one tank on the beach fired at a bunker and was surprised when a salvo from the destroyer *Frankford* screamed overhead and demolished it. Realizing that the ship's range-finder optics could see what he was shooting at, he shifted targets and began identifying targets for the ship's guns, an impromptu forward observer.

Most important, however, small groups of enlisted men were beginning to go over the seawall, cross the flat shelf beyond, and climb the bluff. There was no way to blow the barriers across the draws, as planned, but they *could* climb the slope between the draws, and this is what they did without any officer telling them to do it.

The first to reach the top of the bluff in anything like an organized unit was Company C of the 116th Regiment, together with the Fifth Ranger Battalion, which had come ashore on Omaha east of the Vierville draw at 0745.

But other men made it up between the draws as well, singly, in squads, in platoons. By 0900 approximately six hundred American troops had made it to the top of the bluffs, penetrating the German entrenchments, knocking out emplacements, and relieving the pressure on the men still trapped below.

While the Allied high command worried that Omaha would have to be evacuated, the battle was already being won.

1040 HOURS

"You okay, soldier?"

Joe blinked up at the figure leaning over him, an army lieutenant. "Yeah," he said. "I mean, yessir, I'm okay." Had he fallen asleep?

"The fighting is *that* way," the lieutenant said.

"Yes, sir!" He pulled himself to his feet.

After taking out the machine gun position, Joe had stumbled across a series of interlocking trenches. He vaguely remembered a firefight and killing another German soldier, but he couldn't be sure. Eventually, he'd found the shattered foundation of a stone house and taken shelter there. The next thing he knew, the lieutenant was shaking him awake.

Standing, at the top of the bluff over Omaha, he had his first good look at a stunning panorama, a vision that would stay with him for the rest of his life—a horizon crowded with ships; a beach—shrunken now as the tide raced in—crowded with landing craft, many sunken or burning, but most unloading more troops; and everywhere U.S. troops moving across the beach, crossing the seawall, and climbing the bluffs. Smoke hung heavy beneath the overcast; shell splashes continued to erupt in the water, and he could still hear the chatter of machine guns and small arms fire nearby.

But the men were moving off the beach. A small group crouched behind some empty fortifications a dozen yards away.

"Hey, Lieutenant!" he called. "Did we win?"

"Of *course* we did," the lieutenant said, grinning. An artillery round burst a hundred yards away, and he pointed inland, toward the clatter of gunfire. "Now we just have to convince *those* bastards!"

"We can do that, sir," Joe replied.

They started walking inland.

The Thin Wet Line of Khaki

"Though we could see it dimly through the haze and hear the echo of its guns," General Bradley would write later, "the battle belonged that morning to the thin wet line of khaki that dragged itself ashore."

By the end of D-Day, the invasion's success was secure . . . or as secure as it could be, given the uncertainties of war.

At Utah Beach, twenty thousand men and seventeen hundred vehicles were ashore fifteen hours after H-Hour. The airborne units inland suffered heavy casualties and had been badly scattered in their drops, but by nightfall U.S. troops were within a mile of the critical village of Ste. Mère Église, held by the paratroopers, and elsewhere beach forces had linked up with elements of the 101st.

At Gold Beach, 25,000 British troops were ashore, with 400 killed.

At Juno Beach, the Canadians had suffered 1,200 KIA putting 21,400 men ashore.

At Sword Beach, the British suffered 630 killed landing 29,000 men.

In all, by 2200 hours, and including airborne and naval units, almost 175,000 men were in Normandy, at a total cost of roughly 4,900 killed. The vaunted Atlantic Wall had been breached, the beginning of the end for Hitler's Reich.

The fight at Omaha—Bloody Omaha as it would forever now be known—had been a close-run affair. Of 40,000 men going ashore that day, 2,374 were killed—one in every nineteen. The statistics do not do justice to the horror of those first few hours, for the vast majority of the deaths were among those in the first waves. Of Company A's 210 men, more than 90 percent were killed or wounded. Thirty-four of Company A's men were from Joe's hometown, Bedford, Virginia. Nineteen were killed at Omaha Beach, three more a few days later.

At Pointe-du-Hoc, the Rangers climbed the cliffs and took the German emplacement. The 155mm guns were missing, either moved or not yet mounted. The Rangers moved inland, found the guns later in the day, and destroyed them. By the end of D-Day, they'd suffered 60 percent casualties.

And the men who clawed their way off the beach did so without tanks, without vehicles, without communications with the ships or even with one another, with most of their machine guns and heavy weapons lost, without artillery support save for shells from the ships offshore, with normal command and control functions in utter chaos, and without close air support.

An oral history recorded at the Eisenhower Center at the University of New Orleans perhaps says it best. Sergeant John Ellery, of the Sixteenth Regiment, First Division, would later recall, "The first night in France I spent in a ditch beside a hedgerow wrapped in a damp shelter half and thoroughly exhausted. But I felt elated. It had been the greatest experience of my life. I was ten feet tall. No matter what had happened, I had made it off the beach and reached the high ground. I was king of the hill at least in my own mind, for a moment. My contribution to the heroic tradition of the United States Army might have been the smallest achievement in the history of courage, but at least, for a time, I had walked in the company of very brave men."

A Marine at the Chosin Reservoir

When Hell Froze

BY DOUGLAS NILES

The Korean War began being fought with weapons from World War II and ended with the beginnings of modern technical warfare. It was affected by politics on all levels, down to the selection of objectives and MacArthur's ambitions. It was also the hot beginning of the Cold War. The first proxy war in the fifty-year battle between the United States and the communists. On one level, a very different kind of war, fought in a way that set the pattern of smaller wars that continues to this day.

DOUGLAS NILES is the author of some fifty novels in the various genres of adventure. He has designed award-winning military strategy games and coauthored several military/political thriller alternate history novels of World War II. His board game designs have reflected military strategy and tactics from World War II to the modern era. He has written numerous nonfiction articles about military campaigns of the twentieth century.

[⋆]

KOREA, 1950

"So I heard the LT say we're marching up the MSR. What the hell is the MSR, anyway?"

A glance over his shoulder showed Walt Dane that the speaker was one of the high school kids—probably been in the USMC Reserve for a year or so before the First Marine Division got called up and sent to war. Corporal Dane, who had been in the Corps since Iwo Jima, seven years now, took pity on him.

"That's the main supply route." He kicked at the frozen ruts under his winter boots. "This road, see. The whole division gets its food, fuel, and ammo up this splendid thoroughfare."

"This dirt track?" the kid—his name was Reno—looked skeptical. He stared past Dane, toward the imposing massif of gray, frozen rock rising before them. "And we gotta climb over *that* to get anywhere?"

"Shuttup and keep walking," Dane snapped, his sympathy freezing as quick as spit in this subzero world. As a lofty corporal, he had the rank to issue the order, and as a veteran of World War II he had the presence to inspire these kids to listen.

Even so, he shared some of Reno's apprehension. The heights in front of them were genuine mountains, not hills, and the miserable excuse for a road was heading right toward the highest one of them anywhere to be seen. Thousands of marines had already disappeared into those heights, marching up the MSR with a mission to keep marching until they had crossed Korea, reached the Yalu River, and won the war.

"Ah, these kids," chuckled PFC Conrad James, one of the company's expert BAR men. "They act like they've never seen a hill before."

"Shoot, Conrad. I'm from Bloomington, Illinois," Reno protested. "We got nothing like this around there."

"Join the marines, see the world," Dane observed wryly.

Corporal Walter Dane's unit, Fox Company, Second Battalion, Seventh Marine Regiment—Fox/7, for short—was just one of many companies to start on that march, but Dane, and most other Fox/7 Marines, felt that they were the best company of them all. The men were a mix of World War II veterans and young reservists. Mustered in Chicago, they'd come from all over the Midwest, answering President Truman's mobilization order last summer. There were farm kids and city boys, grease monkeys and ballplayers. There was even a black man, PFC Rupert Jackson from Detroit.

Fox was one of three companies, the others being Dog and Easy, comprising the Second Battalion. The regiment itself included three battalions of three rifle companies each, as well as supporting staff. An additional regiment, the Eleventh, contained the six batteries of artillery dedicated to the Marine Division.

The men of Fox/7 had been left behind when the rest of the regiment had advanced farther into North Korea, moving up the western shore of the huge body of water, now frozen, known as the Chosin Reservoir. Fox/7 spent the night in a crowded little town called Hagaru-ri. It might have been a sleepy little Korean village last week, but now it was a main supply depot and bivouac zone for the better part of a U.S. Marine division, as well as several battalions of the U.S. Army. Hagaru-ri lay at the south end of the reservoir. Dane had sneaked a look at the lieutenant's map and knew that they were starting along the road toward a town called Yudam-ni—and that, on the course of that fourteen-mile route, they'd have to cross a four-thousand-foot elevation known as Toktong Pass.

A familiar, grinding sound of motors growled from behind them, and the more than two hundred men of Fox/7 moved off to the narrow shoulder as a convoy of sturdy M5 trucks, haulers assigned to the USMC Eleventh Regiment, an artillery formation, made slow progress behind the marching men. Much to the marines' delight, the convoy of nine trucks came to a halt and the drivers waved the riflemen to climb aboard.

"Courtesy of Lieutenant Campbell, your forward artillery observer," the nearest driver said to Walter Dane as he climbed into the cab. Other marines pulled themselves into the backs of the trucks, making themselves as comfortable as possible atop the cargoes of artillery shells, food, and other supplies. "We'll give you a ride to the top of the pass."

"Thanks very much," Dane said, with sincere appreciation—appreciation that only grew as he observed the course of the seven-mile drive. The heavy trucks, skillfully maneuvered, turned through a series of switchbacks on the narrow dirt road, climbing higher and higher out of the valley of Hagaru-ri. It took more than an hour to cover that short distance, but Dane knew that they would have been marching far into the night if they hadn't been able to catch the ride.

Finally, in a narrow notch between two looming, rocky knobs, the drivers halted their trucks, right in the middle of the road—there was no shoulder here, even if they'd wanted to pull over.

"This is where you get out," the driver said, not unpleasantly.

"I guess you guys get to guard the pass for the whole rest of the division."

"This place?" Dane said, looking at the barren, snow-covered slopes. A few small, empty houses stood near the road, and some sparse, scraggly pines dotted the mountainsides, but the pass looked pretty inhospitable to him.

"Toktong Pass," the driver noted. He pointed up the road, which began a winding descent almost immediately. "There's two regiments of marines up there. And the only way they're coming out again, or anyone else is moving up to join them, is to come through this godforsaken pass."

This whole campaign seemed like a crazy business. I mean, we were the guys who had won the Korean War a month earlier, when we landed at Inchon, liberated Seoul, and routed the whole North Korean Army. Most of those bastards were killed or captured, and only a few escaped over the border, back into the mountains of North Korea. (Of course, you'd never know the marines had played a key role in the campaign if you saw General MacArthur's victory ceremony—it was all spit-and-polish army brass and South Korean politicians to see President Rhee restored, while we dirty, unshaven marines were shunted off to the side. I guess we didn't fit the picture they wanted for their tea party.)

Anyway, we thought the war was over, but Mac didn't agree. Seems he wanted to take it to the North Koreans, clear the communists out of the peninsula all the way up to the Yalu River. So finally they loaded us on our naval transports again and sailed us around the peninsula to land on the eastern shore, at Wonsan. It took the navy a week to clear the mines in the harbor, but then we came in with a picture-perfect landing: Amtracs and Ducks hitting the beach, marines splashing through the surf, charging onto the land. There we found posters for a Bob Hope USO show—the South Koreans had already captured the town, moving overland. It turned out that Bob Hope had already been through the town, while we were floating offshore. I guess it took General Smith, CO of the First Marine Division, some time to get over that one.

Anyway, once we were ashore, we started moving north, with the intention of going all the way to the Yalu River. The idea was so that the whole country could be united again. We were marching north, and word was we'd be home by Christmas. The war was that close to being over.

But it didn't seem over as we moved up that road, the MSR. There were no civilians around to greet us, no kids begging for candy and chewing gum. Every so often a deer would come running down out of the mountains, like something had spooked it out of the high country. I learned later that General Almond—he was army, not marines, and one of the brass-button types from MacArthur's staff—was in charge of X Corps, which included us. He wanted General Smith to race the division pell-mell toward the north.

General Smith wasn't willing to do that. Instead, he slowed down the advance elements of the marines, and did everything he could to get the division concentrated, instead of strung out to hell and gone along seventy miles of road.

We weren't exactly fighting our way north, but I was plenty uneasy—and so were the rest of the men. And when the deep freeze hit, the temperature dropped to well below zero throughout the whole damned country.

And it was serious business again.

Toktong Pass looked like the end of the world. The 240 men of Fox/7 watched the nine trucks of the How Battery taxi service grind on down the road, drivers shifting into low gear for the long, torturous descent from the pass. Even before the last of the trucks had rounded the next bend, Captain Barber, CO of Fox/7, got his men on the move. At the crest of the pass they broke off the road there and climbed a rocky knob that had a commanding view of the ridgeline, the surrounding summits, and everything else except the biggest mountain in the whole damned place: Toktong San.

This was a rocky summit, separated from Fox Hill by a wide, rocky saddle, and it was the commanding elevation for as far as a man could see in any direction. But the mountaintop was too far from the road, so Captain Barber deployed his men on the lesser hill, where they could command the road as it ascended from both directions. With 240 men, in three platoons, he didn't have enough marines to form a full perimeter, so he deployed them in a horseshoe formation against the most threatening approaches. The sections of mortars, including 60mm and 81mm tubes, he retained near the headquarters tent, which was set up near a small spring that, even in the subzero temperatures, still flowed fresh water out of a crack in the side of the hill. His rifle platoons he dispersed above, and to both flanks of, the command post.

First and Second Platoons took the sides of the hills, while Third Platoon, with Walt Dane and the other three men of his fire team on the left flank, took up a position at the very crest of Fox Hill, overlooking the route that would be taken by any enemy who might approach across the saddle leading toward the massif of Toktong San. Their platoon was bolstered with several of the company's few machine guns, light .30-caliber weapons that were reliable and deadly, even in the bitter cold.

Dane would share a foxhole with his best friend, Conrad James, who was one of the platoon's BAR men, while the other half of his fire team, Privates Cooper and Reno, would excavate a shelter a dozen feet to the right. These were both young reservists who'd gotten their first taste of war at Inchon, and Dane had taken to looking out for them with a rather stern, albeit avuncular, eye.

Even though the men had kindled a few fires, using the wood

of some dead pine trees, Captain Barber ordered them to douse the telltale blazes, and to prepare to defend their perimeter against attack. The ground, of course, was frozen rock-hard, but Dane and his team worked gamely to chisel up the dirt. They scraped up some actual stones as well, and used them to make low barriers, less than ideal perhaps but at least capable of stopping a bullet or two. All the while the wind scoured over the mountains, and as darkness fell the men of Fox/7 felt their complete isolation from the rest of the world.

The only thing that made it even possible for them to survive here was the durable winter gear that, only a week or two previously, had been delivered to the marines as they moved farther into the North Korean winter. Now, at least, each man had a heavy, knee-length parka with an insulated, pile-lined hood. They had wool caps to wear under their helmets, long underwear, thick wool trousers, and winter socks. Flannel shirts and long johns provided an extra layer of insulation, while on their hands they wore wool gloves covered by heavy canvas mittens. The latter were sewn with a single trigger finger extension, so that their rifles could be fired even while the marines were dressed for maximum protection against the cold.

For standard weaponry, most of the marines were equipped with the Garand semiautomatic rifle. This was a light, small .30-caliber weapon that had proved its use during the savage Pacific campaigns of World War II, gradually earning the respect of the marines whose lives depended upon it—even winning over the old school gunnery sergeants who had tended to favor the classic Springfield 30-06. The M1 Garand could be loaded with an eight-round clip, and each man had several spare clips, loaded and ready to use. The rifle could be fired quickly, as a semiautomatic, though it was accurate enough to be deadly with a single shot at several hundred yards of range. It could be fitted with a bayonet, though the marines typically wore these as sheath knives on their web belts.

In addition, individual marines had a few hand grenades, while additional crates of grenades were kept back at the command tent, where Captain Barber and his radioman were posted. The company had several men armed with Browning automatic rifles, as well as a few light and heavy machine guns. The heavy weapons platoon, posted in the rear on the slope descending from Fox Hill toward the pass, was equipped with both 60mm and 81mm mortars. In addition, Private Jackson was carrying one of the new three-and-a-half-inch rocket launchers, with something like a dozen rounds for his bazooka-like weapon.

A ridge of large boulders, some of them the size of a small truck, extended like a spiny backbone down the slope of the hill, right to the edge of the road. Some of the marines used those rocks for additional shelter, while all of them took care to keep a wide open field of fire, wherever they took their places in the line.

The men had enough ammunition for a brisk engagement, though any extensive fighting would require resupply. The company also had several radios, though the cold weather played hell with the batteries, and for the first two hours on the hill Captain Barber wasn't even able to get through to the battalion or regiment to let them know he'd gotten into position.

Walter Dane stretched out on the frozen ground and pulled his sleeping bag up over his legs and the lower half of his torso. Conrad James was right next to him, barely three feet away in the shallow depression, which was all they had been able to excavate. James did chisel up some low, flat rocks, and he used these to form an added breastwork around the rim of their shelter. The BAR man laid out a number of spare clips for his rapid-firing weapon, which—in a hot action—could chew through the ammo like a hungry dog attacking a pile of fresh meat.

With his M1 in his hands, Dane saw that Cooper and Reno were similarly protected against the cold as they settled in for the long night. The men took turns sleeping and watching, as the bitter, frostbitten hours crept past. The sky was clear, and the moon was virtually full, but even the bright light only made the frozen, arctic surroundings look even more barren.

Around midnight Captain Barber came by to check on the deployment. He was accompanied by Lieutenant McCarthy, the Second Platoon CO, and both men knelt beside Dane.

"You staying awake, Walt?" McCarthy demanded sternly.

"Yes, sir, of course!" Dane replied, insulted at the implication.

"Well, you're one of the few then. Too many of these marines are hunkered down like they're on a Boy Scout camping trip. Keep your damned eyes open!"

"Yes, sir," Dane replied, almost growling.

"Any sign of movement out there?" the captain asked.

"No, sir," Dane replied. "Anybody out there would have to be frozen stiff, wouldn't they?"

"Don't count on it," the captain said. "We may not have heard anything from on high, but I have a feeling there's more bad guys out there than anybody wants to believe." The two officers moved on, leaving Dane disgruntled and uneasy. "Coop, Reno—you guys staying alert?" When he got no reply, he pulled himself from his down sleeping bag and, cursing, crawled over the icy rocks to prod the two privates back to alertness.

He didn't feel much better when he climbed back into his bag, and found himself blinking wearily as he looked across the frozen landscape.

This time, he saw movement—*lots* of movement. It was like the whole saddle between the company and the summit of Toktong San had come alive, like the ground itself was sliding stealthily forward. He was not the only one to see it, as somewhere to his right a Garand cracked out. White shapes moved like ghosts, proven real only by the silent shadows moving across the snow.

And the shit hit the fan.

Specks of flame sparked from hundreds of muzzles as a barrage of gunfire opened up, most of the rounds apparently streaking directly at Walt Dane. The nearest attackers were less than a hundred feet away, and there were many more of them behind the front rank. Dane sighted down the barrel of his M1, grateful for the moonlight. He spotted a figure running, ducking low, protected by some kind of hooded parka, and he squeezed off a shot. The man went to the ground, whether hit or seeking cover the marine couldn't tell.

But there were plenty more targets beyond him. A glimpse at his watch showed Dane that it was 0230 in the morning, and then he was firing without pause, quickly emptying the eight-round clip of his Garand. The company's machine guns had opened up, and tracers scored their eerie paths through the moonlit night.

And still the attackers came on. They made noise, blowing bugles and whistles, shooting with a wide variety of weapons. Some of the guns tore off ripping bursts, like burp guns, while others stuttered out deep, staccato blasts, sounding for all the world like U.S. .45-caliber Tommy guns. In the flashes of light the whole mountainside seemed to be moving, and the stark moonlight outlined hundreds of moving figures, mostly dressed in white jackets. Sometimes they blended into the patches of snow layered through the saddle, but when the attackers crossed a swath of rocky ground the pale garments outlined them as clear targets.

Dane took only a second to slam a second clip into the M1. Once again he sighted down the barrel, taking aim at an enemy soldier who was rushing closer at a full sprint. The single shot dropped the man in his tracks, and the marine carefully cracked off two more shots at other white-garbed figures ducking and weaving beyond. A burst of automatic weapons fire chattered beside him, and he knew that James had opened up with the BAR. A sputtering rocket blasted out from the American lines to explode in the midst of a cluster of enemy troops, knocking at least three or four of them sprawling.

"These have gotta be Chinese!" shouted someone, articulating the thought that had been building in Walter Dane's mind. He'd never seen this kind of winter camouflage on the few North Korean soldiers they'd encountered since landing at Wonsan, nor had he encountered the North Korean Army in such numbers, or seen them display such a willingness to charge headlong into a storm of fire.

And the marines of Third Platoon, Fox/7, were certainly unleashing a storm. Grenades sailed out from the shallow foxholes, bursting among the swarm of Chinese, sometimes blowing men right off their feet. Two light machine guns spewed a steady stream of lead into the mountain saddle, dropping so many of the attackers that the men of the follow-up waves would occasionally stumble over the bodies of their own dead. Spotting two men crawling just a dozen yards in front of his position, Walt pulled the pin of a grenade himself, aiming carefully to drop the thrown missile right between them. Ducking his head to shield his face from the blast, he heard the explosion and looked up to see the pair of Chinese tumbling away, thrashing from the force of the deadly bomb.

Something rattled on the ground next to him and Dane instinctively ducked as a Chinese grenade exploded only ten feet away. He felt the flash of heat against his face, and his ears rang as he looked up again, but he wasn't wounded—apparently it had been a concussion, not a fragmentation, grenade. Still, he saw that the wave of attackers was terrifyingly close.

He snapped off the rest of the clip in his Garand and reloaded, relieved when the spray from the platoon's machine gunner swept past the front of his foxhole and sent a score of Chinese to ground. Cooper and Reno sent a couple more grenades into the pack of enemy soldiers, and they exploded with solid bangs. But another shower of grenades came from the attackers, the metallic balls bouncing and clanging across the ground. Once again Dane could only duck and hope to survive the blasts—which, again, he did, escaping even a wound.

But the young men to his right weren't so fortunate. He heard a scream of pain, and a loud "Goddammit!" in what sounded like Cooper's voice. Swinging to the side, he saw a pair of Chinese charging right up to his comrades' foxhole. Dane fired twice, dropping both men, but he couldn't help noticing that there was no more shooting coming from the fire pit sheltering Reno and Cooper.

"Conrad!" he shouted, spotting the BAR man's eyes staring across the ground from six feet away. "Cover me!"

The marine nodded, and squeezed off a quick burst. Dane tried to spring to his feet, only to discover that he was still half-inside of his sleeping bag. Cursing, he fell on his face and kicked the down cocoon off his legs. When he was free, he crawled out of his fire pit toward the foxhole where Cooper and Reno had sheltered. Dane snapped off another round when a Chinese soldier staggered to his feet just twenty feet away, and when the man went down, Dane sprang across the frozen ground and rolled into the shallow pit.

Even amid the cordite and smoke, the smell of fresh blood struck his nostrils with pungent force. He slipped on the slick liquid and came to rest next to a motionless body.

"Oh God, Walter—it's Reno!" cried Cooper, his voice cracking at the edge of hysteria. "The bastards killed him!"

Dane rose to his knees and looked out. For a moment, thankfully, there were no Chinese immediately threatening the position. He felt sick to his stomach, though, as he saw a whole company moving through the position of the Third Platoon's first line of foxholes. One enemy soldier stopped and aimed straight down, firing a burst from what was indeed a Tommy gun, right into the shallow pit that so inadequately protected a pair of marines.

Walter leaned over and barked right into the shaken Cooper's face. "Get a grip on yourself!" he snapped. "Are you sure he's dead?"

"N-no! I just thought—"

"Shut up and check him out!" ordered the corporal. He rose to one knee and sighted over the lip of the shallow hole, snapping off several rounds at the pale, shapeless forms flitting across the moonlit mountaintop. He fired again, and heard the *click* of an empty magazine. Cursing, he ejected the clip and fumbled for another—the last one in his shirt pocket, he realized grimly, though he had several more back in his foxhole.

"Bobby!" Cooper was half-sobbing, leaning down toward his friend. "Bobby! Can you hear me?"

Both marines were heartened by the faint sound of a groan. "Find out where he's hurt," Dane urged, trying to keep his own voice calm. "See if you can stop the bleeding."

"Yeah, yeah, sure," Cooper said eagerly. He touched the injured man and his fingers immediately provoked a grunt of pain. "Oh, shit. He's hurt bad," he continued, his voice a hoarse whisper.

"What about you?" Dane asked.

"What? Me?" The kid seemed confused.

"A grenade went off in your foxhole. Are you hurt?" the corporal pressed, keeping his eyes on the saddle. For a moment, it seemed that the Chinese had gone to ground, but no sooner did he have that thought than fifty or sixty enemy soldiers rose to their feet and charged forward again. Dane couldn't help noticing that there was very little defensive fire coming from the center of the Third Platoon's position.

Cooper seemed puzzled by the question, but Dane didn't wait for him to answer. Inside, he snapped off all the shots in his fresh clip, moderately satisfied as he watched many of the enemy soldiers once again drop prone.

"I—I guess I'm just cut a bit, on my face," Cooper said. "But Reno, he's got a big hole in his side."

"Try to stop the bleeding," Dane urged again. Standard procedure would be to send the two men back to an aid station, but the way the commies were advancing through the line of foxholes, that course of action seemed tantamount to suicide.

"Uh, okay," Cooper said, relieved to have something to do. Dane looked down to see the kid using a spare flannel shirt as a wadding, and at the same time he saw Reno's rifle lying on the ground next to the wounded marine. The corporal snatched up the spare weapon and once again peered from the foxhole, squeezing off a few carefully aimed shots.

The light machine gun chattered again, stitching a line of bullets through a dozen Chinese who were too slow to hit the ground. The attacking enemy troops moved out of the field of fire of the automatic gun, with more than a dozen sprinting right toward Walter Dane. He shot again and again, until the clip was empty.

"More ammo!" he barked, pulling a grenade and throwing the mission while Cooper fumbled for some spare clips.

"Here! Reno had a bunch of them on his belt."

Gratefully the older marine took the rounds and snapped another clip into the Garand. James fired another burst from the BAR, momentarily clearing away the Chinese from his immediate front.

But now the sounds of shooting, of exploding grenades, came not just from Dane's right, but from behind him. He needed no further proof that the enemy had burst through the Third Platoon's position.

There was nothing he could do about that now. He saw white-clad attackers skulking past, only twenty feet to his right, and he shot down two of them with a pattern of quick shots. When more of the Chinese came at him in a rush, he frantically snapped in a new clip, only to watch them fall to another well-timed burst from James's BAR.

A sudden shout cut through the sounds of gunfire and explosions: *"Semper fi!"*

The battle cry of the United States Marines echoed through

the frigid night, followed by a stuttering series of bursts as men from the left flank left their foxholes and closed with the enemy. A shower of grenades tumbled across the crest of Fox Hill, and a dozen marines, bayonets fixed, charged right into the flank of the advancing Chinese. Dane continued firing, shooting enemy troops that rushed toward the melee, unwilling to risk shots into the tangle of hand-to-hand combat. Once more he emptied his clip, and he paused, feeling a sense of profound weariness rise up around him. How could they ever stop this many enemy soldiers?

More guns snapped out from the far right flank, and Walter realized that his hard-pressed platoon was getting help from the other side as well. There was big, black Private Jackson, standing up and firing his rocket launcher right through the middle of the enemy troops. The sizzling, cracking projectile *whooshed* past like a living thing, exploding against the ground with a large blast, sending shards of rock and ice slicing through the charging Chinese.

"Look out!"

Cooper's shout took Dane by surprise, and he whirled, startled to see a Chinese soldier looming right above him at the edge of the foxhole. The man frantically worked his bolt-action carbine, apparently trying to free a jammed round, and Dane reacted by instinct—he dropped his Garand and seized the enemy soldier by his feet, pulling them straight forward. The fellow went down hard, the impact on the hard ground knocking the wind out of him. Dane, his knife in his hand, pounced and stabbed, slicing through the exposed skin of the enemy soldier's neck.

Shaking with adrenaline and fatigue and cold, the corporal slid back into Cooper and Reno's foxhole. Numbly he notched another clip into his M1, watching as the vigorously counterattacking marines killed the Chinese who had breached the line, or drove the survivors back onto the exposed saddle between Fox Hill and Toktong San.

Now mortar rounds began to fall into the saddle as, apparently, a couple of the company's tubes came into play. Marines cheered hoarsely as the thumping blasts knocked dozens of Chinese over and sent shards of shrapnel slicing through the enemy positions. After a dozen rounds, the mortars abruptly ceased, but the quick barrage had done its work. When Walter Dane looked across the bloody mountaintop, the only Chinese he saw were the dead and the dying. And beyond, along the eastern horizon, a pale line of orange light had begun to brighten the sky.

It wasn't until long after the war that I learned what our mission was, up there in that frozen wasteland. Our division was initially intended to move north, to march all the way to the Yalu. We took up positions on that hill on November 27, and neither we, nor anyone else in X Corps, was aware of a key fact:

Two days earlier, about a half a million Chinese soldiers had swept down out of the mountains in western Korea, attacking General Walker's Eighth Army. Walker had a half dozen divisions, and three of them were smashed to pieces in the first attack. By the time we were digging in on Fox Hill, and the majority of the Marine Division had moved through Toktong Pass into the valley of Yudam-ni, Eighth Army was in full retreat. They'd been pushed out of their advanced position and forced back by an onslaught of nearly half a million men.

Yet on our side of the country, we were still moving northward, still striving to reach the brass ring symbolized by the Yalu River. The thing is nobody—not one single brass-strapped officer on MacArthur's or Walker's staff—thought to share news of the Chinese intervention with General Almond, or anyone else in X Corps. We were on our own, and the Red Chinese were in the war to stay.

And, even worse, X Corps was in no position to meet a crushing attack, with the units of the corps being spread all over hell and gone. Two U.S. Army battalions were moving up the east side of the Chosin Reservoir, like us strung out along a miserable road through rugged terrain. They got attacked by several Chinese divisions, and the lead army units never made it out—those men didn't have a chance.

We marines were stopped in our tracks, starting with those attacks on the 27th, but at least we were able to hold the ground we'd already claimed. All along the MSR, from Yudam-ni in the north, over Toktong Pass, and down through Hagaru-ri and the road leading to the coast, we dug in, held on, and waited for orders—orders that, for the first few days of this fight for survival, never came.

Walter Dane had never been relieved by a sunrise so much as he was by that pale brightening in the eastern sky on the morning of November 28. The sun rose into a stark, clear sky—as evidenced by the bright moonlight during the battle, the dour clouds of the previous day had blown off. And to a combat soldier or marine in the armed forces of the United States of America, clear skies meant one very precious thing:

Air support.

The first planes overhead were a quartet of F-51 Mustangs. They snarled out of the southern sky and lashed the flanks of Toktong San with machine-gun and rocket fire. On a second pass, the Mustangs dumped canisters of napalm, the petroleum jelly burning with hellish fury even in the icy cold, scouring whole sections of the frozen mountainside with killing flames. On their way back south the F-51s flew close enough over Fox/7 that the marines could make out the red-white-blue bull's-eye on the underside of each wing.

"Those are Aussies!" Dane said, leaning back and enjoying the show. "The Royal Australian Air Force to the rescue!"

But there was no time to be a simple spectator. Walter helped Cooper carry Reno back to the makeshift aid station by company headquarters. Reno was still breathing, but had gone pale from shock. Then it was back to Third Platoon's sector. Walter and Conrad advanced from their foxholes and, together with other survivors of the Third Platoon, started to walk through the neat ranks of dead Chinese arrayed across the snowy ground of the saddle.

"There must be a hundred of 'em, within a stone's throw of our own foxhole," Dane said, shaking his head. He pointed to four corpses laid out side by side, as if they had fallen in formation. "Looks like you cut these down with the BAR," he added approvingly.

Back in the HQ tent, they found out that the company had been attacked from three sides, including from the road where it crossed over the ridge at Toktong Pass. Several mortars had been overrun, and the others had been uprooted, their crews carrying them up the slope and hastily forming new firing positions before bringing them into action.

Of the 240 men in the unit, twenty had been killed—sixteen from Third Platoon—and another fifty-four, total, wounded. To put it another way, about one-third of Fox/7's men were casualties in the first night on the hill. Conversely, the marines counted more than four hundred dead Chinese around the company's position, most of them in the saddle between the two heights.

Even though the stubborn radios, their batteries so cold they could barely function, provided only minimal contact with the rest of the division, the marines knew they were cut off, since traffic along the MSR, in either direction, had been completely blocked. Second Lieutenant Campbell, the forward observer for How Battery—and the man who had arranged for Fox/7 to get a ride to the top of Toktong Pass—managed to get through to his guns for a brief radio conversation, and was able to agree upon a fire plan to protect Fox/7 with some supporting artillery, but the officer down below refused to authorize any of his precious ammunition to be used in registering the guns onto their designated target zones. As a consequence, when the fire support would finally come, it would be a matter of raw luck as to whether the shells fell on the attacking Chinese or the defending marines.

Later in the morning a pair of USMC Corsairs came over, dropping more bombs and napalm and strafing the surrounding Chinese. By then, the marines figured out they were surrounded by something like an entire division of Chairman Mao's finest. They cheered the rounds fired by the Corsair pilots, but knew that the limited air support could prove, at most, to be a nuisance to teeming enemy forces in the surrounding mountains.

The men of Fox/7 spent the day figuratively licking their wounds, and preparing for the next night on the hill. One man, Private Cafferta, had suffered terrible frostbite. Like the rest of the company, he'd been roused from his foxhole during the first attack, and had raced to and fro across the hilltop, joining in the counterattack, personally shooting dozens of Chinese. Only when dawn gave the men the chance to look around did the private discover that he'd fought the entire night barefoot.

Two tents were set up as shelter for the worst of the wounded, though even within the frozen shelters the injured men were forced to stretch out on the icy ground, insulated only by some ponchos and a few spare sleeping bags. There wasn't enough room for the rest of the wounded, many of whom tried to prop themselves up in sleeping bags right under the frosty winter sky. When night fell and the Chinese came again, many of those men, even some who could only crawl, would add their firepower to defend their battered, depleted company.

Toward late afternoon, the rumble of heavy engines told the marines that more aircraft were on the way. Several four-engine transports, also of the Marine Air Corps, flew past, and a number of supply bundles were dropped by parachute toward the Fox/7 positions. Unfortunately, the wind carried the precious provisions outside of the company's perimeter, bringing them to the ground in a fringe of scrubby pine trees very near the road where it crept through the lofty, windswept pass. Two small, desolate houses stood near the spot, as did the wreckage of the company's jeeps, which had been shot to pieces during the fighting of the previous night.

Walter Dane was watching as the company supply sergeant headed down the slope toward the supplies. A sniper's bullet hit him in the leg, bringing him down. An officer went to the sergeant's aid, and he, too, was hit by the same sniper. That got a group of First Platoon marines motivated. Spraying the forlorn houses with covering fire, they quickly closed in and flushed the sniper out. Dane and a dozen other volunteers raced down the hill and hauled up the crates from the airdrop. Their haul was worth it: mortar shells, radio batteries, and medical supplies.

By the time those supplies had been brought into the perimeter, night was falling again. The able-bodied marines gathered spare weapons from their wounded comrades, and even scooped up a few automatics from the slain Chinese. Then they hunkered down in their sleeping bags, loaded weapons nearby, eyes alert and sweeping the surrounding heights for the next appearance of the enemy troops.

We learned later that the MSR had been severed in many places by the Chinese attack. They hit us with something over a hundred thousand men, and it seemed like the majority of them were looking to do battle with the United States Marines. In any event, our ten thousand were outnumbered at least six to one, and the odds were even higher in the foxholes on the front line.

Up at the end of the road, in the little village called Yudam–ni, the vanguard of the division had been checked in every direction, and pushed back into a vulnerable perimeter. Nearly two-thirds of the division's fighting men were up there, and the only way out from Yudam-ni was, you guessed it, over Toktong Pass.

That first full day we spent on Fox Hill, Marines of the First Battalion tried to reach us. They moved down the MSR, out of the perimeter that had been formed around Yudam-ni, but the Chinese were posted on the high ground to both sides. By the time they got to within six miles of us, they were bogged down but good.

On the other side of the pass, straddling the road back to the coast, was that same little town we had departed two days earlier, the place called Hagaru-ri. It was right at the foot of the Chosin Reservoir, which would lend its name to this whole battle. (I learned later that there were army units going up the east side of the reservoir, with the marines to the west. The poor army bastards got chewed up even worse than we did.)

Anyway, Hagaru-ri was where How Battery, and the rest of our big guns, were placed. I found out that How Battery was actually a little forward of the marine perimeter, because if they pulled the guns back into the lines, Fox Hill would be out of range of their support. Although we didn't get any artillery support that first night, we would be pretty glad later that those guns kept our position in range.

There was another relief attempt launched out of Hagaru-ri, trying to open up the pass and relieve us from that direction. They didn't even get as far as the First Battalion, it turned out. No sooner had they rolled out of town than they met Chinese commanding the heights on both sides of the road. The commies knocked out the lead tank before it had gone a mile out of town, and with the road blocked, the marines of that relief force headed back into Hagaru-ri.

We were on our own again for another night.

The Chinese attacked again at 0200. This time the onslaught was preceded by a mortar barrage, the rain of shells forcing Walter Dane and his fellow marines to hunker down as deep in their foxholes as they could. One round struck a fire team nearby, killing one man and throwing two others across the ground. Explosions shook the earth, and the thunderous blasts of the barrage filled the air with a storm of sound.

After a few minutes, the barrage lifted and the sound of bugles and whistles informed the marines that the enemy infantry was once again charging into the attack. And once again, the marines of Fox/7 met them with every bit of firepower they could bring to bear.

Despite his wounds from the previous night, Cooper was back on the line, and he, Dane, and James fired as fast as they could, still holding the leftmost position on the line across the saddle. Since so many of Third Platoon's men had been wounded and killed the previous night, a squad of First Platoon had been moved in to reinforce the line. Some sixty marines blazed away as the first wave of Chinese came sweeping forward, climbing off the slopes of Toktong San to once again charge valiantly through the saddle.

Somehow, the forward observer for How Battery got his radio to work. As the first of the Chinese were already pushing through the initial line of marine foxholes, a thunderous barrage of 105mm shells poured right into the heart of the saddle. Despite the lack of registering rounds, the barrage was exceptionally accurate, and the entire second wave of enemy infantry was caught in the open and obliterated.

That still left the first wave, more than a hundred men who had pushed their way right into the heart of Fox/7's position. Dane was going through his fourth clip of M1 ammunition when his Garand started to freeze up. The cartridge ejector jammed with each shot, so that he was forced to manually pull back the lever to eject the casing after every round. His fingers were so stiff and cold that he fumbled the spare clip he tried to load, dropping it onto the frozen rocks.

Cursing, Dane had reached down in the darkness, when he felt a blow on his back, immediately sensing that he'd been struck by a grenade. It tumbled onto the frozen ground next to him and he reacted by instinct, throwing himself onto the frozen dirt and covering the back of his neck with his arms. The blast came a second later, smashing the air from his lungs, shredding his mittens, scoring his hands with tiny shrapnel wounds. Fortunately, his heavy jacket and warm clothing had protected his torso from the worst of the explosion. Wincing against the pain in his bleeding hands, he found the clip and methodically reloaded his Garand.

Rising to peer over the lip of the foxhole, he saw many Chinese still milling about in the midst of the company's position. One enemy soldier stood up and started to blow a bugle, the tinny, brash notes ringing out harshly through the night. Drawing a careful bead, Dane shot the bugler through the forehead, and was rewarded by several coarse cheers from his nearby comrades.

The rest of the infiltrators went to ground, where they kept up a desultory fire against the marines for the rest of the night. Thanks to the artillery barrage, the company was spared pressure against the outside of the position through the last hour before dawn. When daylight finally broke, a veteran gunnery sergeant led a squad of the First Platoon to rout the last of the encircled Chinese, killing most of them and sending the final survivors leaping and skidding down the slopes of the mountain toward their comrades below. In the pursuit they overran an enemy machine gun crew trying to set up their weapon right at the foot of Toktong San. The advancing marines quickly turned the captured gun around and used it to spray the backs of the retreating Chinese.

Still, the victory was tempered by bad news when the First Platoon marines returned to the company position. More than a thousand enemy infantry were spotted massing on the far side of the mountain shoulder, clearly preparing for another assault. The cold reality on the morning of November 29 was that more than half of Fox/7's men were either wounded or dead. There was no way the survivors could move themselves off the hill, given the large number who would have to be carried, so there was nothing for it but to wait out another day there.

Captain Barber ordered the marines to take the parachutes from yesterday's supply drop and lay them out to mark the middle of the company's position. More transports flew over, their loadmasters kicking supply pallets out the side doors. They fell right into the heart of the makeshift landing zone. The parachutes opened just in time to keep their loads from smashing into the frozen ground.

Toward midday, the marines heard an unfamiliar chattering sound, and quickly made out the shape of a small helicopter. The pilot of the newfangled machine made a bold effort to steer his little craft through the high winds on these high slopes, and managed to settle down right in the middle of Fox/7's position. The pilot had hoped to evacuate several of the most seriously wounded men, but he was peppered by so much sniper fire from the heights of Toktong San, across the saddle, that he stayed only long enough to unload several new batteries for the company radios. Immediately after, he gunned his engine, took off, and then chattered away into the still clear sky.

In the meantime, Walt Dane and many other riflemen in the front line of the company's position made a cold but practical decision to reinforce their defensive positions. Moving into the flat saddle, which was still littered with hundreds of Chinese dead, their bodies now frozen solid into grotesque positions, the marines dragged one corpse after another up to their shallow firing pits. Stacking the dead like cordwood, they more than doubled the height of their defensive breastworks, using additional bodies to provide protection against attack to either flank.

A flight of USAF Flying Boxcars now flew over the crest of Fox Hill, their loadmasters kicking some large crates out the backs of the planes. But they came over much higher than the marine transports, and the wind carried the drop far outside of the company's position. Some of the supply crates smashed into the ground as their chutes failed to open, and the marines watched in chagrin as one case burst open scattering unexploded grenades over a baseball-diamond expanse of ground.

"I have a feeling we're going to be on the receiving end of a few of those," Dane muttered to Conrad, who could only nod in grim agreement.

Still, the Second Platoon CO, Lieutenant Peterson, who'd been wounded multiple times during the battle already, took a score of marines out across the slope and made it safely to the scattered piles of supplies. They had started slicing at the webbing that held the supplies onto pallets, when they were driven to ground by a sudden burst of automatic gunfire. The marines sought cover behind the very crates they were trying to retrieve as they were raked by Chinese automatic fire. Fortunately, the company mortars laid down a barrage, aided by some accurate shooting from the Third Platoon riflemen. The cover fire suppressed the Chinese shooters long enough for the marines to bring the provisions back to the company.

The latest supply drop included more mortar shells, additional blankets, and a number of stretchers. The latter were a blessing for the wounded men, who'd had to make do before with being placed on blankets upon the frozen ground, suffering great discomfort.

But there was nothing the Marines could do to delay the sunset, which again plunged the heights into darkness, and ushered Fox/7 into its third night on its lonely, frozen hill.

That night, the marines in Yudam-ni made another attempt to break out to the pass. Once again they were stopped by the

Chinese. But as we spent our third night on that frozen crest, we could hear the sounds of battle down on the MSR, and we knew that we weren't going to be forgotten.

If we had known what was going on at X Corps HQ, however, we might not have been so sanguine. As November 29 faded toward the last day of the month, General Almond's office started issuing a bunch of orders that made it sound as if they really didn't know what the hell was going on. For one thing, they tried to order the two regiments surrounded up at Yudam-ni to attack across the middle of North Korea, to try and turn the flank of the massive Chinese army that was rolling up our Eighth Army on the western side of the peninsula.

This was the first order to come out of corps HQ in two days, and it made absolutely no sense. Not only did it ignore the fact that the two marine regiments were surrounded, and fighting for their lives, but it asked those two regiments to march dozens of miles across incredibly rugged terrain to go to the rescue of an entire field army—a field army that was being attacked by a quarter of a million Chinese!

At almost the same time, however, another order came through. This one called for the Fifth Marines to hold on in Yudam-ni while the Seventh Marines were to pull out and start moving southward, clearing the road for the eventual extraction of the whole force. The first objective was to clear about twelve miles of snaky, winding mountain road between Yudam-ni and Hagaru-ri.

In Yudam-ni, the marine officers commanding the Seventh and Fifth Regiments—two light colonels who, in the absence of any coordination from above, had been forced to work out an ad hoc command-sharing procedure throughout the siege—had already decided that they would need to break out. By contracting their perimeter even further, the two regiments were able to give the Seventh the task of holding on up there, while freeing up the Fifth to try and move down the MSR and open up the route for the breakout. A relief force made ready to move out, and this time the marines would cross the open countryside, disdaining the use of the road that had proven so impassable to every previous escape attempt.

The Fifth Marines, under the command of Lieutenant Colonel Raymond Davis, intended to push on at all costs, clearing the flanks of the MSR. And while they were at it, they would try to break through to our little company, Fox/7, still clinging to our hill adjacent to Toktong Pass.

Once again the Chinese came charging up the slopes of Fox Hill in the middle of the night, as the month of November eased into the early, frigid hours of December 1. Perhaps the deadly resistance put up by the Third Platoon, in defense of the saddle connecting the hill to the nearby mountain peak, had at last given the enemy pause. At least, as Walt Dane hunkered in his foxhole, sheltering behind the makeshift breastwork formed by frozen Chinese bodies, he didn't have nearly as many targets in front of him as he was used to. He'd claimed a Thompson submachine gun from the pile of captured enemy weapons, but for the time being the lethal but short-range weapon was just keeping him company.

The artillery support during the fourth night on the hill was again right on the mark, those steady howitzers of How Eleven, miles away down in Hagaru-ri, plunking their 105mm shells right across the saddle. As the smoke billowed and the clouds of snow settled to the ground, Dane saw only a few moving figures in their quilted white parkas. He took a few shots, and was joined by other riflemen and a single light machine gun, and the probing Chinese went to ground and seemed content to return a desultory fire.

On the flanks, however, the enemy seemed to be making a

fresh and invigorated effort. From his vantage, Dane couldn't see the action on the slopes of Fox Hill, but he heard the chattering of automatic weapons, and felt the crump of the mortar shells as the company's few tubes spit out accurate and deadly fire against the enemy infantry scrambling up the slopes.

Dane was startled to find himself waking up suddenly to the sound of battle, and slapped himself in the face as a stern rebuke—and an attempt to force himself to stay awake. Even so, he was surprised to realize that he could fall asleep in the middle of a battle. Dane chalked up his lapse to the fatigue, the numbing cold, the grueling existence that he and his fellow Fox/7 marines had endured for the last four days.

Then Conrad James's BAR rattled into life and Dane was wide awake, rising up to a kneeling position, firing his Tommy gun over the bulwark of frozen Chinese bodies at two score of white-clad figures who swarmed across the snow just a few yards away. The attackers had slipped up close, using the cover of the mountain's shoulder. Walt's Thompson grew hot as he worked the action and used up all four clips of .45-caliber ammo. Finally he threw the empty weapon down, snatched up his M1 and fired that until it jammed. Cursing, he dropped the Garand and grabbed a second one that he'd collected from a slain comrade.

Pumping round after round into the enemy soldiers, he watched one after another fall. Next to him, Conrad blazed away, spinning in his foxhole, shooting at enemy soldiers who had suddenly appeared behind them. The BAR man was burning through his rounds, the fast-firing, reliable old weapon continued to chatter away.

A grenade burst in front of the foxhole, and another one landed right between the two men. Conrad swiped at the weapon with the butt of his gun, but it exploded before he could knock it away. The force of the blast knocked Walt Dane down as a spray of shrapnel rattled off his helmet. Dimly he saw Conrad James falling, too, and then the Chinese swept past. As if from a long distance away, he heard more gunfire, until finally that faded away, with the last shreds of his consciousness.

He awakened some unknown time later with a splitting headache. The hilltop was shrouded in such a complete silence that he wondered if he'd been deafened, until he coughed and heard the sound of his own body. Sticky blood ran in Dane's eyes, and he wiped it away in irritation, until his vision returned, blurry but real.

Conrad was lying nearby, eyes wide open. When Dane prodded his old friend, however, he felt no movement, no warmth . . . no life. Too numb even to cry, he reached over and slowly, carefully closed the dead marine's eyes. Grunting out the words, he somehow called Cooper over from the next foxhole, and the two men carried the stiffening corpse of Conrad James through the cold night air, over to the medical station. Gently, reverently, they laid him alongside the neat row of bodies, the many men of Fox/7 who had lost their lives on this frozen hill. Shuffling, almost stumbling from the effort of walking, the old marine veteran and the young—now unquestionably a seasoned veteran as well—made their way back to their foxholes without speaking.

And when dawn, once again, broke over the cold, barren mountains, the marines were still holding on. They were down to about 85 effective fighters from the 240 men who had marched onto this hill. But the Chinese had been driven back again, and Fox/7 wasn't ready to give up, not at all.

Though we didn't know it, by that night—our fourth on Fox Hill—the relief force from the Fifth Marines had fought its way out of Yudam-ni and was making its way across country, toward the summit of Toktong Pass. Lieutenant Colonel Davis's marines fought every step of the way out of that place, circling around Chinese roadblocks, attacking entrenched positions on the heights. Avoiding the road, the marines crossed some of the worst terrain in the world, passing through chasms and canyons in the darkness, scaling cliffs and mountains, attacking all the way.

Behind them, the entire garrison of the Yudam-ni valley, something like ten thousand men, was made mobile, the able-bodied men marching, the wounded riding in the trucks, on jeeps, in every sort of transport that they could find. With the Fifth Marines clearing the flanking ridges, the road at last was passable—if not easy—and the long column gradually made ready to move. Not one single living marine would be left behind as they started toward the coast.

And all the Chinese in North Korea wouldn't be able to stop them.

The night of December 1–2 passed a little more quietly than the previous four nights. The fifth night on Fox Hill was certainly as cold as any of the others, and the isolated, surrounded marines were even hungrier than they'd been before that, longing for a hot meal, not daring even to build a small fire. But at least the Chinese left them alone, except for a few probing attacks and some long-range sniper fire.

Walter Dane once again hunkered down in his foxhole. The single shots zinging through the air overhead were an annoyance, but the sound of the rifle fire didn't seem particularly dangerous. He was weary, depressed, frostbitten, and discouraged. He would have welcomed an attack of screaming, bugling, whistling Chinese, but that night they didn't come.

When morning arrived, it was the fifth dawn that the company had greeted on top of this godforsaken hill, but at last there was a sense of hope among the men, a feeling that things were going to change. Word spread quickly when Captain Barber was able to contact Lieutenant Colonel Davis, and Fox/7 knew the relief force was drawing close. The company's radios even served to guide air strikes, opening up the path for the battalion of the Fifth Marines as those weary men finally trekked out of a nearby canyon and onto the crest of Fox Hill. They were frost-bitten, hungry, and exhausted from the rigors of their desperate march—but neither more nor less so than the haggard survivors of Fox/7. Two marines had gone mad during the march, and now shuffled along in the midst of the column, restrained by make-shift straitjackets.

"Hell," Dane said, as he looked into the haggard eyes and saw the white, frostbitten face of one of the marines who'd fought his way up to the hill. "You people look as bad as we do!"

"That we do, Marine. That we do," said the stranger, a gun-nery sergeant. He grinned fiercely as he looked around at the rows of stiff, Chinese corpses, the hundreds of still forms lying across the snowfield and piled at the tiny perimeter. Then his smile van-ished as he saw the field of slain, neatly laid out marines by the aid tent. The gunny shook his head and wiped a mittened hand across his face.

"So let's do the right thing by both of us, and get the hell out of here."

The motorized convoy from Yudam-ni crept its way up to the summit of the pass that same day, and the whole force started down the south side toward Hagaru-ri and the coast. The survivors of Fox/7 who could walk fell in with Lieutenant Colonel Davis's Fifth Marines and formed the point of the long column. Before sunset they reached that little town, now a crowded base, at the foot of the Chosin Reservoir.

There, at Davis's command, we straightened up our lines and marched rather smartly into that muddy, frozen place—which had survived a siege of its own over the last five days. We were singing "The Battle Hymn of the Marine Corps," and I don't think I've ever felt so proud to be a part of the USMC.

Even so, there was a lot of work, marching, fighting, and just plain cold survival in front of us. From Hagaru-ri, we still had sixty miles to go before we'd reach the relative safety of Hungnam, the transports of the U.S. Navy, and escape over the sea.

The column only grew larger as we marched. It turned out that there were about a half a dozen concentrations of American and South Korean troops, holed up in pockets of various size along the MSR. Some of these were only a few hundred men strong by that time, and all of them had endured days of siege under the pressure of the attacking Chinese.

For the marines, in particular, the knowledge that we'd been stopped in our advance, and were actually being forced to withdraw, was a tough nut to swallow—not since Bataan, in the early days of World War II, had the United States Marines ever retreated from anything. But we were up against a hundred thousand Chinese, and we really didn't have much choice.

General Smith, CO of the First Marine Division summed it up pretty well when a reporter asked him about that. I didn't hear about it while I was on top of Fox Hill, but by the time the division was moving down the road, his remark was being quoted all through the lines:

"Retreat? Hell no!" he said. "We're just attacking in a different direction!"

General Almond, commanding officer of X Corps, gave Smith permission to leave his equipment behind and just march out with however many survivors could make it. But that wouldn't do for Smith, or for the United States Marines. Not only would we bring out our wounded, and even as many of the dead as could be transported, but we would bring out every truck, every piece of artillery, each prime mover, tractor, and every tank that could still be made to move.

It would be several weeks, each day marked by bitter fighting, before the survivors of the Chosin Reservoir made it to the port of Hungnam, and those navy transports that would carry us away. Fox/7, reinforced with survivors from other units that had been disbanded, led the way for many of these fights. Every few miles there was another ridge top to be cleared of Chinese defenders, or roadblock to be smashed.

Once there was even a bridge to build, as the enemy had blown up the only way across a deep chasm. There, too, it was air power to the rescue, as the air force carried in large sections of treadway bridging material, and the marines erected a makeshift span over the gorge. The treadway bridge was sturdy enough that we could drive over it with our thousands of trucks, tractors, jeeps, and tanks. Naturally, we blew it up after we were done with it.

We were harassed all the way, but we were United States Marines, and we would not be denied. And so, in the end, bringing out our wounded and most of our dead, we made our way down to civilization, to hot food, to steaming showers, and to the sea. The Chosin Reservoir campaign was over, and if it was a retreat it was also a triumph. We had thwarted the enemy in his determined attempt to destroy us. Some of us rotated home—in my case, frostbite cost me most of my toes.

For the rest, the Korean War would last for another two and a half years.

A Navy SEAL in Vietnam

Oscar Platoon, SEAL Team One

BY KEVIN DOCKERY

Guerilla wars were not new. But the modern weaponry munitions, and some units employed in Vietnam were. The term "guerilla" itself is derived from the Spanish for "small war." Gone were the extensive lines or even trenches, replaced by smaller units often fighting much more fluid engagements. Such wars gave a large boost to the importance of Special Forces. Based on extensive interviews with the men who were the Plank Owner SEALs, here is a look at what it was like to be a navy SEAL on one of their first deployments in Vietnam.

KEVIN DOCKERY is a Vietnam-era army veteran who served in a special combat capacity and was later the armorer for the elite Presidential Guard unit. He has written numerous histories and oral histories of the U.S. Navy SEALs, including the three-part *Complete History of the Navy SEALs*, and a number of military fiction novels. He is also a gunsmith and currently works for a military weapons manufacturer.

[∗]

VIETNAM, MAY 1969

The chatter on board the plane seemed to fade away into the background drone of the engines as I started to see a change in the view out the port. That long line of dark filling the horizon was Vietnam. Details were mostly blocked by the cloud cover, but there was a chunk of land, kind of a peninsula with water on three sides of it, coming up below us.

Sam Baggs, chief of Oscar Platoon, had come up to where I was sitting and looked out over my shoulder.

"See that point of land sticking out into the South China Sea?" Chief Baggs said. "That's Cape St. Jacques, with the village of Vung Tau at the end of it. Welcome to South Vietnam."

I didn't really have anything to say, so I just watched the rest of the country pass below us.

"That delightful chunk of crap you see off to port there is the Rung Sat," the Chief continued. "For the next six months, keeping those waterways open between here and Saigon is going to be one of our primary missions."

The Chief got up and went back to where he had been talking

to the older SEALs. Most of them had at least two or more combat deployments behind them. If they had any concerns about going in to combat, they sure as hell weren't showing it.

There were enough breaks in the clouds to give me a good view of the landscape underneath us, and it looked alien as hell. At first glance, it was like some badly done illustration in an old biology textbook, one that showed the human circulatory system. Only on this picture, the colors were all wrong. The big arteries and veins were the rivers, streams, and canals, only they were muddy brown, not red or blue. They twisted and turned, branching out into smaller and smaller waterways until the smallest of them disappeared under the green. And if the rivers and such were the blood vessels, the green landscape was the flesh of the place. Only it wasn't all green; there were open scabs of brown, dead vegetation where defoliants had been used to deprive the enemy of a place to hide. Punctuating the whole place were round craters of all sizes, bomb and shell holes, some of them looking like they could be pretty big.

Looking down at the war-torn land, I wondered how anyone could survive, let alone fight, in such a place. Yeah, I said to myself, welcome to the Rung Sat.

All of that countryside below our plane had seen nothing but conflict for decades. When the Japanese had taken over the place from the French at the beginning of World War II, the local population had fought a long, hard campaign to free themselves. After the defeat of Japan, the French colonial rulers came back, and started another round of fighting. The French were defeated in the mid-1950s and the country split into two. North Vietnam was a communist-controlled "people's republic." South Vietnam was officially the Republic of Vietnam now, and it had an elected government. It was corrupt as hell, but elected.

Now it was the communists from the North and their guerilla counterparts, the Viet Cong, who were continuing the fighting in

Vietnam. They wanted to unify the country under their rule, have total control over the whole place, and it was our mission to stop them.

At the ripe old age of twenty, it was now my turn to join the fight against the spread of communism. I hadn't just volunteered to join the navy. I had worked like hell and earned a spot with the very best, the navy SEALs.

Twenty-six weeks of the hardest single course the navy offered, UDTR—underwater demolition team replacement training— hadn't been enough. My drive to excel, to show my father that my generation could carry the torch forward, had put me in the top 5 percent of my graduation class. That meant I was offered a chance to be even more than a frogman like my dad had been during World War II. I was offered a chance to become a SEAL and operate with SEAL Team One.

Just because I had been offered the chance didn't mean I was automatically going to become a member of a SEAL team. All that was certain was more training, a lot more. Scuttlebutt had it that the navy was going to change the name of UDTR to basic underwater demolition/SEAL training (BUD/S). For me, graduation from UDTR meant going on to army airborne school at Fort Benning, Georgia, and learning how to jump out of airplanes. Once I had completed airborne training, there was SEAL basic indoctrination (SBI) to go through. That meant more weeks of hard work, this time out in the desert of Southern California, at Niland in the Chocolate Mountains. At the training camp at Niland, a very experienced cadre of combat-experienced SEAL instructors taught a bunch of us budding SEALs how to patrol, how to handle a wide variety of weapons, and the effective tactics and techniques that the teams had proven in Vietnam. That cadre's purpose was to have us study and develop the skills necessary to operate effectively, to take on the Viet Cong in their own backyard.

Our mission was to take the war to the enemy, outfight the

guerillas in the shadows and swamps they had considered their own, until the navy SEALs showed up.

The instructors cut no one a break. We had to prove ourselves every step of the way. And they didn't have any trouble telling us just why they hammered us so hard. The instructors were all active SEALs, operators who were teaching in between deployments to Vietnam. It was in their best interests as well as those of the team that each one of us measure up to qualifications that had been written in blood. Those men, those operators, they were the teams, and we wanted to join their ranks. That meant that the next time they headed over to Vietnam as a member of a platoon, we could be operating with them, be one of their teammates. And their lives could depend on us as much as ours would depend on them.

It had been a sobering thought, but not a new one for me. My dad had told me about just how much he had depended on his teammates when he had swum against the Japanese. And he had proudly been there when I graduated UDTR. If anything, he was even prouder when I joined SEAL Team One.

He gave me his knife, the last Mark II that he had carried in the Pacific. It had served him well and now it was going to serve me. That was also when he told me one of the secrets of being a veteran: that I would know I could trust my training. There was no question that I could trust my teammates in Oscar Platoon, and I wouldn't let them down, no matter what.

My ears popping took me out of my reflective mood and brought me back to reality. The Connie was losing altitude. We were heading down to Tan Son Nhut Air Base just northwest of Saigon. Welcome to the war.

* * *

My first impression of Vietnam came to me as I stepped off the plane—it stank. I mean a thick, rich stench that was made up of jet fuel, burned rubber, and hot tarmac, none of which completely blocked the overlaying smell of the tropics, and the fact that human waste was a common fertilizer throughout the country. The hot, humid air helped the smell hit you in the face like a thick, wet towel—one that had been dipped in a roadside ditch.

To say that the air base was busy would be an understatement. Between the scream of jet fighters taking off, the whopping sound of helicopters going by, and the machinery of war running back and forth, it was hard to hear yourself speak. Our arrival was just one of many, and nobody was stopping for us. Instead, our platoon had our own people already in country to pave the way for our arrival. Several members of Oscar Platoon had come over to Vietnam ahead of the rest of us. They were the advance party and would help lay on our transport, housing, and other necessities. So I looked for a familiar face among the milling Americans and Vietnamese.

There wasn't any time to enjoy the wonders of the Orient, so we hit the deck on the move. I expected to immediately see the war. I didn't really know what my first look at the Vietnam War would be. As SEALs, we had some of the most cutting edge weaponry and tools available. So it was something of a shock when the Chief told us to get ourselves on board the bus.

Yup, a bus, a big ugly gray navy bus, no helicopters, no transport plane, a bus. And some trucks to carry our gear. Being one of the new guys, I was told by Chief Baggs that I would be riding shotgun on one of the trucks. After our gear was stowed, I clambered on board the deuce-and-a-half and met the driver.

The predictions of the cadre back at SBI of course proved true. Sitting in the driver's seat of the truck was Hospital Corpsman First Class Conroy "Doc" Puggle, our platoon corpsman and my instructor for combat medicine out at Niland. Now I was operating with one of my instructors. I should be, I had been working with him for weeks as our platoon had trained up for deployment.

"Okay, pile in, Mike," Doc said, "this isn't training anymore, this is the real thing."

I didn't have to be told that twice. There were uniforms all around us, with most of the Vietnamese at least with slung weapons. The American MPs had sidearms, but the weapons we had brought with us were still packed away in our platoon boxes. It was kind of an odd, naked feeling for me unarmed, one I hadn't felt before. Then Doc Puggle pointed out the M16A1 rifle in the rack attached to the dashboard.

"Try not to trip over the rifle," Doc said with a grin.

As I settled into my seat, he reached down and pulled up a familiar green cloth bandoleer. He handed it to me and I felt a reassuring weight.

"Seven loaded mags," Doc said. "We're going to head down to Nha Be along Route 15. Not a hell of a long way, less than ten miles. The area is supposed to be secure, but you never know."

He turned to me, and the grin he had on his face grew wider.

"If the VC were all gone, we wouldn't have anything to do, now, would we."

"Right, Doc" was about all I could think of to say.

Saigon was a bustling metropolitan area, densely packed with people. Traffic was heavy, with military vehicles, civilian cars and trucks, and what seemed like a million little scooter bikes that moved in and out of traffic as if the riders were immortal. But they didn't cut off any vehicle in our convoy. We had a jeep leading the way as well as bringing up the rear, both vehicles packing a loaded 7.62mm M60 machine gun on a central post mount. Settling back for the ride, I stayed alert while also looking around at the first foreign country I had ever been in.

Once we were out of Saigon heading south, the countryside opened up. There were rice paddies with rows of plants growing out of the stinking water. In between the paddies, there were scattered palm trees and a few groves of what Doc Puggle said were banana groves. He continued to say that the real farmland, the breadbasket of Southeast Asia, was to the south in the Mekong

Delta. We were in what was called the Capital Special Zone, Gia Dinh Province in III Corps area. Not far south of us was IV Corps, the Delta, where both SEAL Teams One and Two conducted operations. We were heading down to Nha Be, a big naval facility upriver of where the Long Tau River split off from the Soirap. It was a significant base for us since the Long Tau spread right through the middle of the Rung Sat Special Zone.

The Rung Sat held a special meaning for the men of SEAL Team One. It was the first area where the team had conducted combat operations against the Viet Cong starting back in 1966. Known as the "Forest of Assassins" to the locals, the Rung Sat had been a haven for pirates and smugglers for centuries. It sat on many of the river routes into Saigon. It was a strategic location and one the SEALs had first made their bones in. The VC knew to be very afraid of the men who came up out of the dark and fought against them unlike any other fighters had ever fought before. They had been so impressed that they had given us a special name—we were the "men with green faces." Oscar Platoon was going to keep up operations in the Rung Sat when we relieved India Platoon, already in Nha Be.

The traffic wasn't too bad, but carts pulled by water buffalo just don't move right along very smartly. We didn't really have much trouble, and there was no enemy contact at all, before we pulled up to the gate of the Nha Be base. It had been all of three hours since we had touched down at Tan Son Nhut, and the sun wasn't setting yet.

The first order of business was to unload our gear and put it into the secure area where we would be staying. Doc Puggle drove up to a sandbagged steel shipping container, and we unloaded the gear from the trucks. Mr. Hornady, that is Ensign Peter Hornady, the assistant platoon leader, and the boss, Lieutenant Steve Audree, went off to check into officers' country while Chief Baggs and Henry Mendoza, the platoon leading petty officer (LPO), directed our immediate operations.

Oscar Platoon was twelve enlisted men and two officers, a standard SEAL operational platoon. We broke down into two squads, Oscar One and Oscar Two. Oscar Two was my squad, and our officer was Mr. Hornady. The boss, Lieutenant Audree, was the platoon leader and would lead Oscar One when we went out into the field. Chief Baggs was in my squad and Mendoza was the LPO in Oscar One.

There had been another enlisted SEAL traveling with us, officially making the platoon one man heavy. But Bill Kirtland was part of Oscar Platoon only for administrative purposes. He was going over to Detachment Bravo and would operate as PRU advisor. Detachment Bravo was the SEAL component of the Phoenix Program, an operation that ran provincial reconnaissance units throughout South Vietnam. Each province of South Vietnam was like a state back home, and each one had one of these PRUs. Each was made up of South Vietnamese locals, mercenaries, even ex–Viet Cong. The PRU was paid and equipped by the CIA to operate against the Viet Cong infrastructure in each province.

In no uncertain terms, Bill Kirtland had told me that the PRUs and the Phoenix Program were not an assassination outfit, no matter what I may have heard from the news outlets back in the States. He was there to lead his PRU against the leadership and organizational structure, what was called the infrastructure, of the Viet Cong. Killing the enemy wasn't the best way to fight them, Kirtland had said. A dead VC couldn't tell you much. But capturing a VC, especially a VC in a leadership position, could tell you a lot about what targets were in the areas and what operations the VC might be planning. His PRU would gather intelligence and feed it back to Oscar Platoon to help our operations against the VC.

For my platoon, we were assigned to Detachment Golf, the largest SEAL detachment of the war so far. Task Force 116, the River Patrol Force, had been established back in December 1966 with the express mission of maintaining the security of the waterways of South Vietnam and particularly the Mekong Delta. That mission was Operation Game Warden, and the SEALs had been working in support of it since 1966. Game Warden had been cut back in scale prior to Oscar Platoon arriving in country. Several of the other SEAL Team One platoons that had been deployed to Nah Be were now operating out of Binh Thuy. But there would still be enough action in the Rung Sat to keep the platoon hopping for the six months of our deployment to Vietnam. And Chief Baggs had told me that we could expect to be sent almost anywhere in the country we might be needed or to react to critical intelligence.

* * *

For that first night at Nha Be, we didn't do much more than offload and secure our gear and get our housing taken care of. There was more than enough room for our platoon, even with India Platoon still on the base. They were going to take us out on some "break-in" ops, show us the immediate area of operations and what we could expect in terms of missions and terrain. Most of the platoon had already operated in the Rung Sat at one time or another. For me, it would be my first taste of combat. I couldn't say I was really afraid of what I might be facing, though my dad had told me that anyone who wasn't afraid of combat was a fool. My biggest personal fear was that I might let down my teammates, and that was something I couldn't accept.

In the barracks, we had a row of racks along one side of the building. Screens covered all of the windows on all sides of the barracks. All the windows were normally opened to allow air to circulate through the building, and there were additional vents in the metal roof to let the heat out. The screens kept the bugs out, and there was also heavy wire mesh across the windows to keep anything else out of the building. Along the outside walls was a layer of sandbags also to protect the building. We had a head and shower assigned to us. The mess building was a short distance away.

The base was busy day and night, with boats coming and going on the river just a few hundred feet away from our barracks. Helicopters were lifting off or arriving all the time, with the whopping sound of their blades passing by overhead. The long wooden frame across the far wall from our racks was quickly filled with web gear and weapons. There wasn't any question that we were in a war zone.

Nha Be hadn't been directly hit during the Tet Offensive the year before, but the base had been incredibly busy. Every SEAL platoon had gone out into the fighting for days at a time, and the river patrol boats had come into the docks to fuel and rearm before heading back out. Things had calmed down considerably since those incredibly violent days, or at least that was what the scuttlebutt in the mess had said when we went in for some chow. But the base would be the target of a mortar attack every now and then, one of the reasons behind all of the sandbag protection stacked up all around us. The food was good enough, though I don't think I noticed what I ate at all. Keeping my ears open and my mouth shut struck me as a great way to learn from the men who had been there before me. I had completed my training and was a qualified SEAL, but I had a long way to go to prove myself an operator, both to myself and to the men sitting around me.

First Day—First Op

My first full day in Vietnam came after a night where I had gotten some sleep. After going damned near a whole week without sleep during Hell Week back in UDTR, I thought I would never have trouble getting to sleep at any time or place for the rest of my life. Seems I was a little wrong about that.

Lying there in my rack I could hear the breathing and snoring of my teammates all around me, punctuated by the occasional helicopter passing by. The sound I could hear off in the distance, a muffled kind of thunder, told me somebody was getting pasted with artillery or bombs. There was a battery of 105mm howitzers on call near the base, but if they had been doing the firing, I probably would have fallen out of my rack.

The smell of wet, well, everything permeated the area. And the rotten vegetation stink was much stronger than it had been at the airport. Part of that was probably drifting up from the Rung Sat just down the river a ways from where I lay. The smell was fading into the background a little bit as I joined in with the snoring around me.

The next few days were pretty much filled with just "housekeeping" duties—setting up our pay records, service records and all of the general paperwork that the military seems to live on, as well as lining up supply and such. The money exchange was a little strange to me. We had to go into the disbursing office and exchange our U.S. currency for military scrip. Chief Baggs told me that there was a huge black market in South Vietnam and it ran on U.S. dollars. A sharp operator could play the exchange rates and make himself some good bucks, but in the end, all he would be doing is paying for the bullet that killed him, since a lot of the black market was being run either by the Viet Cong or by VC/communist sympathizers.

With that bit of wisdom handed to me, I decided to just change over my money and hold a few bucks back. As a third class boatswain's mate, even with all of the bonus pay—combat pay, airborne, etc.—I still made less than $300 a month. Scuttlebutt had it that the military was going to see a big pay raise in July, but that wasn't going to affect me now. The military scrip was all paper, bills and coins. The denominations were familiar enough, $1, $5, $10 and like that, but the five- and ten-cent bills seemed a little odd.

The Chief told me that for paying locals for services and especially information, the platoon would be using South Vietnamese piasters. The local currency wasn't given out at the disbursing office, but I was told simply that we would have it when we needed it.

Finally, after several days of "settling in" and sitting on our hands, we had a mission. It was what they called a "break-in" op, in this case a squad-sized ambush. Second Squad would be going out into the Rung Sat to watch over a known VC crossing spot. We would be led out and back on the operation by a veteran operator from India Platoon, QM1 Roger Caitlin. He knew the area and what had been happening with the VC in the Rung Sat since their defeat during the Tet Offensive the year before. It was going to be a real combat operation, not necessarily a cakewalk. And that meant it was going to be my first time out on the edge in Indian country.

The rest of the guys in the platoon told me that we would be going through the full formal procedure in preparing for our first operation. That meant there were going to be two briefings. The first came with the warning order, giving the squad the information it needed to be able to prepare for the upcoming operation. Some of the more seasoned veterans knew most of what was going to be coming out in the orders. This was one of the reasons Chief Baggs told me that the procedures tended to be slimmed down as the platoon gained operational experience. For what was going to be my first combat operation, I wanted to know everything that I could.

My training had proved to me that I had what it took to operate with my platoon, but there was still that nagging worry in the back of my head that I could screw up and let my teammates down. There wasn't any concern about being shot or injured, let alone killed. We were the SEALs, and that meant we were the best. But to let the platoon down, well, I would rather be shot than allow that to happen.

So I paid close attention when Mr. Hornady gave the patrol warning order, which triggered the second briefing. It was really just an abbreviated version of the patrol order that would come later. The format of both orders had been beaten into us both during the land warfare evolutions of UDTR as well as during SBI. The procedures were also repeated during the extensive workup the platoon had gone through as part of our pre-deployment training. For the warning order, we were told that Second Squad was going out on a twelve-hour ambush at a suspected VC crossing. The intelligence was good that the Viet Cong were passing by a small island in the central Rung Sat area that night. It was a spot that India Platoon had scouted out a number of times, noting enemy activity. Roger Caitlin from India would be guiding us on the op to help us get familiar with the area and our supporting units.

Our mission was to set up an ambush after infiltrating across a small island. I was going to be one of the squad's usual two automatic weapons men. For my weapon, I would be carrying a Stoner Mark 63 light machine gun. Steve Dutch, Second Squad's other automatic weapons man, would be packing an M60 machine gun. For this operation, our firepower was going to be augmented by the addition of a second Stoner from India Platoon, Roger Caitlin preferring that weapon.

For the rest of the squad, Mike Cutter would be the grenadier, armed with an XM148 40mm grenade launcher mounted underneath an XM177E2 carbine version of the M16 rifle. Andrew Karpathian was the radioman and would be armed with a second XM177E2 carbine—most of the older SEALs called the weapon a "CAR-15" from the earlier versions of the design. Mr. Hornady would have an M16A1 rifle, while Chief Baggs preferred an Ithaca twelve-gauge shotgun. Ammunition was going to be a standard loadout for an ambush. That gave the squad enough ammunition to put out a very heavy fire for all of about ninety seconds, two minutes tops. It was a good thing everyone had told me that the average firefight only lasted about ten to fifteen seconds before it was all over, except for the cleanup.

But what about the fights that weren't average?

Shaking my head for a second got that kind of thinking out of my mind before I missed anything of importance in the warning order. The patrol leader was Mr. Hornady, and we had Chief Baggs as the second in command of the squad. We all knew that if the shit hit the fan, Mr. Hornady was going to defer to Chief Baggs in a heartbeat. This was the ensign's first deployment to Vietnam, while the Chief had three tours behind him. That kind of experience could make the difference against almost anything we could face out in the bush, and we were all glad to have Chief Baggs in our squad. The leading petty officer of the squad was Keith Dougherty, a gunner's mate (Guns) first class, and that pretty much wrapped up the chain of command for Second Squad.

The patrol order was going to be issued at 1600 hours and the op launch was at 1830 hours. It was only late morning, so we had plenty of time to gather and prep our gear before the final briefing. There were no specific instructions for me, so I pretty much had the afternoon to get ready, even grab a nap. I knew there was plenty of time—because I kept telling myself that. Combat uniforms in the teams were pretty much left up to the individual operator's choice. Watching the rest of the platoon, I had picked up on a lot of what worked and what didn't. I was sticking with a standard tiger-stripe camouflage jacket, heavy green socks, and jungle boots for the most part. The jungle boots were made of green canvas and black leather and were fairly light to move around in. The best part was that they would drain water better than standard footwear and wouldn't get sucked off your feet by the mud when moving through the deep muck. A green T-shirt and swim trunks made up the rest of my uniform outside of what I was wearing for pants. The Levi Strauss Company back in the States never asked the SEALs for a testimonial on their jeans, but a hell of a lot of operators wore their product rather than any issue trousers—at least while in the field. Plain old cotton blue jeans just wore the best while moving through the brush, especially in the heavy thorns that everyone had told me we would run into constantly while operating in the Rung Sat. Plants that would shred even rip-stop uniforms were at least slowed down by Levi jeans. So that was what I was going to wear.

The rest of my gear was pretty much standard issue. I had a military web belt and H-harness to hold my pouches and munitions. At the right rear of my web belt I had the Mark 2 KA-BAR my father had carried during his days in the UDT. That big leather-handled combat knife with its seven-inch bowie-style blade had served him well and would continue carrying on for me. The only difference between how my dad had carried the knife and how I was using it was that I had a Mark 13 Day/Night signal flare taped to the gray hard-plastic scabbard.

Officially the "Signal, Smoke and Illumination, Marine, Mk 13 Mod 0," the fat gray canister held two pyrotechnic charges that you could ignite by pulling on a ring at either end. One charge released a big cloud of orange smoke for about twenty seconds as it burned. The other end had a bright red flare composition, a lot like a car flare, that also burned for about twenty seconds. We had carried the flares on our knife scabbards all during training, where they could be used to bring in help when you needed it. In combat, I was told they would also start fires quickly when we had to destroy structures or enemy stores in the field.

The Mk 13 wasn't my only means of calling for help. In one pocket of my jacket, I carried a Mark 79 signal kit. The Mark 79 kit was made up of an Mk 31 signal projector and a small plastic bandoleer of Mk 80 red flare signals. The launcher was about the size of a thick pen, and the flares screwed into one end of it. The flare would put up a red star that burned for about five seconds and reached an altitude of 250 to 600 feet in the air. Since the whole rig was only a little bigger than a pack of cigarettes, it was easy enough to carry along. Everyone in the platoon called the launcher a pencil flare from it looking like a big, fat mechanical pencil. But it could shoot through the jungle canopy. And it was a hell of a lot easier to stick in your pocket than the big pop flares. Those aluminum tubes were over an inch-and-a-half thick and nearly eleven inches long. The pyrotechnic flare they carried would be punched up by a rocket when hand-fired and go up to 600 feet altitude or more. All kinds of parachute flares and star clusters were available as pop flares, but their use was indicated by unit procedures and not everyone carried them. The pencil flares were a personal emergency item, like the small pocket-sized survival kits we all carried.

We all were wearing Swiss seats under our web gear. Made up of webbing straps, the Swiss seat was a harness that went around your hips, legs, and butt with a carabiner clip on the tag end of the strapping. The seat could be used to rappel down from a hovering helicopter, or you could clip onto a dangling rope and get pulled up by an extracting chopper.

In case of trouble, I had a standard battle dressing in a pouch on my rig, along with three morphine styrettes. These were like little toothpaste tubes. In case a man was hit and in severe pain, you took off the plastic cap, pushed the pin in to break the seal, then pulled the pin out and stuck the needle in. Squeezing the tube would inject a quarter-grain of morphine, enough to relieve pain, calm an injured man down, or even quiet a VC POW when you were extracting with him. Personally, I hated the stuff, but I carried my three tubes taped to my dog tags like they were some kind of religious medal. If I had them, I wouldn't need them. Who says sailors aren't superstitious?

Up on the left strap of my H-harness, I had a standard greenbodies MX-991/U angle-headed flashlight. It looked just like the light I had used back when I was a kid in the Boy Scouts, only on this light I had a screw-in red filter over the face of the bulb. That red filter would let only a little of the light through, enough to let me see at night if I had to, but not so much as to attract attention the way a white light would. Plus, the red filter kept any incoming light from bouncing off the reflector of the flashlight and giving my position away.

A compass was strapped on my left wrist. I would set it to the bearings given to me during the patrol warning order in case we had to "diddy-mau," break contact and run like hell, and conduct an emergency E&E (escape and evasion). My last pieces of equipment were two black rubber UDT life vests. The inflatable vests took up almost no room when folded up and stuck in a cargo pocket or ammo pouch. But if we had to cross open water while packing a load of gear and ammunition, they could literally be a lifesaver. As an automatic weapons man, I was told to carry two vests since my ammunition loadout and weapon were heavy. Just earlier in the month, a SEAL operator from Team One had drowned on an insertion while carrying a Stoner. The directive had gone out that team automatic weapons men would carry two vests and use them both during water ops.

I still had my ammunition loadout, grenades and ammo belts, to draw for the op, but that would come after the final briefing. I sat down on my rack and started to give my Stoner a close inspection, clean, and lube. The Stoner light machine gun was only used by the teams, as I was told by Chief Baggs and others. It was a really special piece of gear, a belt-fed light machine gun that fired the same 5.56mm ammunition as the M16A1 rifle.

The Stoner I carried was my baby, and as such sometimes you had to baby it. The weapon was dependable, but needed more attention than other designs. Stripping down the weapon, I laid the parts out on a brown towel across my rack. With an oily rag, I started cleaning each part, even though none of them obviously needed it.

The Stoner was a compact piece of firepower and worth the extra attention it needed. The model I had was one of the very new ones the team had just received, and I felt lucky to have it. The men who had been to Cadillac Gage, the manufacturer's facility near Detroit, Michigan, had been giving feedback to that company for years. The result of a lot of those suggestions was sitting in pieces on my rack. The new model Stoner had a short barrel and a right-hand belt-feed system on top of the weapon. My weapon could not use the 150-round metal drum found on earlier models of the Stoner. Instead, my weapon had a metal framed hanger under the center of the receiver where I could put the 100-round plastic boxes the ammunition belts came in.

Cadillac Gage called the new model Stoner the 63A1, and it was easy enough to see the name change with the cocking lever being moved from the right side of the weapon to underneath the forestock assembly. The navy wanted to give the weapon an official mark number, but in the teams it was still a Stoner. When fired, one hundred rounds could come ripping out of that sixteen-inch barrel at a cyclic rate of nearly 850 rounds per minute. That meant a full belt would be gone in seven seconds. It was a serious volume of fire to put out onto a target. The only thing the Stoner lacked was power. The small bullet that it fired would tear a man up but would not blast though heavy cover. That issue was taken care of by the other automatic weapon in the squad.

Across from my rack was Steve Dutch, stretched out and relaxed with his cover pulled down over his face. He carried an M60 machine gun, the same kind of weapon he had packed on his last tour in Vietnam. It was a belt-fed weapon familiar to just about everyone in the U.S. military in Vietnam, only Steve had modified his weapon to better fit the needs of the SEALs style of operating. Instead of the standard infantry weapon, Steve's M60 had been "chopped" to make it lighter and handier. The bipod was gone and the barrel cut back to the gas system, then rethreaded to screw the flash suppressor on over the muzzle. That meant the weapon didn't have a front sight, but Steve was very accurate with his aim in spite of that. He didn't intend using the weapon for long-range fire anyway; that's what tracers were for.

The big buttstock assembly had been removed and a small rubber boot from a helicopter door gun put in its place. For a sling, Steve had laced a standard pistol belt to the weapon, attaching the wide piece of webbing with boot laces tied between the sling swivels and belt buckles. A heavy canvas pouch was attached to the left side of the chopped 60, to hold the 100-round bandoleers of belted 7.62mm ammunition.

Steve was a big SEAL, so he carried a big gun and lots of ammunition. Normally, he had told me that he would pack six hundred rounds for his weapon on an operation. That was about the same amount of ammunition I would carry for my Stoner, only his rounds weighed twice as much. But when that big weapon cut down trees and punched through walls, its weight was worth carrying.

Not having paid any real attention to the time, I was wiping down my Stoner for what was probably the third of fourth time when Chief Baggs came into the barracks.

"It's clean, McConnell," the Chief told me gruffly, "put it away and go grab some chow. Then get some rest, it's going to be a long night."

In a softer tone he said quietly, "It'll be fine. Trust your training and follow your teammates. Soon you'll be an old hand at this."

"Thanks, Chief," I said with a small grin. Then I reassembled my Stoner for the umpteenth time and slung it back in the weapons rack. Hungry wasn't the feeling I had right then, more like concern. But back at UDTR we had learned that eating gave the body fuel to keep going, so I got up and headed for the chow hall.

Oscar Platoon was lucky being stationed at Nha Be. We had a real chow hall serving hot food. Of course, there were always C-rations available, and some of the guys swore by them. Some of what came in the little green cans tasted okay to me; I especially liked the fruitcake dessert, and the boned chicken wasn't bad, but that didn't appeal to me right then.

The only rule I had been taught back during tactical training was that before you went out on an op you didn't eat anything you knew gave you intestinal gas. It sounded funny at first, but that humor went away quickly when you had instructors find you in the brush because you or your teammate had cut loose with a fart while you were concealed. So it was some eggs and whatever that gray meat patty was supposed to be for me. That and good, hot navy coffee. Some of the guys said they would only eat local kinds of food while in country. They swore that VC could smell an American beef-eater even in the jungle because of his sweat. I didn't think a hell of a lot about that, especially after learning just how bad the jungle smelled when you were even near it. Besides, screwing up my gut by eating something strange didn't strike me as a great idea before my first op.

After getting some chow, I paid attention to what the Chief had told me and flaked out on my rack to try and get some sleep. My gear was cleaned and prepped, knife sharp without any rust on the blade (boy, had they beaten that into us at UDTR), and in spite of my head spinning about the upcoming op, I managed to get some sleep, or at least a nap of sorts.

1600 Hours

Four o'clock in the afternoon, as 1600 was called back in the civilian world, came up quickly. The little bit of rest I did get certainly wasn't enough to make me late for my first combat briefing. Chief Baggs called us out into the area between our barracks and the next. I hadn't picked up the habit some of the older operators had of calling our place a "hootch." There were a couple of benches and some rough work tables outside of the barracks. Along with a couple of oil drums split in half lengthwise and up on frames to act as solvent tanks, we would use the tables to clean our gear and weapons after coming in from an op. There was also a green chalkboard, just like the ones I had seen for years back in school.

Mr. Hornady had come into the area with some rolls of paper under his arm a little bit before 1600. Using the chalkboard, he taped up one of the rolls of paper he had brought with him. It was a big chart made up of several smaller charts taped together. Though I had never seen it except from out the window of a plane, I knew I was looking at the Rung Sat, our new operational area.

The Rung Sat Special Zone had been called by some infantrymen the "Everglades of Vietnam." One glance at the chart of the area and anyone could see why. The whole area of some four hundred square miles was one big swamp with no dry ground anywhere within its boundaries. A river delta made up of silt and mud that had been deposited over millennia, the Rung Sat Special Zone had another name in Vietnamese: the "Forest of Assassins."

For hundreds of years, the Rung Sat was a stomping ground for smugglers and South China Sea pirates. It was a roughly triangular chunk of South Vietnam, with the South China Sea across its base, and the upper corner pointing toward Saigon some seven miles away. The big river that made up the southwestern border of the Rung Sat was the Soirap. The really bending and twisting main river that went through the middle of the place was the Long Tau, with the Rach Muoi, Co Gia, and Cai Mep rivers making up the northeastern borders. The huge area had been impassible to many military forces for years, and the Viet Cong had taken advantage of that fact. They had camps and hidden bases all over the Rung Sat and were a constant danger to the main shipping channels leading up to Saigon. Only the SEALs had shown up in 1966 and started to take the Rung Sat away from the VC.

After the Viet Cong's serious losses from the failed Tet Offensive in 1968, they were still operating out of the Rung Sat, but in much fewer numbers. Our mission was going to help keep up the pressure on the VC to keep the area from ever becoming a sanctuary for them again.

The squad gathered around the chalkboard, with some of the guys sitting on benches while the others squatted on the ground. Chief Baggs was up near the chalkboard, facing back across the squad. We could see that the other barracks were empty. No one would be able to overhear or see what we were doing. It was operational security at its most serious. Any leaks could get us killed. Things were now as serious as they could get.

The mission itself was a simple one: We would be lining up on an island across from a stream known to be a transit point for VC sampan traffic. Intelligence had it that there was a group of Viet Cong Infrastructure (VCI) suspected to be in the area.

The VCI were the individuals who basically ran the local Viet Cong units. The single VC "cells" were made up of a few individuals, and they really only knew the people in their own cell. It was the VCI people, the commanders, paymasters, and supply types, who would be able to tell us about the Viet Cong units in a particular area.

The intel had been developed from the net set up by the SEAL-led PRU near our area. So this could be a real opportunity for Oscar Platoon to get our feet wet with a big splash. The reason the whole platoon wasn't going out on our op was that First Squad would be setting up the same kind of twelve-hour ambush at another location in the Rung Sat. But we would be far from having our asses hanging out in the swamp without support.

The weather was going to be clear, with a quarter-moon giving some light to the night. High tide was going to be at 1104 hours and low tide at 0238 hours. Sunset would be at 1909 hours and sunrise tomorrow at 0629 hours. The terrain was basically canals, mangrove swamp, and rice paddies, with a lot of nipa palm growing in the area. It was not going to be one of the spots that had not been stripped of vegetation by airborne spraying, so we would have plenty of cover. The only problem was the VC would have just as much cover.

The patrol order listed the friendly forces we would have on call. In spite of our being deep within the Rung Sat, help could be with us, or more accurately overhead of us, within moments.

Among all of the other navy forces at Nha Be, there was a detachment of Seawolf helicopter gunships. There were ex-army Huey UH-1B helicopters on loan to the navy. The birds were supported and crewed by navy personnel, and the SEALs had worked with the Seawolves from the team's first days of operating in Vietnam. Officially U.S. Navy Helicopter Attack (Light) Squadron Three, or HA(L)-3, operated in small detachments, or dets, of two or three birds. The light helicopter fire team (LHFT) we would have on call from det-2 was a pair of UH-1B birds armed with fixed M60C machine guns, a pair of seven-round 2.75-inch rocket pods, and a pair of M60 door guns. That meant fourteen rockets on each bird equal to the impact of a five-inch naval shell, and thousands of 7.62mm ammo for the machine guns.

The best of all was that these birds were Seawolves. They were experienced in operating with SEALs and knew how to come in close, like a dozen feet overhead, and put their ordnance right where it was needed. The Seawolves had pulled the SEALs' bacon out of the fire over and over again so far during the war. I hoped we wouldn't need them, but it was a real comfort knowing they would be available to us.

The other asset Mr. Hornady listed was our method of insertion and extraction for the op. River Division (RivDiv) 54 had a pair of Mk 2 river patrol boats (PBRs) assigned to the operation. The PBRs were part of the Brown Water Navy and their fiberglass-hulled thirty-one-foot boats were the floating equivalent of the Seawolves. The PBRs had a pair of twin .50-caliber machine guns in a rotating sunken tub mounted up on the bow. At the stern was another .50-caliber on a Mark 16 stand, operated by a standing gunner. Amidships, the little gunboats mounted an M60 machine gun along with a belt-fed 40mm grenade launcher, usually a hand-cranked Mark 18 Honeywell that fired the same ammunition as our 40mm grenade launchers. Other than some armor plates amidships and over the gun mounts, the PBRs had only fiberglass between the four-man crew and any incoming fire.

What the PBRs had in their favor, besides the heavy firepower, was speed and maneuverability. The boats could move through very shallow water thanks to their water-jet propulsion system and turn practically in their own body length. Wear and tear from the rivers and canals had slowed the boats down a bit from their top speed brand-new. But they could still move out at about twenty-five knots and pull us out of an area quickly.

The SEALs had operated with the PBRs for years, and Oscar Platoon had worked with them for long hours back in the Salton Sea area of Southern California during our pre-deployment training. The plan was for us to do an underway insertion from the two boats as they passed the island on the main channel at map coordinate YS007618. The squad would make their way to the island and regroup to patrol about half a klick (five hundred meters) to the ambush point at YS003619. That spot was on the opposite side of the island, across from the mouth of the canal that was the suspected VC transit point. We would call in extraction after making contact, or at about 0600 hours the next morning if we had a dry hole. The extraction point was on the western end of the island at map coordinates YS002617. Roger Caitlin from India Platoon would be acting as point man for the operation, leading us into the ambush site and then to the extraction point.

If we were going to be overrun or had to pull out fast, our rallying point was at the southeastern side of the island. The actions on target would be an in-line ambush, with Mr. Hornady initiating with a magazine full of tracers, followed by Mike Cutter illuminating the target with a 40mm flare. The unit standard operating procedure (SOP) then had the rest of the squad open up on their designated fields, with the automatic weapons firing a full belt and each rifleman putting out two magazines. The men on each flank would throw a fragmentation grenade before their first reload. Any intelligence materials were to be gathered by designated individuals (Keith Dougherty and Mike Cutter), while prisoners would be handled by Chief Baggs and Mr. Hornady. Normally, the assistant platoon leader wouldn't be assigned as a prisoner handler, but Mr. Hornady spoke some Vietnamese and gave himself the task. He would also interrogate any locals who came into our area and compromised the operation. If we were compromised, we would call for extraction and withdraw.

This was the SOP we had trained with back in the States, and it had been proven in the field time after time on operations. Andy Karpathian was the squad's radio operator and would carry the AN/PRC 77 radio. Chief Baggs would be carrying a backup radio. There was a SEAL rule of thumb for mission-critical equipment, in which communications was always included: "Two is one, one is none." If you needed it to keep you alive or complete the mission, you better have two of them.

Though Andy had the primary responsibility for communications, we were all told the call signs of our support units. The PBRs were "Butterfly five-six" and "Butterfly zero-one." The Seawolves were "Seawolf zero-two" and "Seawolf one-six." Second Platoon was "Barracuda two" for this operation. Emergency withdrawal to the rally point would be a green cluster flare. Calling in emergency extraction or support if the radio was disabled would be two red flares. The challenge for the mission would be "Ford," the password "Mustang." Each man was to carry his standard load-out along with two fragmentation grenades and a colored smoke grenade. The colored smoke would be used to signal incoming ex-

traction during daylight. Mr. Hornady and Chief Baggs would be
carrying two red and a green pop flare, while Mike Cutter would
have two red and a green flare for his 40mm XM148 grenade
launcher, among his other ammunition.

There wasn't much in the way of questions after the patrol
order had been issued. I certainly didn't feel like I had anything to
say. It was 1635 hours and we had a couple of hours before launch
at 1830 hours. We would be traveling over forty klicks in the PBRs
to get to our target area, though we would be only about twenty
klicks as the crow, or the Seawolf, flies from Nha Be. There was
time to grab some chow or coffee for those who hadn't and still be
able to gear up and draw ammo before our pre-op inspection.

Before we went out on an operation, it was standard practice
to test fire our weapons. The SEAL Stoners and chopped M60s
had a distinctive sound to them, but firing went on often enough
that shooting them into the river didn't draw any particular attention from any VC sympathizers in the area. Along with Roger
Caitlin from India Platoon, I went down to the river and put out
a couple of bursts from my Stoner. I was feeding the weapon from
100-round boxes, while Caitlin had one of the earlier Stoner 63A
models fitted up with a 150-round drum.

The Stoner drums were hard to reload in the field but were
popular since you could move with them in the brush and always
have a fast and dependable 150 rounds ready in the weapon. Caitlin
carried extra ammunition in loose belts hanging across his chest,
reserving the drum for movement in the brush and feeding from
a loose belt for ambushes. The black aluminum drums were getting worn with use, and the back plates of most of them, including
Caitlin's, were held on with green 100-mile-an-hour tape. Card-
board inside the drum helped keep the ammunition belts from rattling. My spare ammunition boxes were kept in a big canvas
pouch secured to my web belt. Five pouches on my rig and one
in my weapon gave me six hundred rounds of ammunition. This

was what I was used to carrying during training and what I drew from the ammunition bunker. I also picked up a pair of M26A1 fragmentation grenades and an M18 colored smoke grenade. The top of the M18 grenade was yellow, indicating it would burn and release yellow smoke. Some of the other guys in the squad were taking green or red smoke grenades among their other munitions.

Keith Dougherty was carrying an additional piece of ordnance, one I personally hoped we wouldn't need. He had an M18A1 claymore mine in one of his pouches. He had it rigged to go off in thirty seconds after pulling the ring on the M60 igniter. That would detonate over a pound of C4 explosive in the claymore, spraying out seven hundred steel balls in an expanding arc. Since we wanted to get some prisoners, we weren't using mines to initiate the ambush. But the "special" mine Dougherty had prepared would be used to break contact if we ever had the VC hot on our tail. In his position as rear security in the patrol, Dougherty would be the last man in line and could plant the mine as we left an area. Any VC following our squad would stand a good chance of running into the sixteen-meter blast radius if the fragmentation didn't get them. Just another trick the teams had developed to move the odds in our favor.

Normally, there were fairly few SEALs involved on a single combat operation. We had our skills and support to help us defeat the Viet Cong in his own backyard, but it was very possible for a SEAL unit to be overrun by a larger enemy force. A squad like mine could put out some very heavy firepower, but only for a short time, a period that could be measured in minutes at most. So we increased the odds in our favor by practicing our actions until they became automatic. I knew where everyone else in the squad would be during an action, which way each man would move and how he would fire. And the others knew the same thing about me. It would be rare to have to even speak on an operation, so we could move silently and communicate with only hand signals. I knew I was the result of some of the best, and hardest, training the U.S. military had available, and now was going to be the first test of that training.

We assembled for a fast inspection at about 1800 hours. Everyone in the squad was fully kitted out and armed. We had camouflaged our faces and hands with green, brown, and black cosmetic paint. The camo had two advantages. The first was the obvious one, it helped us blend into the foliage and darkness. The other was that it scared the hell out of the Viet Cong. Some of the guys called the VC "Charlie"; Chief Baggs used the cruder "slopes" or "zipperheads." I still hadn't found out where the hell zipperhead had come from, didn't care really. But in spite of the derogatory names, each and every member of the squad respected the enemy we were fighting. Chief Baggs had told me during pre-deployment training that when you underestimated your enemy was when he would kill you because you would be unprepared for whatever he might pull. Those were some of the words I thought about as we underwent inspection by Chief Baggs and Mr. Hornady.

Even when a man would jump up and down, his gear wouldn't rattle. The squad may have been an unusual-looking military formation, each man wearing the uniform that worked for him and most of us having nonstandard weapons. The Ithaca 37 Featherlight shotgun that Chief Baggs carried was one of the fifty special China Lake models that had been made for the SEALs early in 1968. It had an extended magazine giving it an eight-round capacity rather than the normal five. On the muzzle was the split-beaked "duckbill" shot diverter than changed the pattern of shot from a circle to an oval. With the XM25 #4 buckshot ammunition that the Chief carried, the twenty-seven lead pellets in each shot would go out in a pattern ninety-six inches wide and only twenty-four inches high at thirty yards. The Chief may not have been the best shot in the teams, but with that chainsaw of his, he didn't have to be.

There was no question to any outside observer that we were professionals at what we were about to do. And what we were going to do was take the war to the enemy. The squad walked down to the docks and climbed aboard the two PBRs that were assigned to us, four SEALs to a boat.

The boats pulled away from the docks with a quiet roar of their engines. Chieg Baggs had told me that the boats were quieter than they had been during his earlier tours, but they still seemed plenty loud to me. We settled amidships, securing ourselves for the long haul ahead of us. The rule was to stay the hell out of the way of the big gun tub up in the bow, same thing for the stern .50-caliber. Those guns were the big punch of the PBR, and we didn't want to get in their way if they had to open fire.

It wasn't too crowded a ride with four SEALs and all of their gear on the boat, along with the four-man crew, so we were all reasonably comfortable. On board the "zero-one" boat (the hull number of the PBR was 101, which was where the 01 had come from) with me were Chief Baggs, Mike Cutter, and Steve Dutch. For most of the early part of the trip, Chief Baggs talked to Chief Radcliffe, who ran the zero-two boat. The two PBRs cruising down the Soirap River did not stand out from all of the other military and civilian traffic along the waterway. It was about a twenty-five-klick trip down the Soirap before we had to make a port turn into the mouth of the Vamsat River.

Even with the foliage stripped away from some of the banks we passed, the swamp closed in around us. We had entered the Rung Sat proper and you could feel the tension level rise in the boat. The boat's weapons were manned and each SEAL had his personal weapon. Each of us turned and looked outboard, over the gunnels and out to the jungle. Just because we were heading out to ambush the Viet Cong didn't mean they couldn't be waiting in ambush for a target just like us. There was no talking at all on the boat as the two PBRs slowed down a little from our cruising speed out in the main river.

The Song Van Sat was a twisting, bending waterway. We were only going into the Rung Sat about ten klicks from the Soirap River, but we traveled over thirteen klicks on the Vamsat alone. After a long, almost straight stretch of river, we made another port turn into the mouth of the Dinh Ba River. It was up ahead about five clicks that the Dinh Ba split into two tributaries. At that split was the island that was our target.

Insertion

A few klicks up the Dinh Ba and we lined up for our insertion. Doing an underway insertion meant that we would be rolling off the back of the PBR as it continued up the river. Without the boat slowing down and with us slipping into the water without splashing, there would be very little indication to anyone on the shores that something had happened. The quarter moon had risen, but the jungle had also closed in. It was dark, very dark, and the only thing I could hear was the rumbling of the two PBRs as they moved along.

Chief Baggs came over to me and poked me in the chest to make sure my two UDT life vests were inflated. I took no offense since I was not only new, and he was the chief, but also because he did the same thing to Steve Dutch on the opposite side of the boat. Both Steve and I would have sunk to the bottom with the heavy load of machine guns and ammunition, taking with us a big chunk of the squad's firepower. So making sure would could at least float a bit was part of the Chief's job, I guess.

The island loomed up ahead of us as the PBRs made a pass around the eastern end. As the island was slipping by our port side, we lined up on the fantail. I knew that the rest of our teammates on the other boat were doing the same thing, but for the moment, all I had eyes for was Chief Baggs in front of me. On the opposite side of the stern machine gun mount, I knew that Steve Dutch and Cutter were lined up the same way. Seeing the men going over the side of the other boat, Chief Baggs turned to me and signaled with his thumb. No thoughts, no concerns, it was time to go. I rolled off the back of the PBR without the boat slowing at all. The water was warm when I hit it and it closed over my head.

The water-jet propulsion system of the PBRs made the fantail roll-off an easy and safe insertion method. There were no propellers or prop wash to pull us into the blades, and all we had to do was orient ourselves in the water and ease up to the surface. I knew the water was dark and brown with suspended silt and organic matter. There wasn't any time to concern myself with what might be in the water, we had all received a long series of shots and immunizations back in the States to prepare us for just such exposures. The blood-warm water surged around me as the wash from the PBR tugged at me. I could hear the roar of the engines much louder than when I had been on board, because of the magnifying effect of sound underwater. Then my head broke the surface and I was treading water while managing not to splutter or cough.

Orienting myself on the surface only took a moment or two, then I could see the head of Chief Baggs a few meters away as he turned and looked at me. Steve Dutch and Mike Cutter joined up with us without a word being spoken. With our weapons cradled in our arms and protected from the muck, we struck out toward the shore close by.

The sounds of the PBRs were fading in the distance as I felt the soft bottom of the river under my boots. The river bottom was just mud and muck, so it was faster for us to still partially swim along while moving forward. The water quickly shelved off and we foundered on a mud bank surrounding our side of the island.

Mud is not a barrier to a SEAL. During part of our training at UDTR and especially during Hell Week, the instructors had taken the class down to a particularly repulsive field of mud at the mouth of the Tijuana River. There, groups of happy students frolicked in the worst, stinking, filthy, gray mud most of us had ever seen. And it was more than just games. We rolled in the stuff, swam in it, ate in it, and learned how to move through it. It was off that miserable little island in the Rung Sat that I realized just how important some of what seemed to be just harassment during training could really be.

Moving through that mud was difficult, even for us. To the average Vietnamese, or more importantly Viet Cong, it would probably seem impossible for big, heavily armed Americans to move through such a barrier. Which is one of the reasons the SEALs used such avenues of approach—no one would expect us to.

There was a small stream on the island just a little to the left of where we were heading in to shore. Mr. Hornady and the rest of Second Squad had joined up with us, and we all made it in. For a long ten minutes, we just lay on the beach, just inside the lines of vegetation, not doing anything after having wiped most of the mud off our weapons. Now was a silent time. We listened, each of us pointing our weapons in another direction, boxing the compass even to covering the river behind us. We secured the area, and there was a far shore on the other side of the river. Insertion is one of the most dangerous parts of a mission—that was something that had been beaten into me over and over again during training. So you immediately secure the insertion site, stop, and listen.

Sound carries for a long way at night, even in the jungle. If we had caused anyone to suspect what might have come off the passing boats, we had a better chance of hearing them before we could see them in the dim moonlight. Minutes passed and all I heard was my own heartbeat. The plastic grip of my Stoner felt warm and slick in my hand; it had mud on it, but I still held it in a firm grip, ready to be fired. Sounds were rising up from the jungle and swamp all around us. The noises were mostly insects and the plopping, gurgling sound of the water passing by behind me. There was nothing man-made that stood out, only the jungle, the mud, the water, and a horrible stench.

I thought Vietnam had stunk the first time I smelled it after arriving in country? That stink was nothing compared to the rich, heavy methane- and rot-laced perfume we were right in the middle of. The stink didn't make my eyes water, but it sure made me wish my nose was plugged up with the river water I had just climbed out of.

Finally, Caitlin waved a hand signal for us to get ready to move out. We got up and slipped through the brush with him out on point. We only traveled for a few dozen feet before we came on to that small stream I had seen on the way in. We stopped, and each man in turn took a moment to rinse off his weapon if it needed it. We had protected the weapons as best we could when crossing the mud bank around the island, and most of our equipment was waterproofed as well, but it was still a good idea to take a moment to clean them off before we might have to use them.

Once more we lined up in patrol formation with Roger Caitlin on point. The hand signal to move out was passed back, and I signaled the man behind me in turn. We were patrolling deep inside Indian country, and for the moment, we were very much on our own. Up ahead of the squad but still in sight, Roger Caitlin moved slowly through the brush. He was very good at his job, being able to slip through the brush without making much of a sound at all. Behind Caitlin came Mr. Hornady with Andy Karpathian and his radio. Chief Baggs was next in the patrol, with me following him. Behind me was Steve Dutch, along with his M60, and Mike Cutter and his grenade launcher coming up next. Finally, in drag position and maintaining rear security was Keith Daugherty. He had one of the harder jobs next to the point man's. Rear security had to walk almost backward much of the time to maintain a watch on our six o'clock position and make sure no one could come up behind us.

He was also tasked with trying to cover any signs of the patrol's passing through an area. As the leading petty officer of the squad, Daugherty was second in rank to Chief Baggs and a very experienced man, just the kind of person you wanted covering your tail when moving through enemy territory.

In his position on point, Caitlin had the freedom to move as he felt best while he maintained the patrol's heading and chose our path. It was his movement that determined the speed of the patrol. Mr. Hornady covered the right side of the patrol path with his weapon, and each man behind him went alternately from side to side. That meant I had my Stoner pointing out to the left and Steve Dutch had his chopped M60 pointing out to the right of our line of march, just as we had practiced so many times before.

It was an eerie feeling to move through the dark jungle, but I didn't have any time to think about it. My teammates were depending on me to keep watch over my sector, and I wasn't going to let them down. I just hoped no one could hear my heart beating as loudly as I could. That thumping in my ears threatened to drown out every other noise around me. So I crunched down on myself and just ignored it, concentrating on the task at hand, one of the most important jobs I had held in my life up to this point.

The island was about seven hundred meters long from end to end. We had inserted about three hundred meters from the eastern tip of the island and had about four hundred meters to patrol before we had to cross the two-hundred-meter-wide island and get to our planned ambush site. The brush and vegetation on the island was thick but passable. I didn't see any sign of the Viet Cong, or any other humans for that matter, but there was almost no land to speak of. The whole island couldn't have been a foot above high tide, and the ground was one big sponge. The VC and locals would build platforms out of bamboo to sleep on in the jungle, but this ground was so wet I didn't think even bamboo could hold any weight on it.

India Platoon had operated in this specific area of the Rung Sat before and had gotten results on several of their ambush missions. This was one of the reasons Roger Caitlin was on point and showing us the way in. The point position was too far off my spot in the patrol for me to see what was going on, but any hand signals Caitlin would put up would be transmitted from man to man down the squad.

My eyes were sweeping to the left of the patrols line-of-march, but that didn't mean I missed the Chief's hand signal when he stopped and snapped it up. Chief Baggs had his left hand up in a clenched fist, the signal for an emergency stop. I immediately went down on one knee and put up my left hand in a fist to pass the signal along. Didn't know what was going on, didn't really care. My heartbeat went up a notch or two, but I kept my cool and my attention on the area in front of me and to my left.

After what may have been just a minute or so, but seemed like a hell of a lot longer, Chief Baggs got up and swung his arm from rear to front with his hand down below his shoulder in the "advance" signal. Getting up from where I was crouched, I passed the signal back and started to move forward slowly. I hadn't gone very far when Chief Baggs stopped again. He waved me forward and pointed at something on the ground.

Following the Chief's finger, I saw he was pointing at what looked like just a stick propped up by the crotch piece of another stick. It wasn't much to see and anyone not looking for it would have missed it. It was obvious the propped stick meant something because when I looked up at the Chief, he had his hand in front of his face with the fingers spread, our "danger" sign.

Following the SOP we had established back during training, the Chief moved forward while I waited for Steve Dutch to come up to me. Repeating the signals and pointing to the stick, I "told" Steve what the Chief had communicated to me. Steve nodded and took up his position to wait for Cutter. The Chief was waiting for me just a few meters past that propped stick. Same signals as before, danger and follow his finger, only he wasn't pointing at a stick this time. It was an old green metal C-ration can secured to a small bush. Stuck in the can was a U.S. hand grenade, the same kind of M26A1 fragmentation grenade as I had attached to my H-harness. Only this grenade had the pull ring missing and a length of vine was tied to the fuse. Anyone stepping on the trip-wire vine would pull the grenade from the can, releasing the safety spoon and detonating the frag.

Being more than a little familiar with that kind of grenade from my training, I stared at the deadly little booby trap for a moment. Then the Chief poked me in the shoulder and looked at me when I turned my head. He gave me a thumbs-up sign and I returned it. Then he moved back out on the patrol and I waited for Steve.

It was a simple, deadly little device, one that had taken many soldiers unaware in Vietnam. And it was my first "encounter" with an enemy who was trying to kill me. It wouldn't be the last, of that I was certain. But when I moved out along the line-of-march with the patrol, I have to admit that I was paying even closer attention to the ground around me, while still maintaining my watch along my sector of fire.

It wasn't more than fifty meters past the VC booby trap that the patrol once more came to a halt. Only this time it was because we had reached our objective, the ambush site on the northwestern side of the island. The brush grew all the way down to the water-line, and there was no place for us to take up a linear ambush position and still have a decent line of sight. We were upstream and on the opposite side of the island from our insertion point. Our line of travel had been in a curve rather than a straight or staggered line, so as to throw off any enemy following us. The only sign of VC any of us had seen so far was that booby trap and the VC signal that indicated it existed. Other than that, we could have been almost anywhere, anywhere that was in the middle of a stinking swamp and on a boggy island.

Now it was time to lay out the ambush SEAL-style. With Roger Caitlin at the upstream point of the line, the squad took up positions along the downstream side of his position. Right across from us was the mouth of the canal or stream that was the suspected crossing point. To hide as completely as possible, we all got into the water and crouched down as we reached our positions. The only member of the squad to stay up on "dry land" was Karpathian. As the radioman, he stayed close up behind Mr. Hornady to keep him in communications with support. He also acted as our rear guard to make certain no one came up from behind us, a place none of us could see over the brush and thorns.

Normally, one of the two automatic weapons men in a squad would be separated and close to either end of a linear ambush. That would allow the automatic weapons to completely cover the kill-zone of an ambush. But with Caitlin carrying a Stoner, we had three automatic weapons men, so Steve Dutch and his chopped M60 were right next to me in line. We settled down into the blood-warm water and became still and quiet. The last movement of the patrol was the passing of a line down from the upstream end of the ambush. The line was just some parachute cord, a simple object with a simple task. I very loosely wrapped a turn around my left wrist and passed the coil on to Steve just a short reach to my left side.

The night grew still, and the only sound was the buzzing of insects and the gurgle of the river. Our eyes had long been used to the darkness, and I could see the far shore as a shadow in the darkness. Mr. Hornady had an AN/PVS-2 starlight scope attached to his XM177E2. With it, he could see in the darkness, sacrificing his night vision when he did so. The starlight scope amplified available light some thousands of times, making the darkness appear bright on the green screen of the scope. The electronic sight was expensive and nearly as big as a man's forearm. The squad only had one and Mr. Hornady was using it, since he would be the one to trigger the ambush. All I had to do was settle in, keep still, and remain alert.

Even in the middle of enemy territory, you would think that it would be easy to stay awake. After all, if you fell asleep, you could not only get yourself killed, but your partners who were depending on you would pay a price for you slacking off as well. One of the big lessons during UDTR was that you could go a hell of a lot longer without sleep than you might think you could. And I knew how to do that. But it was still boring as hell crouching there in that dirty water. Far off in the distance, so far it was hard to tell exactly what direction it was in, came the thump and rumble of artillery. Or it may have been a bombing attack for all I knew. I was still a bright, shiny penny compared to nearly everyone else in the squad. I would do my job, and depend on them to guide me with their experience.

Months and months of training just to sit in the water and be leech food, such was the adventurous life of a navy SEAL, I thought to myself. For the most part, I tried to keep my mind blank but attentive. You learn very quickly that the mind can play tricks on you, especially in the darkness during a high-stress situation. If you allowed yourself to imagine something, chances were that you would see it out there in the darkness. That was how some of the guys had their better hallucinations during Hell Week in UDTR, when we went for five days without sleep. Where I was now, there were no instructors to pull you out if you screwed up, so you just kept watch and moved nothing but your eyeballs.

Ambush

Looking at a watch doesn't help during a long wait, besides I wasn't wearing a watch, and wouldn't have paid any attention to it if I was wearing one anyway. I had other, much more important things to pay attention to during that long wait in the water. There was enough repellent in the camouflage paint we wore to help keep off the worst of the insects, but sweat combined with the river water had helped wash off a lot of that protection. We were still well hidden along that bank deep inside the Rung Sat. If anyone had looked at us, they wouldn't have seen anything but shadows. If they had come close enough to see the whites of our eyes, or the water gleaming on our weapons, well, that was one of the reasons we all carried at least one knife.

The moon had moved most of the way across the night sky before I heard something besides what I now considered the normal noises of the Rung Sat at night. It was a soft splashing sound, intermittent, and coming from somewhere in front of us. At first, I thought it was just the sound of the river splashing on some log or whatever. But the sudden tug I felt on the line around my wrist told me it was not a natural sound.

Smoothly, or at least as carefully as I could, I passed the signal on down the line. It took a serious effort of will not to lift up my Stoner, especially not to check it. I knew it was loaded, I knew the bolt was drawn back and it was ready to fire. In spite of all that, there was a very strong urge to check my weapon. I choked it down and remained still and ready. There was a plastic cap over the muzzle of my weapon to help keep water out of the barrel. The first bullet fired would shatter that cap and put the fragments downrange. My Stoner was ready and so was I, and it seemed the wait might be up.

The splashing sound grew a little louder, and now I could see a shadow coming out of the canal across the river from us. There was about thirty to forty meters between us and the mouth of the canal, and I could now see the outline of a sampan moving from the mouth out to midstream. It couldn't have been more than twenty meters in front of where I crouched, but Mr. Hornady hadn't fired his tracers and initiated the ambush yet. There was something more going on, maybe the target wasn't a proper one, or we were waiting for someone else to come along.

The tension got pretty high for me over the few moments after I made out the sampan. My heart was beating so damned loud in my ears that I knew Steve or Chief Baggs had to be able to hear it. Outwardly, I was calm, prepared, and ready. Inwardly, I was wondering what the hell was going on. Then I made out the second sampan, and then a third. It was a damned waterborne convoy of VC.

There wasn't much question that these were bad guys. I could make out the barrels of weapons slung across the backs of two of the silhouettes in the second sampan. The first boat looked like it held two targets, the second three. Before I could make out how many might be in the third sampan, the night split wide open.

With a stuttering roar, Mr. Hornady opened up with his XM177E2. The short-barreled version of an M16 rifle spit out red tracers at a cyclic rate of about eight hundred rounds per minute. That first twenty-round magazine was empty in less than a second-and-a-half. But we had all opened up long before that burst was done.

The streak of red tracers from Mr. Hornady's position was almost instantly joined by the fire from six more weapons. The crashing roar of Steve's short-barreled M60 nearly drowned out the sound of my Stoner firing. There had been a thump from off to the left, but I hadn't heard it over the huge sound of Chief Baggs's shotgun and Steve's M60.

Suddenly, a light bloomed on the far riverbank, backlighting the sampans with a brilliant actinic white light. It was the 40mm M583 white parachute flare fired from Mike Cutter's XM148 grenade launcher. In preparation for the mission, he had taken the cap off the flare round and removed the cloth parachute, cutting the chain that held it to the magnesium flare. When he fired the modified round into the far riverbank, it illuminated the enemy sampans, making the people within them look like moving silhouettes on a target range back in the States.

But these targets were shooting back. For the first time I heard the zip-zip sound of bullets passing close by over my head. And in front of me was the deep booming sound of an AK-47 fired on full automatic. In spite of the return fire, I kept my aim within my field of fire, the twenty-degree arc directly in front of me. That was how we had trained back in the States, in UDTR and during pre-deployment training. It was an ambush firing technique that had been developed and proven out by the combat SEALs who had come before me. The only thing that had changed from our standard SOP for an ambush was that no high-explosive grenades were thrown or fired by any of us. With the bulk of the squad down in the water, the shock wave of the nearby explosions could have injured us besides taking out the enemy. But the lack of those explosions didn't lessen what was taking place across the surface of the water.

The river in front of us became a hell zone of streaming projectiles. The three sampans and return fire meant that we weren't going to try quite as hard to capture prisoners, it was more important for us to stay alive. The 7.62mm bullets passed well over where we were down in the water. It was common for soldiers to fire high at night, and we were lower targets than most would have been anyway, given our position in the water below the banks.

My weapon's fire hadn't been undisciplined spraying of a solid stream of bullets. I had been firing bursts rapidly, one after the other. It was a 100-round belt, but the inevitable happened. The bolt of my Stoner snapped forward on an empty chamber. My weapon was out of ammunition.

Without conscious thought, I pulled back the cocking handle underneath the front grip. From suggestions coming from the more experienced operators, I had pushed a piece of metal conduit up onto the round cocking handle, making it several inches longer than standard. That had made it much easier to cock, and I hung onto that handle as I popped open the feed cover by pushing the back latch forward.

My fingers felt like they were thick and useless as I pulled the empty plastic ammo box from the hanger underneath the Stoner and tossed it away in the same moment. From the pouch at the right rear of my web belt, I pulled out a full box of ammunition and slipped it in place. A sudden calm settled in over me as my hands did what they had practiced over and over again. There wasn't any fear, just concentration. I pulled the tag end of the fresh belt out and slapped it down into the feed tray. Of almost its own accord, my hand slapped back on the feed cover, closing it and prepping the weapon to fire. It only took twenty seconds for me to reload and get back into the fight, only the fight was over.

In front of the squad were three bullet-riddled sampans, the middle one already awash and sinking. Some bodies were floating in the river. The current was starting to take them downstream. Mike Cutter and Keith Dougherty were already heading out to the boats to gather up any materials they could find. My job was to provide cover for them as well as the Chief and Mr. Hornady if they had to take charge of any prisoners. The Chief was standing up next to me, stuffing twelve-gauge shells into the underside of his shotgun to reload it, so it didn't look like he was expecting any prisoners. Mr. Hornady was on the radio calling back to the PBRs, telling "Butterfly" to come to the extraction point.

The whole situation took longer to describe than it did to happen. Then was a ringing silence on the river with the sound of firing gone. The stink of the Rung Sat now had another smell, the sickly sweet smell and taste at the back of the throat from burned smokeless powder. I could smell that, but the stench of the Rung Sat had gone away quite a bit.

But the danger we were facing sure hadn't. The far side of the river started to crackle with small arms fire. Muzzle flashes popped into being as the Viet Cong we hadn't suspected were there opened fire.

Dougherty and Cutter were already heading back to the bank when the VC opened up. Their fire was sporadic and very little came our way, but the volume of fire was growing. It was time to get-the-heck-outta-Dodge, as the Chief would have put it. I held my fire since we had men downrange. But the urge to shoot back was tremendous. Didn't matter, training held and so did my fire, along with everyone else's in the squad. Once our men were out of the line of fire, we all opened up on the far banks with everything we had. It was like the ambush had been, only more so, at least that was how it appeared to me. Chief Baggs had grabbed up Dougherty and practically pulled him bodily out of the river. I stood almost right over the two men as I poured the fire from my Stoner back at the far bank. Chief Baggs took something from Dougherty and pointed at the bank. I couldn't hear what he said or what he was pointing to, I had my hands full manning my weapon.

Again, there was the heart-stopping clank as the bolt went home on an empty chamber and my Stoner went dry. Smoke was rising from the steaming barrel as I knelt down and quickly reloaded. As I started to fire back at the VC, the Chief smacked me on the shoulder and bent down to me.

"Withdraw!" he practically shouted in my ear. "Break contact and withdraw!"

That was when the squad started to get the hell out of that hornet's nest. We had our men out of the river, and it was time to start peeling away in order, just as we had practiced. As the rest of the squad pulled back, the automatic weapons men would fire long bursts before they, too, pulled away in order. The situation changed as a pop flare went off across the river.

The VC had the habit of picking up every piece of dropped ordnance and equipment lost by the U.S. military, and they bought stolen gear off the black market. Wherever it had come from, the pop and whoosh of a rocket going up told us that things were about to get very dicey indeed.

Far overhead, there was a fainter pop and a sputtering white flare ignited, dangling down from its parachute. Whoever the hell had been in those sampans, the VC were seriously pissed that we had taken them out. They never used nighttime illumination in the Rung Sat, from what I had been told by the veterans in the team. The night hid them as well as it did us, but this situation was different. How different we heard moments later as there were a couple of deep booms quickly followed by sharp explosions off to our east. These sounds were punctuated by the deep, thundering booming of several .50-caliber machine guns opening up. The PBRs were taking fire, and giving it back.

We cut into the island, moving away from the shoreline and heading to the western end. It was not a panicked run but a disciplined, practiced maneuver. We were in the shit but so was the enemy. Just how much trouble the VC was in became apparent as we cut into the island, moving fast and hard.

Back behind us, there was a violent explosion as a pound-and-a-quarter of C4 plastic explosive detonated on the riverbank we had just left. Whatever the number of VC were on the other bank, they were suddenly faced with a sleeting storm of high-velocity steel balls moving at thousands of feet per second. Keith had placed his claymore mine and pulled the igniter as we broke away. That blast was going to discourage any following enemy forces for a couple of precious minutes. As we headed toward the primary extraction point, we had reversed the order of march. Now Keith

Dougherty was in the point position and Roger Caitlin was pulling rear security. With Caitlin being the other Stoner in the squad, that seemed like a great idea. He had fired his Stoner from a loose belt, breaking it off as we pulled out. Snapping the tag end of the belt in the feed tray to the end of the belt in his drum, he now had a full 150-round belt to defend our tail with as we pulled out.

But the biggest gun in the squad wasn't the Stoner, or the M60, or any firearm. The biggest, most powerful weapon we had was the radio, and the support that was at the other end of our communications line. Mr. Hornady was on the radio as we moved, calling up Seawolf. The overhead flares had long burned out as the sound of approaching helicopters grew louder.

I couldn't hear what Mr. Hornady was saying to the birds as they came in, or what they were telling him. But it was an amazing sight as two helicopter gunships came roaring in, right down on the deck. Chief Baggs popped a pencil flare to mark our position, and the Seawolves opened up as soon as they knew where we were.

Rockets roared out of the pods as the four-foot-long motors pushed the seventeen-pound explosive warheads out to their targets. Explosions erupted behind us, and sounded not too far behind us, as the impacting 2.75-inch rockets smashed into the approaching VC. There was a pattering sound all around us as the Seawolf gunships hovered almost right overhead. It was the sound of the empty brass ejecting from the six M60 machine guns firing from each bird as the door gunners and mounted weapons put out their fire. Then the swooping death machines moved out for another pass at the enemy, never leaving us but not staying still and making a bigger target of themselves.

We had kept moving as the Seawolves dumped hellfire onto the pursuing VC. In spite of the heavy firepower smashing them in the face, they were still chasing us. The only thing that was keeping the squad alive was not standing still, and the heavy metal being put out by the Seawolves overhead. Those helicopters wouldn't leave us, but they also couldn't extract us. The birds were heavy with ammunition and weapons, plus there was no place in the brush- and jungle-covered island for them to safely set down for a pickup. We had taken the war to the enemy and hit them hard, now we had to get out.

Funny thing was, I didn't feel any fear during that pullout. I had thought I might be scared, worried about it. But my dad had told me to trust my training. He had been right, and I think we had a little of the luck with us that comes with being prepared. Dougherty may have been keeping an eye out for booby traps, but I don't think so. It was just a risk we had to take as we pulled out.

Nothing exploded in the jungle that we didn't want to blow up as we broke out onto the shoreline at the end of the island. This was where we were going to make our stand. My Stoner was still pinging hot from the fire I had put out during the ambush and extraction. I had reloaded another box while we were on the run, barely remembering that I had done it. The squad spread out to secure the extraction site as Mr. Hornady was on the radio with Butterfly Five-six and Zero-one.

The Seawolves were still doing a lumberjack of cutting down mangroves, palms, brush, and Viet Cong as the two PBRs came roaring up from the south of our position. The boats came up to the mud banks and slowed down suddenly. The spotlights on the forward .50-caliber guns showed them the border of the mud bank. They were there to pick us up, but we still had to get to them and they were a dozen meters away from the shore.

We moved into the mud as Chief Baggs shouted for us all to keep low. We practically swam across the mud as the bow guns on the PBRs opened up. Facing a firing pair of .50-caliber guns is awe-inspiring, but only if the weapons are on your side. To the VC in the jungle, they must have seemed like monsters as the huge bullets ripped through trees, mud, and flesh. The shock wave from the muzzle blasts of the guns smacked into my face as I ducked past the bow gun tub and moved to the side of the boat. Strong hands grabbed me to help pull me out of the mud and on board. As soon as my feet hit the deck, I turned to add my portion of fire to the weapons opening up on the Viet Cong. Then the PBRs pulled back away from the mud and out into the main stream of the river.

The agile little craft spun around quickly. Now it was the turn of the stern-mounted .50-calibers to keep the pressure on the enemy behind us. In spite of the efforts of the Seawolves and the PBRs, there was still some fire coming out of the jungle, though very little of it seemed to be aimed at us. The spotlights were out as the boats went to full-ahead and started back toward the Soirap River, Nha Be, and the safe haven they offered.

We took a different route back to the main river, but moved along at a much higher speed. It wasn't very long before the waterway we were on opened up into the main river and we turned north toward the base. We could relax a little and put the safeties back on our weapons. Chief Baggs pulled up a dented and beaten ammunition can I hadn't noticed him carrying. There was some kind of writing on it, but I couldn't make it out in the dim light coming from the control panel of the PBR.

Popping the lid, Chief Baggs pulled some wads of paper from the can and looked at them.

"Maybe this is why the gooks fought so hard," he said with a grin, looking over at me. "We either took out a paymaster or a tax collector. Either way, we've got a couple of cans of documents and piasters.

"So, Teammate," he said looking at me, "is your first op everything you thought it would be?"

It was the first time I could remember that the Chief had called me a teammate. There wasn't any question that I was a member of the teams now. I looked at him and the smile spread across my face, smeared green makeup and all.

uin Random House LLC
Broadway
Y, 10019

://www.penguinrandomhouse.com
)-733-3000

authorized representative in the EU for product safety and compliance is

uin Random House Ireland
son Chambers, 32 Nassau Street
YH68

://eu-contact.penguin.ie

9780425230138
se ID: 150393642

Printed in the United States
by Baker & Taylor Publisher Services